In a Sun Scorched Land

Yielding to the yearning for Africa, Leona and Cyril Lane left the comfort of family and friends in the Canadian north and took up the challenge of a volunteer assignment with C.PP.S. Mission Projects in Central Tanzania.

They lived in Africa only three and a half years: chronologically, a very short time. But, the happenings there registered a much greater influence on their lives than could be expected in such a short period.

It was not an easy time for them. They often felt isolated and unappreciated. They missed several family milestones. They were not in Canada for the birth of six of their grandchildren. They missed attending the wedding of one of their sons, were not present to give care to an ailing daughter, nor to attend Leona's brother's funeral or offer sympathy to his family following his untimely death.

They suffered from malaria and various, often violent, stomach ailments, were tormented by mosquitoes, driver ants and flies, and faced injury every time they drove on the horrendous roads.

Yet, in spite of those difficulties, it was, for them, one of life's most affirming experiences. They have been fulfilled by the knowledge that they helped to make a positive contribution to the lives of the Tanzanian people, been blessed by the new friends they made and broadened by the cultural knowledge that they gained.

Experience Africa with them. In Leona's words, "To be involved in the daily rhythm of African village life, and to savour the wonders of the animal kingdom while on safari, is to see life lived in its most fundamental way: to witness the timelessness of ages."

In a Sun Scorched Land

An African Experience

Compiled from letters home

By Leona Lane

First Paperback Edition – June 2009

ISBN: 978-0-9813078-0-0

This book is dedicated to:

Brother Anthony Canterucci C.PP.S. (Bro)

Isaiah 58:10

And if you spend yourselves on behalf of the hungry and satisfy the needs of the oppressed, then your light will rise in the darkness and your night will become like the noonday. The Lord will guide you always. He will satisfy your needs in a sun scorched land and will strengthen your frame. You will be like a well watered garden; like a spring where waters never fail.

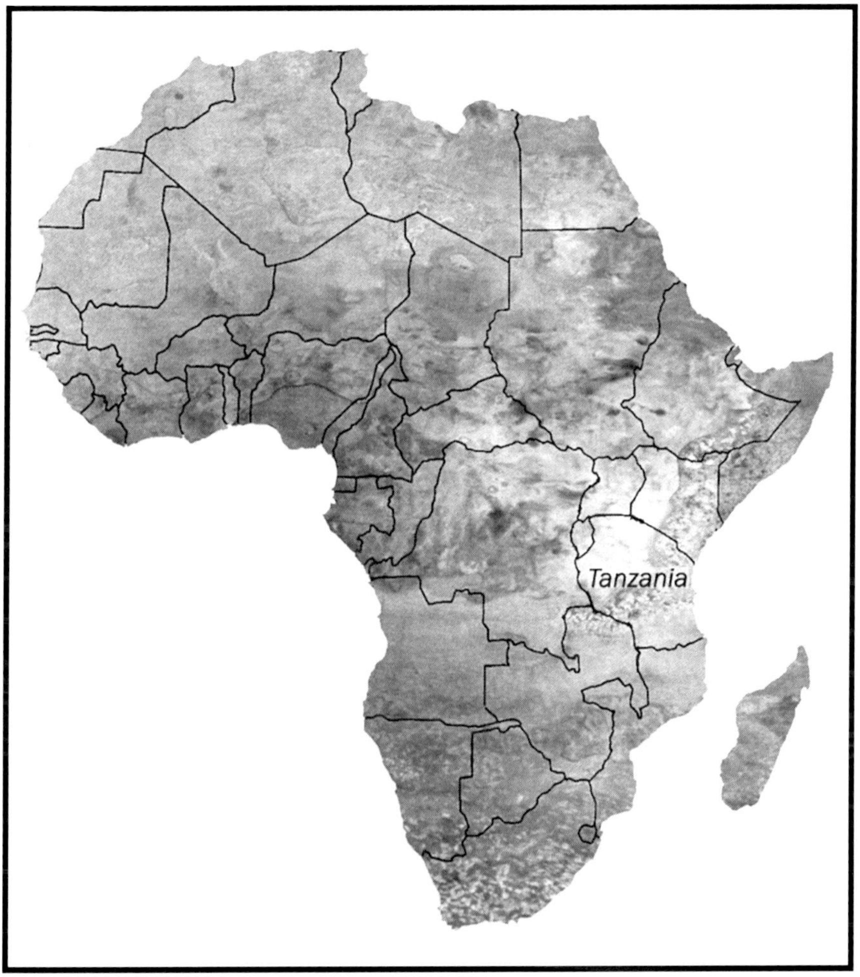

Map of Africa

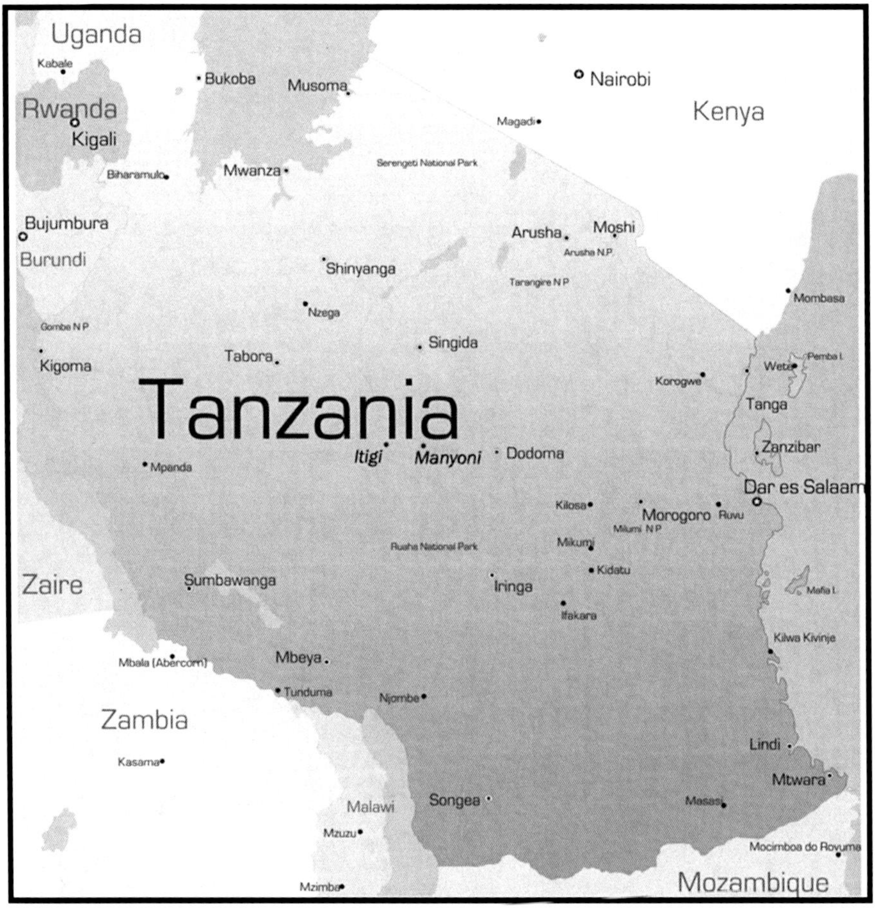

Map of Tanzania

Introduction and Acknowledgements

This book is a true account of events that my husband and I experienced during our time of service as support workers with C.PP.S. Mission Projects in Tanzania, East Africa, from 1987 to 1991.

The characters are real. Except in a few instances, I have not disguised their names. Some are living examples of courage and holiness who have dedicated their lives to the raising up of the less privileged. Others, flawed by human failings - and I include my husband and myself in this - have nonetheless tried to make a positive contribution to African society.

Many Tanzanians and fellow missionaries have become lifelong friends. Without their support, we surely would not have been able to fulfill our mandate. Thanks to: Ted Van der Zalm, Girish and Menoj Vishani, the Lamb family, Baldwin, Alex and Darcy Isinika and C.PP.S. Fathers: Dino, Domenic, Francis, Gianni (John) and Vincenzo.

Thanks also to: our accountant and 'right-hand man' Laurenti Ntiruhungwa, our mechanic shop foreman Mzee Kimome, our carpentry shop foreman Mzee Peter Msaga and all those in the mission who helped guide our steps toward understanding the richness of Tanzanian culture.

Thanks, everyone, for saving the original letters that we'd written you from Africa. They have served as a valuable guide in developing the book. Thanks also to those who offered suggestions for improvement on the early drafts, and for allowing the use of your African photos. I would like especially to thank George Moore for giving his permission for the enhancement of one of his finest shots for use as the cover photo.

Special thanks to: Virginia Dansereau and Muriel Moore who gave so generously of their editorial skills, Bluff Hollow Editing for their work on the early drafts, Roger Wilkinson of www.customslideshows.ca for compiling the maps and photos in readiness for print, James Mmbando for his help with the Swahili translations and Ted Van der Zalm who contributed to this work by supplying reports of his two harrowing flights.

To our son Dave, thank you for your patient technical support in preparing the manuscript for publication, and to our daughter Laura, thank you for your keen sense of drama. Your tireless rereading and editing of the manuscript brought vitality to what would otherwise be listless pages of prose.

To all our other children and their spouses; thank you for your ongoing support, even though there were probably times when you doubted our sanity.

I would like to give special recognition to our friends Loverna Armstrong and her late husband Bob who, by passing on carefully-chosen biblical passages, provided strength for us during difficult times.

To Cyril, my husband, without whom these chapters of my life would not have been lived: thank you for taking me with you on the "grand safari" that our life together has become.

To Brother Anthony Canterucci (Bro), our friend and mission director, who never lost confidence in us, this book is dedicated to you. You continue to be an inspiration.

Leona Lane
June 2009

Prologue

As long as I can remember I've been in love with Africa. As a child in our one room schoolhouse on the prairies, I'd spend hours poring over the school atlas pronouncing the exotic names of places such as Tanganyika, Zanzibar, Mozambique and Madagascar.

Tanganyika, as Tanzania was once called, was featured in a vibrant orange on the map. I felt drawn to it and promised myself, "One day, I will go there."

My husband and I will never know whether it was a fulfillment of this "calling" or an endless craving for excitement that led us from our comfortable home in Canada to serve as volunteers in the East African interior. Or, was it was simply a quirk of our personalities that drew us into this strange yet intriguing adventure?

Cyril and I were both in our 50's and had raised a family of nine fantastic kids (some of whom had already married and given us grandchildren while one daughter had passed away at the age of twenty-one.)

Cyril's expertise was in the field of mechanics and general trades training. Not only did he have practical "hands-on" experience of the trade, he also had supervisory and teaching experience. And, after retiring from his work involving mechanics, he further prepared himself for service in development work by taking a ten-month course in basic carpentry.

I was a qualified teacher, free-lance broadcaster and professional singer. Both of us had acquired local and national experience in leadership and organizational roles in a number of volunteer groups. All in all, we felt we had much to offer.

It was almost a year before we were able to find a situation abroad which would suit us. We registered with numerous volunteer agencies and waited for the calls to roll in. Some offers were totally inappropriate; the recruiters often misinterpreted our qualifications. For example, a UN agency offered Cyril a job operating bulldozers on a Bhutan mountainside! There were numerous other ‘nibbles’ and tentative offers which never came to fruition.

While waiting for a foreign assignment Cyril volunteered to help out at the transient men’s house at Madonna House (Maryhouse) in our hometown of Whitehorse, Yukon. After each day of work he’d drop in at the kitchen where the teapot was always on. Like the old-fashioned Russian ‘listening houses’, there was always at least one of the staff of lay missionaries who would take time to visit. It so happened that on one occasion Maryhouse was entertaining an illustrious guest, Monsignor John Knight, the person in charge of “home missions”. When the conversation between Cyril and Monsignor turned to missions, Cyril expressed his frustration in trying to find a suitable spot for us. As it turned out, Monsignor Knight was exactly the right person to vent to. He heard Cyril out, then said, “A friend of mine, a member belonging to the religious order, The Society of the Precious Blood, is in charge of a mission project in Tanzania. Have I your permission to mention this conversation to him?” Cyril readily gave his OK and next day bundled up our résumés and rushed them over to Monsignor who stuffed them into his briefcase before leaving for the airport to catch his flight back to Toronto.

Astonishingly, within two weeks, we received a call from Toronto. Brother Anthony Canterucci, director of C.PP.S. Mission Projects Tanzania was on the line. (C.PP.S. is the acronym for the Italian name of the organization.)

“This is very curious,” Brother said softly. “I have just returned from the field in Tanzania where I received a request to find someone to look after a workshop and trades training centre and someone who would teach English and here your résumés are on my desk. If you agree, I would like to interview you.”

So, arrangements were made for "Bro", as Brother Anthony is affectionately called, to visit us in Whitehorse. At that meeting, we learned the background of his organization's work. "Nineteen years ago," he said, "at the invitation of the local bishop, a group of missionary priests and sisters travelled from Italy to the central part of Tanzania to establish small mission stations. They found that the local people in that rough and arid place lacked primary health care, educational opportunities and access to clean water for drinking and cooking. So, as well as offering spiritual guidance, the missionaries set to work drilling water wells and setting up clinics and schools. Support was needed from Europe and North America, so nine years ago, I set up an office in Toronto to raise awareness and funds for the development projects. From the beginning my vision was to encourage young people to get involved and after a year of hard work, seventeen students travelled to Tanzania to see the work for themselves. They erected one of the first windmills in the mission field enabling people to have access to fresh clean water right in their village rather than having to walk many kilometres to a dirty pool of ground water."

Bro explained that as a result of this experience, a wonderful bond was formed between the people of Tanzania and the people of Canada. Every year since then he has taken a group over to help with a project. Some of these young folks, he told us, have become so totally committed that they have returned. In fact, he said, two of them had returned to work side by side with the Italian missionaries.

"What exactly do you have in mind for us?" Cyril asked.

"Well," Bro replied, "the mission operates many projects such as clinics and schools and a hospital that need the technical support of mechanics and other trades people with a working knowledge of English. There are vehicles and water pumps and electrical generators all needing repair and maintenance. The demands on the workshop have grown so large that we need someone to manage it full-time and we'd want you to build up the training to a level where these young Tanzanian students can find jobs anywhere in the country."

We were stunned. After finally finding an organization that wanted our help, doubts began to creep into our minds. Did we really want to leave our family and friends behind? Could we really tackle such an assignment? Knowing it would take some time for us to digest the enormity of it all, we convinced Bro to take us to Tanzania on a five week fact-finding visit to all the mission stations of the Society of the Precious Blood: Dar es Salaam, seaport and major city where the Society has a procurement centre and guest house; Dodoma, where it was building a seminary for the religious education of young men; Itigi, where a modern hospital was nearing completion; Chibumagwa, where the Canadian contingent was setting up a maternity clinic; and Manyoni, the headquarters for the organization where Bro's water project, the workshop and training centre, the mission farm, and the Italian Sisters' home craft school were all located.

Seeing the need for our services during that preliminary visit we agreed to take up the challenge of a three-year commitment.

The circumstances of our position were complex. We were immersed into a situation where we had two cultures and two languages to adapt to; Canadian lay people such as ourselves were called to work alongside Italian missionaries for the advancement of the people of Tanzania. At the beginning, we had trouble understanding each other. It was not only language that presented a problem. Our three variant groups differed in philosophies of development and in the expectations of each other. Our way of life was different from the Tanzanians and from the Italian priests and nuns who lived a monastic life. But, in the fullness of time, we learned to work together. Many have become life-long friends.

Life was often difficult for us. We missed several family milestones: the birth of six new grandchildren, the wedding of a son, and, when my brother died unexpectedly, we were not at home to give solace to his family. When bureaucracy, inefficiency and indifference thwarted us in accomplishing our goals, we would yank our suitcases out from under the bed in fits of pique and pack our things in readiness to catch the next plane home.

When we were felled by malaria or driven from our beds by an army of ants, we would sink into despair until our spirits were enlivened by an invitation into the home of a Tanzanian friend for sweet lemon-grass tea and true tales of witchcraft or as simple a thing as a smile of appreciation from one of our staff. Then we would talk of prolonging our stay.

And what exotic benefits we received when we ventured far afield! In Musoma, where we were sent to Swahili language school, we took pleasure in watching the lantern fishing fleet working the black waters of Lake Victoria on a moonless night and, while on safari, felt the rush of primal instincts as we witnessed the daily parade of animals to the waterholes or heard a pride of lions brushing against the guy ropes of our tent. At times like those, we would look at one another and think, "How could life be lived more fully than this?"

My husband and I worked in Africa only three and a half years: chronologically, a very short time. But the happenings there registered a much greater influence on our lives than could be expected in such a short period.

"In a Sun Scorched Land" is our story. Compiled from and written in the style of letters home, it tells of the challenges and rewards that we experienced as volunteers in Tanzania from 1987 to 1991. The reality of living in a developing country has indelibly altered our perspective on the world.

Leona Lane

To our son Greg:
Dar es Salaam, Tanzania
June 14, 1987

Dear Greg,

We've had four action-packed days since leaving Canada for our first glimpse of "Assignment — Mission Africa." But, before launching into a description of the sights and sounds of this exotic land, I must tell you how we arrived at this place, an ocean and a continent away from home.

Our orientation began in Toronto at the mission offices where, surrounded by bright batiks and graceful ebony carvings, we were drawn ever closer to Africa. Later, while Bro, the mission director, finalized our bookings on Air France, we browsed through the literature, familiarizing ourselves with the concept and scope of this extraordinary mission.

The first leg of our flight took us to Paris. At the outset there was a festive atmosphere on the plane when word spread that the young couple in front of us were on their honeymoon. Bro called the steward and ordered champagne for the young folks which they shared with those of us seated near them. (I suppose Dad and I are also on a honeymoon of sorts. Certainly we're as nervous today as we were on our wedding day many years ago.)

While the flight to Paris was most enjoyable, our eight-hour layover turned out to be especially onerous. After slogging around the airport for an hour or so we decided to take a taxi to a small hotel where we hoped to have a shower and stretch out for a bit. What a hassle! By the time we'd endured the rudeness of a pompous security guard and our bad-tempered taxi driver we were well and truly put off by the Parisians even before we reached the hotel.

Even the concierge was a snotty little twit. With an irritating Gallic shrug, he claimed there was no space and turned to busy himself with other matters. But, when Bro, brown eyes flashing, leaned his portly frame against the desk and pointed to the rows of room keys hanging there, the concierge relented, handed over two of them and, without a word, waved his arm in the general direction of the rooms. Good grief! One wonders what satisfaction these people gain by being difficult.

Anyway, we freshened up and caught a few winks before making our way back to the airport for our final leg to Dar es Salaam with a stop in Saudi Arabia.

Because this flight carried many Muslims en route to the Arab states and Tanzania, the airline exhibited sensitivity to diet and cultural mores. A card on our dinner tray proclaimed, "Air France guarantees this meal is free from pork," and, before landing at Jedda in Saudi Arabia, the stewards locked up all the liquor and gathered up the magazines in respect for the Muslim disdain of worldly distractions. However, as soon as we left Saudi airspace, we were surprised to see some of the sheiks happily imbibing, while many of the women had shed their hijabs.

At Jedda, it was interesting to watch the Muslim workers dressed in their traditional *kofia* (round caps) and *kanzus* (long robes), bustling about on the tarmac loading and unloading cargo. Dad, camera in hand, stepped out onto the landing at the top of the airplane steps intent on photographing the scene; that is, until an Arab security guard carrying an automatic weapon curtly ordered him back into the plane.

After supper the steward distributed pillows and blankets, and we settled down to pass the night in some measure of comfort. The cabin lights dimmed, quiet descended, and we were lulled by the gentle throbbing of the Boeing 747 engines. I leaned back into my pillow and, through the window, watched the silver threads of lightning that flashed intermittently, breaking the inky blackness of the African night. Bro roused us as we passed over Mt. Kilimanjaro, its snow-capped cone clearly visible. My excitement was rising! It was almost time to deplane!

I squeezed into some summer clothing in the tiny washroom before the plane swooped low and swung over the curving palm-studded sands of Dar es Salaam, Arabic for "Haven of Peace". A wall of heat and humidity swept over us as we deplaned and walked across the tarmac toward the terminal. Although it was only 6:00 a.m. the hot wind blowing from the Indian Ocean whipped up the grit from the tarmac and flung it against my bare legs.

We followed Bro's black-clad figure into the airport building. We were expecting a modern air-conditioned facility, but found it shabby, muggy and mosquito-infested. Thankfully, we were met by a Tanzanian government official who escorted us directly into the VIP lounge where he spared us the troublesome duty of going through passport and immigration, health checks and baggage control along with the rest of the hapless passengers. (Hanging out with Bro has its privileges.)

Bro, who is a personal friend of Past President Julius Nyerere, and has been travelling here on mission work for 17 years, reasoned that he should not be subjected to the everlasting hassle endured by the ordinary Joe on entering the country. *Ergo*, a government-sanctioned greeting!

While we sipped tea, Challamilla, our escort, took care of our entry requirements. When all was completed, we squeezed into his double-cab pickup for the 35-minute drive to the mission. Dad and I sat with a Toyota window stretched across our knees, a replacement part which Bro had brought along with his luggage from Canada. Bro, himself, carried a toilet seat on his lap: a gift for the wife of an influential friend. Our work had already begun.

We followed the road north toward Bagamoyo. On our right, from time to time, we could see the azure blue waters of the Indian Ocean sparkling through the palms.

These roads are incredible! We used to think the gravelled Alaska Highway was rough and dusty, but it's a superhighway compared to this. At times Challamilla's driver (all government officials have drivers) took to the ditch to dodge the potholes in the broken pavement or to avoid falling through washouts left from recent rains.

The smell of dust and diesel lay heavily in the air. Black exhaust spewed from the horn-honking vehicles that charged along scattering frightened pedestrians, chickens and goats.

Dump trucks laden with commuters careened perilously. Men, women and children alike stood packed tightly in the dump boxes.

Local markets were already in full swing. Fruits and vegetables were being unloaded from hand carts onto makeshift wooden stalls under rusting corrugated iron roofs where bits of ragged gunny sacking hung separating the stalls.

Baskets and bundles were being filled by haggling women who hoisted them up onto their heads for the walk home. Indeed, one woman, in a remarkable balancing act, managed a full wooden caseload of Coke on her head. Ouch!

At length we reached the mission retreat and procurement centre. Tucked away behind the tiny village of Tegeta, with its thatched and mud-stuccoed huts, we found a veritable Garden of Eden. Every type of tropical fruit tree and flowering shrub seems to have been planted among the red coral paving stones that surround the common rooms and guest quarters. We were struck by the array of colour and beauty in the hibiscus, bougainvillea and yellow trumpet flowers and by the exquisite fragrance of the white frangipani. We saw, for the first time, bull's heart, mangoes, papayas, passion fruit and guava. It all made me think of that great old hymn, "My Lord, What a Morning".

Brother Tim Coday, the gentle and earnest young Nebraskan in charge of this retreat and procurement centre, was the first to greet us. Then, bouncing along on the balls of his feet came dynamic Father Domenic, the parish priest.

It was still early, but lunch had been prepared for us, and we were invited directly into the dining room. Tanzanian staff stopped their chores and greeted us with outstretched hands and cries of, "*Jambo, Jambo*!" Light flooded across the oilcloth-covered refectory table through the lightly curtained windows. Ceiling fans whirred with a steady "whump, whump, whump" cooling the room and keeping flies from alighting on the place settings.

Damas, the cook, had prepared spaghetti and small whole fish (called tilapia). A wire basket of fruit from the garden sat in the centre of the table. I chose a mango, but had no idea how to eat it. Fr. Domenic came to the rescue and gave me my first lesson in "Tropical Fruits Preparation 101". Taking the mango and a sharp knife, he sliced it through on either side of the flat pit, scored the slices in a grid pattern, inverted them and ate the flesh right off the skin.

When we had finished lunch, Bro took us to our quarters to freshen up and relax. The room was beautifully clean and cool. The overhead fan gently pushed the ocean breezes through the louvered windows. We stretched out on the twin beds and fell asleep almost immediately, waking just before the evening meal.

Next morning, even before the first shafts of daybreak entered the room, we were awakened by a rooster's raucous crowing. We got up, eager and ready to explore.

Life in any mission always begins with prayer. Here, prayer takes the form of daily Mass celebrated at sunrise. In preparation for this, we showered, dressed and stepped out into the courtyard to join Bro and Fr. Domenic. Together we took the short walk to the village church.

Large iron gates, separating the retreat centre and warehouses from the village and parish house, were opened for us by Andreas, the elderly *mlinzi* (guard). Walking along the curving red path through the village, we skirted a blue lily pond on our right and Fr. Domenic's bougainvillea-draped house and parish centre on our left. All along the way cicadas chirred noisily in the mango trees that lined the path. In the village the African women were already out and about, sweeping the hard-packed ground in front of their huts. Hens and chicks foraged, pecking for seeds and grubs through the sweepings. The women gazed at us, the newcomers, with curiosity but greeted Father and Bro with the traditional greetings, *Jambo* and *Habari za Asubuhi*? (How are you this morning?)

The village church was surprisingly cool. The corrugated tin roof and the half-walls of ornamental breeze block allowed the morning air to filter among the worshippers who had taken their places on the backless wooden benches.

Fr. Domenic presided at the Mass in Swahili. After introducing us to the congregation, prayers were said for us and for our "Mission". It was humbling to be honoured in such a way.

A shrunken, bird-like old woman stopped to greet us on the way out of church. Years of drudgery had bent her brittle body almost in two, causing her to peer up at us from beneath her brightly coloured head covering. Her coal-black leathery face crinkled into a broad toothless smile. Then, taking one of my hands in her gnarled and calloused ones, she began speaking in animated Swahili. Her words were unintelligible to us, but we could feel the warmth of welcome in her voice and in the sparkle in her eyes, black and bright as a sparrow's.

Partially embedded in the indent between her nose and upper lip was a button. We were puzzled by this and wondered if it was some type of ornamentation. As we strolled back to the mission retreat house, Fr. Domenic explained that during the days of slavery parents of young girls often disfigured them in such a way so they would be unattractive to the slave traders. This, then, was one lady who'd been spared that degrading fate.

After breakfast of toast, local honey and papaya, we ventured out with Bro. His first chore was to deliver a package to the Carmelite Sisters at their convent on the outskirts of the city.

High concrete walls with broken glass set in along the top surround the convent compound. Even so, during the night someone had scaled the barrier, broken into the chapel and made off with the silver chalice and ciborium. The evidence had not yet been cleared away and Mother Superior showed us the place where iron security bars hung twisted and bent on the chapel windows. Rocks which had been used to smash the windows lay among shards of broken glass on the floor.

Bro had two more chores to tend to in the area. While we waited in the car he stopped at a friend's home to drop off the toilet seat that he'd brought from Canada and then popped into a shop to pick up an English language newspaper. When he finished, it was lunch time so we drove directly to the Kilimanjaro Hotel to eat. The Kili, as the locals call it, was once very posh. Spiral staircases and marble in the main lobby attest to that. Now, however, it shows signs of decaying grandeur. We took the creaking old elevator to the rooftop restaurant where a uniformed waiter seated us at a table draped in blue linen and ornamented by a bouquet of bougainvillea. From there we enjoyed magnificent panoramic views of the city and harbour. An Indian naval ship was in port and we could see the dark-skinned sailors clad in immaculate white uniforms being transported on small boats to the main ship after their shore leave.

We ordered the tilapia - a mistake. The dry, bony fish was served with the head on and, unlike the tilapia Damas had served the day before, was not at all appetizing. Bro cautioned us to drink only pop or beer. "Definitely no water," he said, "unless you know it's been properly boiled and filtered." For dessert, Bro recommended the caramel custard which was superb and more than made up for the unappealing main course.

On the way back to the mission, we took the scenic coastal route past the gleaming white facades of the embassies, grand homes and the gardens of ambassadors, high commissioners and wealthy merchants of Dar. We spotted the American flag, the Union Jack and the Maple Leaf fluttering over their respective abodes. What a contrast to other parts of town!

Well, Greg, I see that this has become a very long epistle, so I'll close now while it can still be sent by letter rather than parcel post. Please share this with all the family and friends and keep us in your prayers.

Til next time,

Love,

Mom and Dad

****

To our son, Dave:
Dar es Salaam, Tanzania
June 15, 1987

Dear Dave,

Our unique experiences in and around Dar es Salaam (that the locals call simply "Dar") continue apace; each escapade being more exotic than the last.

Bro took us to out dinner at the Bahari Beach Hotel one evening and even along the rural pot-holey route that skirts the northern suburbs of the city, we witnessed a fragment of African night life.

Darkness had fallen and as we passed a scattering of huts we could see, through each open window, a lone light bulb emanating an amber glow. The feeble light fell across the hard packed earth and reflected off the bronzed faces of the families who sat outside on stools grouped around charcoal braziers, preparing the evening meal. Nearby, food stalls illuminated by softly flaming oil lamps offered a "fast food" equivalent. Enveloping the scene, African rhythms, blending modern technology with traditional sounds, throbbed from boom boxes.

The hotel, owned by a German safari group called "Bushtreckers," is lovely. It comprises several thatched coral cottages which surround the main dining room and lounge of the same architecture. Red, mauve and white bougainvillea wrapped around the lattice and half-walls of coral, separating the walk from the gardens.

We were lucky enough to be seated at a table close to the seawall, where we could enjoy the effect of the full moon playing on the gently lapping Indian Ocean.

On Sunday, the church service was set to begin at 10:00 a.m., but when we arrived half an hour early the little church was already filling up. Worshippers were squeezing themselves eight or nine onto benches meant for six. We found a bench with five already seated, so accommodated ourselves there. Then, along came another worshipper and, with a swing of her "Bantu bum" nudged Dad farther along the bench, crushing us together and forcing us all to sit sideways to accommodate elbows and shoulders.

Our discomfort vanished as soon as the choir began to sing. Male voices, rich and resonant with overtones fell naturally into harmony with the women's high shrill tones. The singing, marked by the steady rhythms of shakers and drums, created an African sound experience of almost unbearable poignancy.

Fr. Domenic's homily in Swahili went on and on, seeming to last at least an hour. It was quite a trial for us, not knowing the language, but the congregation appeared to be enjoying it, occasionally breaking into gales of laughter

When time came to take communion we observed an unusual cultural practice. Rather than proceeding orderly row by row, as we do in our churches, worshippers got up whenever the spirit moved them and walked to the front. Shuffling in and out of pews they pushed by and stumbled over each other's feet on the way back and forth to the communion rail, but no one seemed to get annoyed or impatient, except us.

In the afternoon Bro suggested we drive to Kunduchi Beach. Before we piled into the vehicle, he checked to make sure he had an up-to-date permit to drive on a Sunday afternoon. (All fuel has to be imported, so the government enforces a fuel-saving regulation that prohibits driving on Sunday after 2:00 p.m. without a special permit.)

This beach is indescribably alluring: the curving coastline, white with sand and dhows bobbing at anchor or in full sail on the shimmering blue of the Indian Ocean present a stunning view. It is, I think, the most beautiful beach in the world.

In the distance, Mbudya Island, ringed with white and blue, added perspective to the vista. (This island is part of a coral reef, and far beyond the reef sits Zanzibar, the spice island.)

Here on the beach, desert roses bloom among the coconut and fan palms that have been planted just so for perfect balance. Under them, small palm-thatched shelters provided shade to the patrons seated on the cane chairs. As we sat there enjoying a Safari beer, beach boys, illegally selling shells and ebony Makondi carvings, surreptitiously approached us.

To get to the beach we walked past a growth of huge banyan trees with their aerial roots trailing to the earth, and then through the lobby of the Kunduchi Beach Hotel. The hotel architecture is magnificent; sweeping white arches in Swahili and Arabic style express a mood of pure exoticism.

Once privately owned, this grand establishment was taken over by the Tanzanian Tourist Corporation (TTC) and now sits sadly neglected. Its white paint is peeling and turning black from the salt sea spray and its shabby interior is in need of refurbishing.

At one point, I went in search of the washroom which wasn't easy because the signs were in Swahili. The sign on one door said *Wanawaki*, and on the other, *Wanaume*. I haven't had any Swahili classes yet, so this was a mystery to me. I hovered around until I saw a lady come out from the "*Wanawaki*" door, so in I went. The washroom was in a disgusting state! Most of the toilets were out of order. Even so, they'd been used, leaving urine and feces reeking in the stained bowls. I tried cubicle after cubicle until I found one that was functioning. Then, wanting to wash my hands, I could not coax a single drop of water from the rusting taps at the cracked sinks. What could be done? Luckily I'd saved a "handiwipe" from the aircraft, so the "day was saved".

We were anxious to return to the mission house in time for supper. (Sunday's meals are always special.) There was a new cook whose name is Pius (they pronounce it "puce"). Small and delicate and sporting a Ho Chi Minh beard, he's an unforgettable figure. He had obviously taken quick control of the kitchen and "wowed" us with barbequed swordfish.

The mission often receives donations of good used equipment, which explains why they have a Heinz variety of vehicles. We've ridden in three types already. An ambulance had just been delivered from Italy for the mission hospital up-country and Bro decided he'd like to take it for a spin the next morning "Get ready," he said, finishing the last of his espresso. "Today I'm going to show you the real Dar es Salaam."

When we arrived at the centre of the city, Bro directed the vehicle toward St. Joseph's Cathedral compound to fuel up. (That's right, there are fuel pumps in the Cathedral parking lot.) The Bishop has provided a safe and secure supply of fuel as well as parking space for visiting missionaries. Bro left the vehicle under a huge cashew tree and we followed him onto the broken, dusty pavements.

The natural harbour at Dar es Salaam made it an ideal choice for a trading centre. The Sultan of Zanzibar had great plans to develop the harbour way back in 1866, and the German colonists continued with the plan 21 years later. Arabic, German and British influences are in evidence everywhere. Even though many of the stone and cement structures are crumbling and nearly in ruins, it has a magic like no other city.

As we followed Bro, who set a brisk pace in spite of his burly build, we were careful to avoid stepping into holes in the broken pavements. We were also mindful of the beggars, some without arms or legs, others damaged by the ravages of leprosy. Bro tossed a few coins to one old leper, who was sitting at the Cathedral corner, his face, hands and feet badly disfigured. A mother, her sickly baby wrapped in rags, looked up piteously as we passed. She, too, captured Bro's compassion and he pressed a few shillings into her hand. These scenes seemed to have stepped out of a Biblical epic film, yet here they were in real-time 20th century.

The streets were grey with dust and dirt. Scraps of paper and blue plastic bags littered the city. Sand had sifted in from the sea covering doorsills and stairs, and the once grand whitewashed buildings were flaking and mottled.

We were fascinated by the people, mostly black and Asian, who surged through the streets. Most of the men sported Western dress (white shirts and dark trousers or safari suits), but a few Arab men were attired in long flowing robes — *kanzus* and round caps — *kofia*. Most of the women wore *kangas*, simple lengths of colourful cotton wrapped around and knotted at the waist, topped by a T-shirt or simple blouse. Others, Muslim ladies, were dressed in the more traditional *hijab* or *burka*.

Street vendors had set up wherever they found a free spot on the pavement. Used books and magazines, gum, candy, carvings and other goods were being sold in direct competition with the established *dukas* (small Asian shops). Shoeshine stalls were everywhere; just another branch of private enterprise at work in Dar's inner core.

But, most engaging were the food stands where the smell of roasting corn on charcoal braziers, the fragrance of freshly peeled oranges, the pungent aroma of curries and deep-fried samosas mingled with the pervasive smell of rotting vegetation that lay beside and under the stalls.

Dodging the diesel-belching vehicles to cross the street to get to the ice cream shop, where Bro treated us to cones, took some lively stepping. "The Ice Cream Shop" (its real name) is run by an American couple. (Who other than Americans MUST have their ice cream?) By the time we manoeuvred our way back to St. Joseph's compound, the intense heat had melted our ice cream and it was running down our hands and up our arms.

Adjacent to the Cathedral sit the Chancery offices, and around the corner is St. Joseph's Bookroom, run by the same Sisters who'd had the break-in at their convent. This is the "missionaries' meeting place" in Dar. We popped into the cool interior to finish our cones and to have a brief chat with the Sisters while browsing through some of the book titles before wending our way back to the coolness and calm of the retreat centre.

It's been a remarkable learning experience and we wouldn't have missed it for worlds. Dar es Salaam in all its contradictions: the good and the bad; the beauty and the ugliness.

Please share this with all the family and friends, and remember to pray for us.

Love,

Mom and Dad

****

To our son Kurt, daughter-in-law Carole and family:
Dar es Salaam, Tanzania
June 17, 1987

Dear Kurt, Carole, Brittany and Ben,

Our fascinating experiences are becoming one great big saga, and we've been here only one week.

Last night, Andreas, the old *mlinzi* (gate guard) was taken ill and Brother Tim rushed him off to Muhimbili Hospital where he paid 1,500 shillings to secure a bed for him. With a hint of disillusionment in his voice, Brother Tim said, "I'm afraid we could go back tomorrow and find him on the floor if someone came along and offered more". We were thunderstruck that such an attitude should exist among health care workers, but it seems this type of thing is not at all unusual.

Some Italian nursing sisters run a clinic and dispensary that is tucked in right behind the parish centre. Sister Piarosa, the director, invited us over on "well-baby clinic" day and, judging from their cries, the babies didn't appreciate the attention one bit. Many of the moms had walked a long way carrying their babies in cloth slings on their backs. Now they were resting patiently under the shady mango trees. All had been given numbers and as their turns neared they moved, in an orderly way, closer and closer to the treatment rooms.

A young mom, perhaps 15 or 16 years old, had reached the clinic step where she sat, tattered blouse pulled up exposing one breast, encouraging her pathetically emaciated baby to nurse. Sister stooped and pulled down the child's lower right eyelid. "This baby is very sick," she said. "He is anaemic and needs to go to the hospital right away." Then turning to the mom she spoke in Swahili telling her that his anaemia was caused by malaria, and that he urgently needed a blood transfusion from one of his parents. We wondered how this teenaged mom was going to transport herself and baby to the nearest hospital in the city. We hoped she had enough shillings for bus fare. If not, maybe she'd have to ride standing in a dump truck box, as we've seen others doing. Seeing firsthand the effects of malaria and other tropical diseases plaguing these children makes us truly grateful that our grandchildren are so blessed to live in Canada.

After lunch, Fr. Domenic took us on a tour of his house and the parish centre. This energetic and charismatic priest arrived here from Italy years ago and has gained the confidence of the local people. They absolutely love him. He's fluent in Italian, Swahili and English, all of which he speaks with rapid-fire precision. One can't help but be drawn to this stocky, dark-complexioned fellow so obviously suited to Africa.

He has a fantastic collection of ebony carvings. As well as the usual assortment of African animal figures, he owns some stunning historical depictions of the Arab slave trade. One of his carvings features the political motif, *Ujamaa* (family) that is unique to Tanzania. The statue, an intricately carved cluster of human figures clinging together with arms and legs intertwined, one figure climbing onto and supporting another, depicts the interdependency of family. (*Ujamaa*, was the watchword of Past President Julius Nyerere's socialist idealism.)

The Makondi tribe, originating in Mozambique, is famous for these crafts that are sold throughout East Africa and the Arab states. We were delighted when Fr. Domenic gave us a splendidly carved nativity scene with 16 pieces. The set would sell for a small fortune in the classy shops of Nairobi or Dubai.

Fr. Domenic was the one who'd set up the Manyoni workshop and training centre that Dad may be going to manage. We three are certainly "on the same page" when it comes to building up a first-class trades training centre, but how much can be done will depend on the mission's priorities.

The Canadian High Commission was closed on our first trip into Dar, so we took another foray downtown to "sign in", always a good policy to follow when visiting a developing country. We entered the city from the east, which took us along Ocean Road past the embassies. Close to town there's a bustling waterfront fish market called the Kivukoni. Dhows were pulling up to the shore and discharging their catch of the morning. As we passed, we couldn't help but wrinkle our noses in response to the pervasive smell of gutted fish, exacerbated by the tropical heat. Seabirds and crows drifted lazily around and around, hovering above the operation watching for the chance to swoop in and carry off discarded bits of fish. Sellers and buyers were bargaining for the best deal before exchanging seafood and shells for shillings. This is THE place in Dar to buy the freshest red snapper, barracuda, squid and prawns. From a point on the shore the Kivuko ferry was busy shuttling people, produce and vehicles back and forth across the bay to Kigambini, a large fertile peninsula. Further on, we drove past the former Sultan's palace, now the home of an Order of Catholic Priests, the White Fathers, and swung into St. Joseph's Cathedral grounds.

Again, with Bro as our guide, we walked along busy Samora Avenue, passing the old leper at the corner of Cathedral Square. Walking briskly in the oppressive heat, we ignored the sidewalk sellers and took care to avoid the pitfalls of the disintegrating streets. What we didn't notice on our previous visit, we took in now: the churning air conditioners spewing condensation onto the side walks and the electrical wires that dangled spaghetti-like from the walls of buildings and overhead power lines. We veered away from those that just hung, connecting to nothing; it was impossible to know if they'd been severed from the electrical source or were alive with potentially lethal voltage.

We arrived at the Canadian High Commission offices, walked up the winding staircase, and were admitted into air-conditioned coolness where we signed the registration book. Copies of the Globe and Mail and Maclean's magazine were spread out on the waiting room table. Bro wanted to introduce us to the High Commission nurse, but in order to get into the "inner sanctum" he spoke to the receptionist through the aperture in the thick bullet-proof glass. She picked up the phone and in a moment tall, regal Elizabeth Shaba appeared. We followed her along the cluttered corridor to her office passing stacks of tires, batteries, spare parts and a stripped-down refrigerator. (It seemed a curious place for storage.)

To hear Elizabeth's soft African voice above the noisy air conditioner, we moved our chairs closer to her desk. Conversation revolved around mission work in health care and eventually turned to the growing problem of AIDS in Africa. Our visit was concluded when Elizabeth gave Bro a can of Paludrin tablets for malaria protection. We left then, stepping reluctantly into the steaming streets and returned to our vehicle.

The leather car seats were hot from the blistering sun, so I perched myself carefully on the edge of the seat to avoid burning the backs of my legs. When we were settled we drove off along Ocean Road. Bro wasn't yet finished showing us the finest that Dar had to offer so he stopped at a restaurant on beautiful palm-studded Oyster Bay. A magnificent six foot replica of an Arab dhow, complete with tattered sail was the dining room centre piece. Here we sipped cool Safari beer and enjoyed the tasty Indian buffet while drinking in the ocean scene. What can I say but, "Wow!"

In Swahili there's only one word to describe "nice" which is *nzuri*. If it's REALLY nice they add the word *sana*. Therefore *nzuri sana* describes everything that's really nice. How simple that would be. Here I am, working in English, wearing out my mental thesaurus trying to come up with superlatives to describe the beauty of this particular place. How many synonyms are there for "nice"? So far, in these letters, I must have used: lovely, beautiful, splendid, gorgeous, stunning and magnificent. Help! I'm running out of adjectives. "Wow!" will simply have to do!

We're really getting the "honeymoon treatment" with all this wining and dining, and we wonder when reality is going to set in. Perhaps when we get up-country to Manyoni?

Brother Tim is taking us north to Bagamoyo tomorrow so I'd better wrap this up and get some rest in preparation for another adventure.

Please continue to pass these letters around and keep praying for us, your very foolhardy parents who haven't yet a clue what we're getting into.

Special hugs to all those lucky, lucky grandchildren who live in our part of the world where we don't have to worry about them getting malaria or worse.

Love you guys,

Mom and Dad

****

To our son Chris:
Dar es Salaam, Tanzania
June 20, 1987

Dear Chris,

We're most definitely being "courted" into accepting the assignment of managing the workshop and training centre up-country. At the moment, the prospect is very intriguing, but time will tell.

On Thursday Brother Tim drove us to Bagamoyo, 72 km. north of Dar es Salaam. Deep ruts and washouts kept Brother busy battling for the smoothest part of the road, which, believe it or not, was often in the ditch.

Brother gave us a capsule history of the town as we swayed and jolted past the thatched and wattle huts scattered among the fields of banana and coconut palms.

"Bagamoyo," he said, gripping the wheel tightly, "was once the slave port and terminus for the caravans that brought slaves from the interior. From there, they were transported by sea to Zanzibar, where they were traded and transhipped to foreign lands. In fact, the name Bagamoyo is said to mean "Here I Lay Down My Heart"; probably the last desperate cry of the captives before being packed into vessels for their voyage to unknown lands."

Brother also told us that the Holy Ghost Fathers had established the first Christian mission in Bagamoyo and were the first group to buy back the slaves from the traders.

When we arrived at the mission he drew up and parked under one of the largest and oldest baobab trees in East Africa and said, "There's a museum here I'd like you to see".

We were fortunate that Fr. Fritz, the founder and curator of the museum was free and willing to take us for a private tour where we saw the actual instruments of bondage: the yokes, chains and shackles. Photos of enchained slaves and of the Arab-African, Tippu Tip, infamous slave and ivory trader of East Africa were posted on the walls along with displays of faded and moisture-stained Certificates of Freedom printed in German. (Just 100 years ago, Germany and Britain divided parts of the Sultan of Zanzibar's territories between themselves with Germany acquiring this part of Africa that we now call Tanzania.)

Bagamoyo was also the departure point for explorers of the African interior, such as Burton and Speke, and for Stanley in his search for Dr. Livingstone. When we left the coolness of the museum we walked out into the blistering heat toward the old tin-roofed adobe Anglican Church, through which Dr. Livingston's body had rested at the close of his medical mission to Africa.

"When Dr. Livingstone died near Ujiji on the shores of Lake Tanganyika, his devoted followers removed his heart and buried it there," Brother Tim explained. "Then they embalmed his body and, embarking on an 11-month journey, carried it all the way back here, where it lay before being shipped back to his final resting place in Westminster Abbey."

We'd learned from our history lessons in school about Dr. Livingstone, but had no idea that this was the place where he'd landed in Africa and from where his body was taken at the close of his mission. It was like visiting a shrine.

From the little church, we walked to the cemetery where iron crosses marked the graves of early missionaries. We moved between the markers and read the inscriptions that told us that many had perished after only a few months in this unforgiving, disease-infested area.

Everywhere on the hot humid soil, thousands of ants scurried, anxious to climb up our trouser legs. But it was a six-inch, poisonous, red-bellied centipede that caused us to move along more quickly than we had intended.

The crumbling adobe structure where the slaves had been held sits near the beach. A lone tree has grown up from a collapsed corner near the roof, but the building is still in use as a police station. From this historical place tunnels had been dug to move the precious human cargo directly to the sea, where waiting slave ships sat at anchor.

Bagamoyo has been designated a UNESCO heritage site, and reconstruction work has already begun. This is definitely a place for all you history buffs to visit in a few years.

We said goodbye to Fr. Fritz and climbed into the vehicle for our return. But before we left the site, we stopped to visit the gigantic granite cross erected to honour those early missionaries whose actions saved thousands from being victimized by the slave trade. From there we drove to visit the Kaole ruins of the ancient Swahili town and the remains of what is believed to be the oldest mosque on the East African mainland. Children were chatting and playing on the ruins, seemingly oblivious to the history they were trampling on.

It was dark before we reached Tegeta and the retreat centre. Brother drove more slowly on the way back to avoid hitting pedestrians who were walking in the roadway. Kerosene lamps glowed softly from the thatched huts, casting shadows across our path. No one spoke: we were quiet, not wanting to intrude on each others thoughts. In Bagamoyo, we had touched the shadowy face of humanity.

Next day, Bro took us to pay a courtesy call on Cardinal Rugambwa, the first African to be named to the office of Cardinal in the Catholic Church. An African Sister with dark dancing eyes and a welcoming smile met us at the door of the Cardinal's palace and seated us in a large cool living room. In keeping with the practice of African luminaries, he kept us waiting for a rather long time. When, at last, his slender white-robed figure swept into the room, we became instantly aware of the presence of confident grace. Sister served tea and cookies on Japanese china and we engaged in small talk until, at the appropriate moment, he and Bro excused themselves and went into the study to conduct official mission business. Few are privileged to be invited to take tea with the Cardinal and, while we sat waiting for them to return, we found ourselves wondering what we had done to deserve such an honour.

Having taken photos of ourselves with Cardinal Rugambwa, we drove off to the State House where Bro conducted business with one of the government dignitaries. We waited, again for a very long time, in a cluttered office where filing cabinets bulged with yellowed documents and secretaries typed on clacking old Remingtons or sat languidly doing their nails. A huge low-hanging fan wobbled dangerously above the brown cracked-leather sofa where we sat. At one point Dad turned to me and whispered, "If that thing lets go, we'll all be decapitated."

The International Telephone Exchange office in downtown Dar was our next stop. Bro spoke to one of the operators seated at a switchboard behind the counter. The operator nodded, and, as in a scene from a 40's movie, proceeded to work the plugs and wires of the telephone exchange.

We became aware that something very big and worrying was on Bro's mind. While the operator worked to establish contact, he sat beside us and filled us in. "I'm very concerned about Ted Van der Zalm, my young volunteer," he said, wiping sweat from his forehead. "Normally, he'd be here in Tanzania drilling water wells and looking after the windmills. But now, he's half way round the globe. His family raised money and bought an airplane, a Cessna 206, for the mission. He went back to Canada, took flying lessons and is flying it all the way to Tanzania. Thank God, his flying instructor is with him. Can you imagine such a journey? If all has gone well they should have landed in Italy. I'm trying to reach Ted there, as prearranged."

"I have your party on the line," the operator called out and directed Bro into one of the telephone booths. After a few moments, he hung up the receiver and rejoined us. "All's well at this point," he said, decidedly relieved, "but it was a rough trip over the Atlantic. They should be landing in Dodoma in five or six days providing the rest of the flight goes smoothly." Then he added, "This calls for a treat."

Bro drove directly to the Kilmanjaro Hotel, where we ate lunch at the bruncheria on the main level. Mmmm, another taste experience - hot, spicy deep-fried samosas with pork and vegetable fillings!

Well, those were two action-packed days. Again, please share these letters, and, would the last person to read them, put them away for safekeeping? In years to come the grandchildren may find them interesting reading.

Love,

Mom and Dad

****

To our daughter Kelly, son-in-law Don and family:
Dar es Salaam, Tanzania
June 21, 1987

Dear Kelly, Don and kids,

We haven't been taken out to any intriguing places since Brother Tim took us to Bagamoyo. We've been staying here at the guest house trying to get a perspective on the vast scope of the work of the mission.

Yesterday two shipping containers were delivered from the port in Dar es Salaam. One of them was hoisted onto the mission transport truck and driven to Manyoni while the contents of the other (boxes of medicines and medical supplies, clothing, foodstuffs, plumbing supplies, spare parts and stacks of tires) were off-loaded into the warehouse. The mission tries to buy locally, but it's not always possible. Many things are unavailable; others simply too costly. It's Brother Tim's job to receive goods from Canada, the U.S.A. and Italy. He has to deal with the port authorities to release the containers and arrange for them to be brought here. (Each branch of the mission in all three home countries has a "procurator" whose job it is to procure items that are sent to the Procura - which is what the Italians call this section. Simple once you know the terminology.)

The Church is still very much at the centre of life here in Africa, so mission work tends to encompass not only spiritual needs, but also practical and social ones. Life is hard for ordinary folks, and no opportunity is missed to make an event special. Today was one of those days. It's Corpus Christi Sunday (if you've forgotten your Latin that means "Body of Christ") and was chosen as the day the young people of Tegeta and outlying villages were to receive their First Holy Communion.

To accommodate everyone who was expected, Fr. Domenic arranged for the celebrations to be held outside on the wide tree-lined boulevard beside the parish centre where overhanging branches cast dappled shadows on the red earthen path. When we arrived at the site, we saw that most of the chairs were already occupied. But we needn't have worried. Bro reached for my hand and, with Dad striding two paces behind, led me to the front. I admit to feeling some embarrassment at being singled out for this honour, but, like reluctant royalty, I fell in alongside Bro and swept up the aisle, the hem of my long blue caftan lifting and falling with each step. Three places had been reserved for us directly across from the choir where we could hear the nuance of every voice and the intricacies of each rhythmic phrase.

On the white-draped altar, central to the worship service, sat the tabernacle, a miniature roundavel with a beautifully carved tiny ebony door. On either side, bouquets of red, white and mauve bougainvillea provided a blaze of colour. Shafts of light glinted off the golden chalice and cup that rested on the side altar and, beside the golden vessels, two simple grass baskets had been placed to receive the offerings. An African sister in a simple blue and white sari, her hands cupped gently, stood demurely by, ready to assist Father.

The First Communicants, like miniature brides and grooms, made their entrances after everyone was seated. They walked up the aisle two by two: the girls radiant in long white dresses and the boys, trying hopelessly to look angelic, in crisp white shirts that refused to stay tucked in.

Fr. Domenic stood in front of the altar and began the Mass by making the sign of the cross, *Kwa Jina la Baba na la Mwana na la Roho Mtakatifu* (In the Name of the Father, the Son and the Holy Spirit). On cue, the choir director took up his baton and the singers, accompanied by drums, cymbals and shakers, 'opened up' with such exuberance it was as though they intended to "storm the heavens" with their sound. I switched on my small Sony tape recorder and, holding it in my lap, began to record. Although the Mass was in Swahili, it followed the same formula as Catholic Masses all over the world.

The only exception to Swahili happened during the taking of the offering. The choir did not sing at this point. Instead Brother Tim held a tape recorder to the mike, switched it on and played Schubert's *Ave Maria* from the recording that Loverna and I had made. It may have been the first time people had heard a type of music different from their own.

At the conclusion of Mass, Father gave each First Communicant a medal and a rosary. Then, carrying the Blessed Sacrament in the ciborium, he led the procession down the long drive and into the church. The First Communicants, strewing bougainvillea blossoms along the way, were the first to follow. Then the choir, continuing to sing, proceeded, and behind them came the general congregation.

The throng then gathered in the parish hall for a simple meal of rice and beans made special by the addition of a dollop of imported canned tomato soup.

Well, tomorrow we're finally going to leave for Manyoni to have a look at the workshop/training centre. But, it seems, we'll not be going there directly. Bro has promised us yet again another diversion - a stopover in Mikumi Game Park. We're absolutely thrilled with the idea!

We'll write again once we're upcountry. Keep sharing these letters and remember to keep us in your prayers.

Love,

Mom and Dad

PS: The recording of the choir turned out well. You can hear it when we get home, so be ready for a cultural treat.

****

To our daughter Kim, son-in-law Blair and family:
Mikumi Wildlife Lodge,
Tanzania
June 22, 1987

Dear Kim, Blair and David,

I'm writing this from our room at Mikumi Wildlife Lodge as the sun sets over the hippo pool. Here in the tropics there is no dusk; the sun simply goes down. In fact, one can see it descending; at one moment it's hovering, like a fiery red ball, above the rim of the earth, then, touching the horizon, it spreads a rosy glow onto the clouds, and is gone. Darkness comes quickly unless the moon is shedding its reflected light. There's a full moon tonight, so we can see the silhouettes of the flat-topped acacias across the park. A pair of elephants was sparring in front of the hippo pool just before sunset, and we can still hear them grunting and crashing among the branches. This is a magical place.

We left the mission station in a brand new Peugeot 4x4 after the morning's routine, with Fr. Domenic at the wheel. I don't know if the sideswipe of our vehicle just five minutes out of the village of Tegeta bodes ill; we sincerely hope not! We had left the village and were awaiting our turn at the beginning of the detour around a big washout when an approaching dump truck crowded into our lane, crushing the Peugeot's right outside mirror. There was much shouting and waving of arms as Fr. Domenic and the bleary-eyed truck driver exchanged names, license numbers, etc. What a volatile mix; Africans and Italians embroiled in a conflict! Although no lasting harm was done, it took some time before Father ran out of steam. "Probably on *bangi,*" he fumed. "They smoke a lot of that."

Veering west toward Morogoro, we passed through the coastal area lush with tropical vegetation.

Colourfully dressed women and girls walked on both sides of the highway. Some were wearing *kangas* designed with a large circle motif on the back centred directly over their ample backsides. Every step emphasized the motif. This was not a problem for wearers of *kangas* printed with an African symbol, such as an animal or a flower, but it may have been something of an embarrassment (if they were to think of it) for those wrapped in *kangas* bearing the likeness of the president's face whose eyes seemed to wink in rhythm with their swaying buttocks.

Many women carried babies on their backs, their tiny bottoms snuggled round with slings fashioned from *kangas*. Others balanced baskets and bundles on their heads while toddlers trotted alongside, grasping a free hand or the hem of a *kanga*.

Young boys herding goats and cattle along the roadsides stopped now and again to let them munch on fresh grass and rotting fruit and vegetable peelings. Outside the thatched and corrugated iron-roofed huts, the hard-packed earth had been swept clean to clear off debris that snakes might hide in. Small children were being bathed in plastic basins, and females of all ages sat on the ground, legs straight out in front, giggling and braiding each other's hair.

It's said that in these countries more deaths are caused by traffic accidents than by disease. This is easy to believe. The vehicles are often in poor mechanical repair; brakes are defective and tires are bald. Many trucks coming toward us were "dog tracking". (That is to say, the axles were improperly aligned, causing this peculiar crablike movement.) The buses were the worst, loaded to the hilt, every seat seeming to be taken twice. Other passengers were packed in the aisles or hanging from the doorways. Bags, bundles and baskets of chickens were loaded on the roof until it could hold no more. (Then, and only then, it seemed, would the driver move off.)

The cabs of many of the trucks and buses were festooned with tinsel garlands that swayed as the vehicles hurtled along. Some sported catchy phrases on their bumpers. One had *Mungu atakuja*, which means, "The Lord is Coming", painted on the grill. Is that prophetic or what? Who knows if the vehicles and drivers were properly registered and licensed, or was some corrupt official was bribed to give his imprimatur on the whole procedure? Many were broken down by the side of the road; the driver camped nearby, keeping watch until spare parts could be found and the vehicle repaired.

Our first stop was at a phenomenal market in the village of Chalinze. We walked along absorbed by the smells and sights of tropical fruits piled in pyramids: oranges, tomatoes, papaya, mangoes, tangerines and pineapples, and next to them, gunny sacks of potatoes, rice, red onions, sweet potatoes, corn and long reddish carrots; all grown in abundance in this region of fertile soil. The handcarts, baskets and empty paraffin tins used to bring the fruit and vegetables to market rested under the stalls.

Youths in tattered shirts and shorts weaved among the stalls selling *samosas*, *mandazi* (doughnuts) and hard-boiled eggs from trays that they carried aloft on hands, wrists bent, like waiters in a fancy restaurant. Yellow mongrels with tightly curled tails trotted alongside them, sniffing and snarling over fallen morsels.

Fr. Domenic bought peanuts from a little boy who was scooping handfuls of them into homemade newspaper cones.

As we left the coastal area it became cooler and the countryside changed. The tropical fruit trees and palms were gone, replaced by enormous baobab trees that stood in the midst of sisal, millet and sunflower fields. To our left a series of clapboard buildings marked a prison farm. (In Tanzania, prisoners raise all their own food and have become some of the best farmers in the country.)

In the distance we could see the ragged Uluguru Mountains, the lower slopes covered by miombo woodlands where mahogany, ebony and mninga trees grow. Beneath this picturesque setting the town of Morogoro sits; the dome of a mosque dominating the city square. Father Dominic told us that the religious population is roughly divided into thirds: one-third Muslim, one-third Christian and one-third Hindus, Sikhs, animists and others.

"By and large," he said, "there is respect for religious differences. A few radical Muslims have tried to lobby for a Muslim state, but this has been met with stiff resistance by moderates. As one of my Muslim friends said to me, 'There is no way we're going to let those radicals disturb our peace!' In fact, the government is constructed so if the president is Christian, the prime minister will be Muslim, or the other way around. Usually the Muslim is from Zanzibar, which is heavily Arabic, while the Christian leader will be from mainland Tanzania."

Fr. Domenic stopped to gas up the vehicle while we took advantage of the 'toilet facilities'. This was my first experience with an Asian toilet - a hole in the floor. A bucket of water and dipper had been provided in lieu of toilet paper and for hand washing.

We left the main road there and turned south toward Mukumi. Sorghum and cotton fields predominated the area until we reached the outskirts of a 47,000-square-mile tract of wilderness bounded on three sides by hills and mountains and lush with high grasses and flat-topped acacia trees. Ahead, a prairie fire was sending great billows of smoke across the roadway. As we drew nearer, we saw that the flames were climbing up the ditch and threatening to cross the road. Fr. Domenic did not even slow down. Flinging the vehicle headlong into the smoke and flames, he drove on the wrong side of the road to get away from the encroaching firestorm. Visibility was nil! For a few seconds we were obscured by the dense smoke and in real danger of colliding with another vehicle. Bro shouted repeatedly in Italian for Father to move over. All I could think of was, thank God, that we had made our wills before leaving home so you kids wouldn't be faced with decisions in the event of our demise. (Funny what comes into one's mind at a time like this.) God was with us. As you see, we emerged unscathed, from good luck rather than good sense.

Soon we entered Mikumi Wildlife Park where herds of Grant's gazelles, zebras and wildebeests were grazing. Elephant moms, their babies almost hidden in the tall grass, munched their way along like live lawnmowers. Wrapping their trunks around bunches of vegetation they pulled them up and stuffed them, dirt and all, into their mouths.

The lodge sits near the entrance to the park. Like many others, once privately owned, this one has been taken over by the Tanzanian government. Lacking currency and know-how, it's been allowed it to fall into disrepair.

We gained access to our rooms from an outside un-swept corridor. Gigantic spiders and their prey, an assortment of flies, lodged in giant webs in almost every corner along the walkway. Monstrous cockroaches scurried into hiding as we approached. Although the rooms are well situated to look out over the park, they are sorely in need of a good scrubbing or a fresh coat of paint. Threadbare sheets covered the twin beds that stood side by side against a grungy wall where dried blood smears and squished mosquitoes reminded us to take our anti-malarial medication. On the nightstand was a mosquito coil, a packet of matches and a can of insecticide spray. No mini bar here!

We stopped just long enough to splash water over our dusty faces before we were off on a pre-dinner game drive. Observing animals in their native habitat is surely one of the most thrilling things in the world, and I felt I could watch them forever. However, as the light began to fade, we reluctantly returned to the lodge and settled ourselves in the lounge, where we enjoyed a Safari beer and an unexpected last glimpse of Mikumi's wonders.

A superb starling in metallic green and blue plumage lighted on a branch of whistling thorn just outside our window. A giraffe stretched her long neck to nibble on leaves from the highest branches of an acacia tree while two warthogs scurried by. What could be more perfect?

It will soon be time to go to dinner. I think it will be charming and so colonial! We saw the stooped and greying waiters moving about in the dining room in their shiny well-worn uniforms with frayed cuffs. Bro says he thinks they're serving warthog tonight.

We expect to reach Manyoni tomorrow. Then we'll see how the "other half" lives. Good night and God bless everyone.

Keep praying for us, eh?

Love,

Mom and Dad

****

To our daughter Kelly, son-in-law Don and family:
Manyoni, Tanzania (Part 1)
June 23, 1987

Dear Kelly, Don, Vanessa, Dyana and Nicholas,

Anticipation for the day's adventures woke us long before dawn. We showered, using up the last of the tepid water in the solar tanks, dressed and stepped out into the corridor of Mikumi Lodge for the walk to the dining room. Father Domenic and Bro were a few steps ahead of us. We were all anxious to get an early start on our final day's drive upcountry. Our breakfast menu, a holdover from British Colonial times, consisted of eggs, baked beans, bitter marmalade and toast served cold and unbuttered from a battered silver toast rack.

The cool of the early morning is absolutely the best time for game viewing and our drive through the park was glorious. Huge herds of wildebeest and their zebra companions lined the roadsides. A few of the flightier zebras, startled by the approach of our vehicle, whirled around and prepared to take flight. Turning their fat butts toward us, they looked back over their shoulders and warily watched our movements. Two warthogs were fighting and squealing in the ditch and some of the younger gazelles, both Grant's and Thomson's gave "pronking" demonstrations. ("Pronking comes from the Africaans word, "pronk" meaning "to show off".) It's an amazing thing to see how they can leap so high and so far forward with each bound. With gracefully arched backs and all four legs held stiffly, they vaulted into the air, touched back down to the ground and sprang back up again. They repeated this performance several times; bounding as though each tiny hoof were on a coiled spring. It was terrific fun. We parked for a while and sat quietly watching these wonders of nature. There in the stillness, insects and birds hidden in the long elephant grass whirred and warbled in chorus. And overall was the ubiquitous song of Africa: the coo-coo-coo of laughing doves.

We had a long journey ahead of us, so our respite was brief. But, moments later, we stopped yet again to take pleasure in an even more magnificent sight. A pride of 16 lions, faces still bloodied from having gorged on their kill of the early morning were lying bloated by the roadside. A wildebeest carcass lay beside them, stripped to the bone; a rack of ribs was the only thing left. Vultures perching on nearby thorn trees cocked their heads and, fixing their penetrating eyes on the prize, waited patiently for the lions to leave before moving in to peck off any remaining shreds of flesh.

We'd travelled only a few kilometres beyond the unfenced boundary of the park before we again encountered human activity. Women and children were standing by the roadside selling basketry that hung from the branches of scrawny thorn trees. Father Domenic stopped the car and we got out to admire the handiwork of intricately woven dyed grasses. Fr. Domenic told us that all the pigments had been obtained by boiling down natural vegetable matter, except for the purple; for this, they made use of potassium permanganate, an antiseptic found in the village clinics.

At Morogoro we swung west toward Dodoma onto what is, by far, the best road in Tanzania. A gift of the Brazilians, it had been recently upgraded and paved. Father could really try out the new Peugeot now. He sped along like a silver bullet in true Italian fashion scattering chickens that half ran, half flew, squawking into the bushes. Pedestrians walking on both sides of the road leapt from the pavement into the safety of the ditches. We were terrified, as other vehicles were approaching us in like manner, and were relieved when the road worsened and he had to slow down.

The blue-green Uluguru Mountains were now behind us and ahead, to our right, was the low silhouette of the Nguru range, darkly ragged against the sky. At the village of Magole an attendant sat at a toll booth inside the shelter of a triangular canvas tent. While Father paid the 20-shilling toll, we watched the village scene. The huts here, like many on the coast, are made of sticks and mud or adobe brick. Some of the roofs are thatched; others are of *mabati* (corrugated iron sheets) or rusting paraffin tins hammered flat and held down with heavy rocks and old tires. Huge termite hills, some at least 12 feet tall, stood up everywhere. Hollow and conical in shape, they ventilate and enrich the soil. We peeked into one of the smaller ones to watch the bodies of the transparent termites at work and felt the heat radiating up from the red earth. Deep down, hidden from view, lay the queen like a fat yellow slug, popping out baby termites at a formidable rate.

A row of burlap bags stuffed with charcoal stood at the curb ready to be picked up and carted to the cities. A charcoal-making facility was at work and, from that site, men in ragged clothing blackened by soot were bringing more bags and setting them down alongside the others. As they trotted along, each carrier balanced two bags of charcoal, one on each side of a flexible pole that was slung across their shoulders as a yoke. With shoulders sagging and knees bent, their bodies formed curious "S" shapes as their heavy bags bounced up and down in pliant rhythm with each step.

Father Dominic informed us that the traditional method of making charcoal is still being used whereby wood is put into an earthen pit, lighted and then covered with dirt. The combustion of part of the wood produces enough heat to carbonize the rest which becomes charcoal.

Women walking with their burdens are ever-present in Africa. Here in rural areas with no plumbing, water must be fetched from water holes, from who knows how far away. Yet hardly a drop is spilled from the tin vessels or the gourds they carry on their heads. The women don't bend under their burdens as the charcoal carriers do, but walk erect and stately on the well-worn paths.

Further on, the soil deepened to dark red. Women and children were selling sweet potatoes that were piled high into *debes* (square tin containers that hold about four gallons of liquid measure). The plains here are broken by grassy rolling hills dotted with acacia trees. It seemed one could see forever from this lovely spot. I wanted to stay longer but lack of time dictated that we to carry on.

Only a few kilometres along we abruptly "fell off" the end of the pavement into a giant bowl of grey dust. We were approaching Dodoma - officially the capital of Tanzania. Bro told us that, in order to relocate government services to the geographic centre, all government offices are expected to move here from Dar es Salaam once the infrastructure is in place. But, he doesn't think this is likely to happen soon. There is an incredible water shortage here. Huge ditches have been dug around the town to transport water that is expected to be piped in from distant mountains. There is tremendous resistance from the government personnel in Dar, who understandably are reluctant to leave the beaches and amenities of the coast for this desolate spot. Except for some well-constructed upscale homes occupied by professionals and merchants, the houses here are no different from those in the villages.

We had some difficulty passing through the dusty narrow streets that were partially blocked by rubble from building projects. (Whether the buildings were going up or coming down was hard to tell.)

Goods being sold in the Asian *dukas* spilled out onto the narrow sidewalks. Cheap Chinese-made tools and building supplies vied for space with galvanized pails and brightly coloured polyethylene tubs.

Barefoot mechanics plied their trade at the side of the road carrying out complicated procedures such as engine and transmission replacements on the spot. Vehicles were simply tipped on their sides at a 45-degree angle and leaned against a bulwark of old tires to expose the undercarriages. No hoists? No grease pit? No problem! There are no workers' compensation regulations here.

Father Domenic aimed our vehicle toward the site of a slowly turning windmill. The first of many in this region, it was erected by C.PP.S. mission (our group). This one pumps water for the Italian Misericordia Sisters, who live and work in this spot. The Sisters served us lunch in the cool dining room of the convent where we met Father Ernesto, another of the priests with our mission. (Dad refers to him privately as Father Sad Sack because he's so earnest and intense.) He was transporting the ambulance from Dar es Salaam to the hospital mission in Itigi, west of Manyoni.

We said goodbye to Father Domenic, who was returning to Dar es Salaam. "I'll get up to Manyoni to see you before you leave," he said. "You'll need some support in revitalizing the workshop. In the meantime, take it easy." Then, turning the Peugeot around in a cloud of dust, he was gone.

Bro seemed preoccupied. Looking westward toward Manyoni, he mused as if to himself, "Brother Luis and Ana left the mission early this morning to pick us up. Maybe they've had car trouble or were forced into the ditch." Then turning to Father Ernesto, he said, "It's providential you're still here. If you're carrying on to Manyoni today, I think we might need your backup." Father agreed to wait and drive in tandem with us.

While waiting for Brother Luis and Ana, we walked with Bro in the Sisters' orchard and talked about the mission work and personnel. "Ana," he said, "was one of the kids among the group of young people in Toronto who helped raise funds, pack containers and promote the mission in general. Every year, for several years, I've been bringing a group to see the work for themselves. Ana was one of the first to come. After she finished her nursing degree and midwifery training she begged to return to Africa. She was born in Kenya, and I think Africa has stayed in her blood. The Canadian side of the mission agreed to set up a maternity clinic at the remote village of Chibumagwa in the Great Rift Valley, about a 45-minute drive from Manyoni. Ana has been there for a year, organizing the clinic. She's staying with some of our Italian Sisters."

Then, after pausing to pick an orange, he continued, "And, I've told you about Ted Van der Zalm, who's also been in Manyoni for a year. I've put him in charge of the water project. I tell you, if I had half a dozen like him, I could revitalize the whole economy of Tanzania. As you know, he's flying the mission plane over. I expect he'll be arriving soon."

"And, who," I asked, "Is Brother Luis?"

"Luis works with me in Toronto," Bro explained. "He's here for the summer to help out."

As we strolled back to the Sisters' house, a white Toyota Hilux double-cab pickup rolled into the yard, and Ana and Brother Luis stepped out. Luis unfolded his long slender frame from behind the wheel with a look of consternation on his youthful face.

"We were forced off the road, the pickup stalled, and I couldn't get it going again," Luis rushed to explain even before introductions could be made. "We waited for a long time before somebody came by to give us a boost."

Ana looked equally miffed. "The Toyota just came out of the workshop," she said with a toss of her short, dark hair. "It was supposed to be roadworthy." She turned to Dad, "You'll soon see how badly you're needed in that workshop."

Dad and Father Ernesto cleaned and tightened the battery cables; it was the best that could be done at this time and place, and we regrouped for the final leg of the journey. Before tossing our cases into the back of the pickup, Bro stuffed them into black plastic garbage bags and threw a tarp over them. "Even with this," he said, "you'll be lucky if your belongings aren't covered in red powdery dust by the time we get to Manyoni."

The Toyota refused to start, so Dad got behind the wheel while the rest of us pushed until the engine coughed into life with a plume of black diesel smoke. "Keep it revved up," Dad shouted to Luis as he moved over, making way for him to take the wheel. Ana and I climbed into the crew cab and we were off on a bone-jarring, neck-wrenching ride. The short wheel base of the Toyota added to the rough ride on a road that is unbelievably bad. Huge rocks projected from the sandy soil and giant potholes left from last season's rains threatened to throw us into the ditch.

Passing out of the Great Rift Valley, conditions worsened. The narrow, winding road became little more than a trail as we ascended the tortuous hills. Smoke from brush fires burning in the distance created cover for the setting sun, turning it into a bright red orb. Visibility was very poor. Once the sun had set, it was hard to see the boulders that lay haphazardly on the road.

Ana explained how they came to be there, "Truckers who stall on the hills place rocks behind the wheels of their rigs to prevent them from rolling back. Then, when they are able to continue, they simply drive off, leaving the obstacles where they are." Luis was very quiet as he fought to keep the vehicle on the road. As we drove, we got to know Ana a bit. She promised to stay in Manyoni for a few days to help us get oriented and through her answers to our questions we learned more about local customs and who's who in mission work.

Suddenly, we were stunned into silence by the scene of a fast-approaching lorry in the middle of the road, its headlights blazing. Luis jerked the pickup as far as he could to the left to avoid a collision and bogged down in the deep reddish sand. The engine stalled, and Luis could not get it going again. Everyone piled out of their vehicles, including Bro and Father Ernesto, who had pulled up directly behind us in the ambulance. "I told you it's like driving on ice," Bro said crossly. Luis looked chastised. As a "city boy," he'd had no experience with such things.

Dad got behind the wheel again to show Luis how to "push start" the Toyota by manipulating the clutch and throttle expeditiously while the rest of us pushed. It fired and we were off, this time with Ana's short chubby frame behind the wheel.

I wish I could tell you that that was the end of the car trouble but, in fact, we were forced off the road yet again by a dog-tracking lorry on the crest of a hill. Facing uphill as we were, our pickup refused to start no matter how hard we pushed. We simply could not muster enough momentum to get it in motion, so there we sat, kicking the red sand out of our shoes until a kindly Asian trucker came by and gave us a tow. And that is how we entered the mission of Manyoni, "kicking and screaming" on the end of a chain.

Through the gloom of night we were dimly aware of the outlines of buildings and huge mango trees of the town. The homes and streets were in darkness, but on the other side of town, on the outskirts, the lights of the mission glowed faintly.

It was almost 10:00 p.m. when we arrived at the main mission building, unloaded our cases and walked through the gate along the concrete walk to the dining area. A huge square table large enough for 12 sat in the centre, at which six place settings were laid. Francis, the cook, bustled from the kitchen, carrying covered platters of food, his white teeth shining in his ebony face. "*Karibu, karibu*, welcome, welcome," he called and motioned for us to take our places on the benches. Then the parish priest, Father Tonino, rushed in. "What kept you?" he asked, nervously puffing on a cigarette. The Italian speakers lapsed into their native tongue in an animated discussion of our mishaps while the platters were passed around and we each took our share of pasta, potatoes and fried chicken.

Fatigue came quickly after dinner. Bro gave us each a flashlight and showed us to our single rooms side by side in the corridor adjacent to the entrance. "The power plant will be shut down soon, so you'll need these lights," he said. Then, wishing us good night, he left for his own room further up the aisle.

Our cases had been taken out of their protective plastic bags and were standing in the corridor. In spite of the protection, red dust had settled into the seam ridges of the blue Samsonite. Dad and I said good night and, picking up our cases, went into our respective rooms. Once in my spartan quarters, I fished out my toiletries and nightgown and made my way to the washroom. A quick wash and brush-up was all that could be done. No relaxing hot bath or refreshing shower today.

I flaked out from sheer exhaustion, and I guess Dad did the same, because neither of us remembered the power plant shutting down.

Well, I'm going to take a break now, since I've run out of space on this air-letter. It's enough for one letter, anyway. I'll continue this saga later.

Love you guys.

Keep praying for us, and God Bless.

Mom and Dad

****

To our daughter Kelly, son-in-law Don and family:
Manyoni, Tanzania (Part 2)
June 24, 1987

Dear Kelly, Don and family,

I could hear Brother Luis before he arrived at my room. Starting at the end of the corridor, he moved along giving three sharp raps on each door while calling out, "six o'clock, six o'clock, six o'clock!" It was almost dawn; time to get up for the monastic routine of early morning Mass.

Still groggy, I threw back the plain grey blanket and swung my feet onto the bare cement floor. The coldness of it surprised me and jarred me awake sufficiently to pull on my robe, grab my toothbrush and head to the washroom.

Dad has always had an abhorrence to getting up before sunrise, so I sympathized with him as he emerged bleary-eyed from his room and stumbled down the corridor rubbing his stubbly chin and mumbling something about "not wanting to live this monkish lifestyle" - probably in reference to the early rising and the loneliness of his bed last night.

Returning to my room, I raked a comb through my dust-encrusted hair, donned a long skirt and blouse and looked around me. The only decorations in the grey, monastic cell were pictures of Pope John Paul II and St. Gaspar, the mission's founder. I flashed my torch around and spotted a blood-engorged mosquito half hidden by the curtain. Suddenly, I realized I had forgotten to take my anti-malarial medication the previous night. In a panic, I fumbled through my bag, found my Paludrin tablets and took them with a swig of water from the recycled whiskey bottle on the windowsill.

Dad and I walked out together through the courtyard lined with palms and red hibiscus where Bro, Luis and Fr. Tonino were waiting for us. It was still dark and cold when we arrived at the modern Swiss-built church in downtown Manyoni. Fr. Tonino pulled on his surplice and alb and said Mass for the faithful who had braved the early morning gloom. The young African women who are postulants (Sisters in training) sang the Mass parts beautifully. By the time Mass was over, dawn had broken and we returned to the mission house for breakfast. In the daylight, I could see that the dining room walls were decorated with batiks featuring images of cutout dolls holding hands encircling stylized windmills featuring the motto of the Water Project, "Helping People Help Themselves". Tiny geckos scooted along the walls in search of mosquitoes. Sometimes they slipped their transparent bodies beneath the batiks and sometimes they hunted out in the open, darting out their little sticky tongues at potential prey.

After breakfast Bro took us for a walk in the mission yard. At the back of the main house, a neat row of 40-foot steel shipping containers stand under a shade canopy of tin. Goods imported from Canada, Italy and the U.S.A. had arrived in them and once the products were unpacked and sorted, the containers were kept and put to use for the storage of spare parts, food stuffs, used clothing and medical supplies for the dispensaries. Each one is numbered and securely padlocked.

In a corner of the back yard, among mounds of chipped rock, women were sitting straight-legged on the ground. Their *kangas* were hiked up around their thighs, and between their knees each held a melon-sized boulder that she vigorously attacked with a chipping hammer. This was the rock crushing crew preparing gravel for new construction projects.

A border of eucalyptus trees marks the periphery of the mission yard and beyond that, toward the town, leafy, beautifully-rounded mango trees identify this place as one of historical significance.

Bro gave us a brief history of the area. "Manyoni," he said, "is along the former slave route and the presence of the mango groves indicates that this was a place of encampment where mangoes were eaten by the traders and fed to their consignments of human chattels."

As Bro spoke, my mind's eye conjured up images of caravans camped here. I could visualize the Arab traders, heads swathed in burnooses, squatting and chatting around open fires. A hunting party, I imagined, had successfully brought down an antelope that was being roasted over glowing coals and, somewhat apart from the cooking, I envisaged the head traders conferring, tallying up their potential gains and losses. Many more miles of trekking lay ahead to Bagamoyo and not all of the slaves would be expected to survive the journey.

At a distance, away from the warming fires, I pictured the naked captives huddled together. I wondered if they were still yoked and shackled at this point, or had they been given relief from the chafing bonds while they ate their mangoes and tossed the pits onto the ground?

And what of the African accomplices, who, for pay, willingly rounded up their fellow countrymen and were now supervising their transport. Did any have the grace to feel ashamed?

Early adventurers had also followed this route and I wondered if perhaps Dr. David Livingstone, on his medical mission to the interior, had himself camped on this very spot.

My mind was drawn back to the reality of the moment as we walked through the mission *shamba* (garden) where bananas, oranges, lemons, pompelmo, tomatoes, avocados and eggplant formed a colourful mosaic of yellow, red, orange and purple edibles against a background of green foliage and white blossoms.

At the end of the *shamba*, lay the barnyard where staff was attending the livestock. Pungent smells coming from piles of steaming manure overpowered and obliterated the fresh fragrance of the garden. Huge pigs snuffled at the trough, which the farm workers were filling with *pumba,* the ground husks of maize plants. In another part of the barn were the cows. A cross between Swiss Brown and native African cattle, they'd been specially bred to produce large quantities of milk and beef and yet be resistant to debilitating tropical diseases. The milking had already been done and the cows were munching contentedly on their share of *pumba.*

A huge *kopje* (a jumble of enormous boulders) rising several hundred feet to its apex stands just beyond the barnyard. This collection of rocks consists of a central, mammoth thumb-shaped rock surrounded by other rocks of lesser dimensions. Scrub bushes grow in the deep crevasses between the rocks. Hazarding a guess as to the circumference, I would say that it probably occupies the space of a soccer field. Atop the largest rock is a gigantic cross, a symbol of peace and unity. From its four points, solar lights radiate into the darkness highlighting the shape of the cross announcing the presence of our Lord in East Africa.

The tour was over as Bro looked at his watch and announced, “Time for an espresso.” We turned then and strolled away from the farm, out through the mission’s main gate and down the driveway toward the Sisters’ complex.

There are five Italian Sisters here, and a few Tanzanian postulants. Sweet elderly Sister Angelina, the Sisters’ cook, immediately dropped what she was doing, hugged us all in Italian fashion and put on a pot of espresso. Sitting at the round table draped in a soft white cloth, we drank espresso and nibbled on homemade biscotti. Sister Angelina speaks no English, but through Bro’s translation we learned about the Sisters’ work in Tanzania. We enjoyed their bright and sunny home. There is definitely a woman’s touch here which can be seen in the choice of the bright curtains, paintings and batiks. The floors are of gleaming terrazzo, unlike the painted concrete in the Fathers’ house, and the furnishings are much more comfortable.

The Sisters run a clinic and dispensary in this location and provide an outreach service to neighbouring villages. In addition to the health services, they run a home craft school. About 15 Tanzanian girls attend classes in basic Math, Swahili and English, as well as learning practical homemaking skills such as cooking, sewing and knitting.

There is a rocky outcropping behind the Sisters’ property also, but it’s not nearly as imposing as the one behind the main mission house. Beneath this smaller jumble of rocks the Sisters and their Tanzanian students raise rabbits and chickens and grow cassava and maize. So, you see, between the two missions, almost all basic foodstuffs are provided.

All this was very interesting, but I was anxious to see the house we’d be expected to live in and asked Bro when we could see it.

“Ana is coming soon and will take you there,” Bro said.

Moments later, Ana announced her arrival by calling out *hodi* at the door and Sister Angelina responded with *karibu*, the customary welcome.

(A person calls *hodi* when arriving at a Tanzanian house, rather than knocking at the door. Etiquette demands that one calls no more than five times. If the host does not wish to admit you, you must politely go away. This practice comes from the fact that some homes don't have doors to knock on. A piece of tattered gunny sacking is often the only doorway covering.)

"Ana will show you to your house now," said Bro. We finished our coffee and left with Ana, retracing our steps back toward the mission. We passed through the main gate and stopped directly in front of the red stucco, tin-roofed bungalow immediately on our right. "This is really a duplex; your quarters are on this side," Ana said. "The other side is occupied by Tanzanian seminarians."

My hopes for quarters as bright and sunny as the Sisters' were immediately dashed. I was devastated!

It's almost windowless. Luis had tried to make it cheery by painting the cement walls in three of the four rooms. However, colour choices were limited to whatever he could find in the storage container. He painted one room purple, another bright blue, yet another emerald green. The furnishings in the green room are a handmade desk, one straight-back chair, two low handmade stools, and a brown peeling leather easy chair with broken springs. In the bedroom there are two cots and a wardrobe. Single 40-watt light bulbs hang from the centre of each room, uniquely anchored at the ceiling by a half coconut shell through which the wire is passed. The only one muted by a shade is the one in the bedroom where light passing through the patterned cut-out design cast eerie shadows against the purple walls. There is nothing but lower cabinets and a sink in the blue room that is to serve as the kitchen, and in the bathroom no water comes from the pipes leading to the toilet, shower and rusting sink.

Ana explained what will be expected of us in this regard, "There's a pump at the cistern around the back where you can get water for hand washing and toilet flushing. You'll have to shower at the Fathers' and, of course, you'll take all your meals with them, at least until Bro can get the kitchen outfitted."

Ana left us then, and we sat dumbly on the thin, lumpy mattresses. I know I'm more disappointed with this accommodation than Dad is. He will have many more pressing things to engage his interests, but for me, making a comfortable home is paramount.

"Well, let's do something," Dad said at length, so we took the folded sheets from the desktop and proceeded quietly to make up the beds.

"You know," I said finally, "there is no way I can spend three years in this place."

We'll see what transpires during the next three weeks we'll be here. I will definitely need assurance of better accommodation before I would agree to return.

I'm really quite exhausted relating this, so please keep us in your prayers. While I feel drawn to be involved in some type of mission, I realize I'm no Mother Theresa.

God Bless.

Love,

Mom and Dad

****

To our son Mark, and daughter-in-law Christian:
Manyoni, Tanzania
June 28, 1987

Dear Mark and Chris,

Although we've been here in Africa only two weeks, we've already sampled its exotic charms along with its maddening frustrations.

To be fair, the frustrations are not so much Africa's doing, but stem from the curious blend of the three cultures — Italian, Tanzanian and North American — which make up the mission personnel. We'd heard of "culture shock" before, but had no idea how it might affect a person and now; here we are, caught in its grip.

We spent the last four nights in our quarters, which we're already referring to as "the bunker" because of its depressing gloom. We've been trying to rise at 6:00 a.m. to join the other mission folk for morning Mass. It's so cold and dark at that hour. Bro gave us a kerosene lamp to use during the dark hours when the generator is not working, but because we're not yet familiar with our surroundings, it's even hard to locate the lamp. Amidst our fumbling around this morning, Dad gave his elbow a vicious crack on the headboard, which sure didn't put him in a prayerful mood. We also forgot to fill our water bucket from the cistern pump last night, so had no chance to wash or brush our teeth before Mass. (I'm not sure if we can be flexible enough to adapt to the realities of this situation.)

A few days ago we toured the workshop areas and training centre located beneath the smaller rocky outcropping by the Sisters' station. Close to the workshop gates, at the end of the sandy road, a cluster of women, partly obscured by billows of blue smoke, squatted around cooking fires preparing tea for the workers' midmorning break. Jonas, the gate keeper, crippled by polio, crawled toward us on his calloused knees. With a broad smile and friendly greeting, "*karibu*", he unlatched the gate. It swung open and we walked through. Every pair of dark eyes was on us as we sauntered along with feigned nonchalance through the various areas. This is the sector Dad will be expected to manage, so his eyes and ears were wide open to the operations going on.

Under a huge acacia tree to the left of the small gatekeeper's shelter sits the corn grinder, another service the mission provides. Folks bring maize from their *shambas* and for a token fee it is ground into flour, ready to prepare *ugali,* a porridge that is the staple diet in these parts. Bringing the maize is a task largely done by women and children. As we watched, a girl of perhaps ten struggled toward the grinding site, carrying her little brother on her back. Two other siblings were clutching at her *kanga* and, on her head, she carried a large basket of maize. "Truly amazing," Dad quipped.

We followed the sound of the whining and ripping of saws to the carpentry area where we were surprised to see tried and true techniques from a hundred years ago being used alongside 20th

century technology. In one section two sawyers were wielding a whip saw with astonishing precision. One sawyer stood in a deep pit and another on the squared log above that had been laid along the length of the pit. Between them, they manipulated the saw up and down in rhythm, slicing the log into neat even boards. Both were shirtless and glistening with sweat and every stroke of the saw set the muscles in their coal-black arms and shoulders to rippling. We couldn't see what footwear, if any, the one in the pit was wearing, but the one on the log was shoeless; his bare toes exposed to within inches of the movement of the saw. In another zone, on a long open-fronted cement building roofed with tin, we could see carpenters operating power thickness planers and table saws among piles of lumber and sweet smelling mounds of shavings and sawdust. Dad was stunned to see all this activity going on without the benefit of eye, ear or limb protection.

We moved on to the mechanics area next where the offices and workshop are built around an oil-sodden unpaved quad. Confusion was everywhere. Dozens of men were milling around. Several were in the grease pit under a vehicle, others were bent over an open hood, but many appeared to have no job at all and stood visiting in groups in the centre of the quad. Rusting chassis, axles, engine parts with wires hanging out and bald tires were dumped into one of the work spaces. An old tractor sat waiting for parts; we were told it had been there for eight months.

The classroom space is merely a tin-roofed shed open to the elements. It's located at the back of the shops beside the power generator that was running at full throttle. All conversation was blotted out by the din and vibrations that rattled the roof and set the rows of desks dancing about on the cement floor. It will be impossible to teach here under these conditions.

Back in the quad, large numbers of men were swarming about near the "Workers' Store". Small incidentals are sold there, presumably for the convenience of the workers. Dad is not terribly happy with it being located in the workshop, where it most certainly is interfering with the work at hand.

"That'll be the first thing to be moved if I'm in charge," he growled. "Clearly all those folks hanging around are not mission workers. Something else is at play here."

There are scarcely any hand tools in the tool room, and those that are there are not tagged or organized in any way. Dad picked up a chisel and felt its edge. "This thing has been abused," he said tersely. Then, moving on, he examined the machinist cutting tools that had been tossed haphazardly into a box. "This is no way to treat precision tools," he snapped.

As we walked out, I asked him if he thought things could be turned around and made efficient. "It would be a challenge, but, if I get the support of the Fathers, I think it could be done."

We've spent some time alone in "the bunker," trying to digest the happenings of the last few days. Dad seems to be rising to the challenge of reorganizing the workshop and training centre, but I'm still focused on how to broach the subject of the unsuitability of this accommodation.

Apart from the gloom of the place is the problem of its location. Because it's right at the mission gate, we are constantly disturbed by vehicle and pedestrian traffic passing within 30 feet of our door. Yesterday, being Saturday, was especially onerous. That's the day of the week set aside for the "*pumba* for clothing swap" when villagers bring gunny sacks of *pumba* (corn husks) for the mission livestock and, in exchange, receive bundles of used clothing. It was only 4:30 a.m. when we were awakened by the steady murmur of first arrivals who came and squatted right outside our bedroom window. From there the lineup extended all the way back to the Sisters' quarters. The exchange doesn't begin for hours, but I suppose this is taken as an occasion to catch up on the latest gossip.

A voluptuous gate girl with wonderfully large "come hither" eyes has taken to stationing her buxom body on our front steps. She's often surrounded by giggling Lotharios, who take obvious delight in watching the fluid movements of her large hips whenever she rises to open or close the gate. Sometimes she sings in her high shrill voice as she moves languidly about, reminding me of "Prissy" in "Gone with the Wind."

Every day a tormented lady, her face contorted with anger, comes and stands shouting at the acacia tree that grows outside our window. We never know what time she will come, but she has never failed to show up. The shouting continues for 30 or 40 minutes, then, spent by the effort, she quietly leaves. Cerebral malaria has left the wretched soul demented. Those who understand what she says believe she is under the illusion that her dead husband has been reincarnated into the tree. If it's true, the poor man is not going to get any rest, at least not as long as she keeps scolding him so mercilessly every day.

Ted Van der Zalm and his navigator, Malcolm Murray, arrived yesterday evening, having flown the mission plane all the way from Ontario. It was, according to Ted, a horrendous trip. Some days, he said, they flew as long as 12 hours at a stretch. They faced death daily in the cold, cramped cabin as they battled icing and low cloud conditions. Delays and frustrations with authorities at various airports had also taken their toll on the two fliers. Although Ted had filed the required documentation for landing in Dodoma, the airport authorities claimed they had not received it. There was further irritation when the police confiscated Ted's rifle even though he had a permit. He surrendered the weapon, but not before wrapping it around a pole, bending the barrel and rendering it unusable. The details of the flight and the logistics of planning the route and outfitting the plane for such a long, arduous flight will have to be told by Ted himself. Malcolm and Ted were so tired they retired early after supper and a celebratory glass of champagne.

Ted is already becoming something of a legend here in Tanzania because of his heroic exploits. If he'd lived in an earlier era, he would surely have been among the ranks of explorers such as Burton, Speke and Livingstone. Imbued with the Dutch work ethic, he's been able to accomplish some amazing feats, given the complexity of the three cultures. And his blond good looks and strikingly handsome physique also make him 'one of a kind' among the populace.

Malcolm will be returning to Canada soon. As one of Ted's flying instructors, he agreed to take up the challenge of the African journey with him. There were probably times en route when he doubted the wisdom of that decision.

Bro is so relieved they have arrived safely. Perhaps he'll be in a better mood now. He's been awfully testy, so we've not mentioned a word about our discomfort with "the bunker."

Ana, Dad and I climbed up "Manyoni Mountain", the huge mass of boulders behind the main mission. From there we had superb views of the surrounding area. In the distance, on the flat scrubby plain, a few vehicles, looking as small as Dinky Toys, crawled along the main road kicking up puffs of dust. In the town, the sun glinted off the corrugated iron roofs of the concrete and adobe buildings that were nestled here and there among the groves of mango and cashew trees. The mission house, the *shamba*, the farm buildings and the row of neatly organized storage containers lay almost beneath us. Off to the right we could see Ted's workshop. Beside it a windmill circled lazily, pushed by a light breeze. We took spears and clubs on the climb and walked heavily, doing the "Tanzanian stomp" to flush out any snakes ahead of our path. We sat for several hours at the summit under the giant cross where Ana briefed us on the political and social milieu of the country and the mission.

Every Sunday we all go to the Sisters' for meals. Sister Angelina is in charge of their kitchen and the food is excellent. But we're finding communication very hard at these large get-togethers. When all the Italian speakers come together, they naturally talk in their own language.

Bro has sent both Ana and Ted to Italy to learn some Italian, and if we agree to come back to this mission, he will send us also. Ana says it's not made much difference to her understanding because the Italians all come from different parts of Italy and speak in their own dialects.

It's like getting a Yorkshireman, Alabaman, Newfie, Aussie and East Indian together. They'd all speak English, but each in one's own dialect and peculiar accent. They would understand each other, but it would still sound like the "Tower of Babel" to a foreign speaker trained in classic English.

We have incredible admiration for both Ted and Ana, who must feel so isolated in that they are the only single, lay, non-Italian, English speaking missionaries in their respective locations. The Sisters and Fathers have their own communities and their religious life, but the laity is left to float on the fringes of missionary society. Dad and I have each other, but Ana and Ted have no one. This is a tough situation.

More letters to follow as our experiences unfold.

Love to all,

Mom and Dad

****

Although the following report relating the risks and rewards of the daring flight that Ted and his flying instructor undertook from Canada to Tanzania was written some months after the event, I've chosen to include it at this time to give continuity to the story.

In the African countryside without navigable roads, ferrying spare parts and medicines was difficult. It was problem that often resulted in delays, and occasionally, in tragedy. The Precious Blood Mission's solution was to fly. They bought an airplane in Canada - a Cessna 206 - and sent Ted Van der Zalm, their young Canadian missionary, back home where he earned his pilot's license. Then, together with his flying instructor, Malcolm Murray, he flew the plane from St. Catherines, Ontario to Dodoma, Tanzania.

In this letter to Father Nick Arioli, the Father Provincial, Ted describes their flying adventure.

Manyoni Tanzania
September 10, 1987

Dear Father Nick,

Words will never be able to describe the feelings of fear, exhaustion, frustration, excitement and victory that Malcolm and I shared in trying to get ourselves and the Cessna 206 to Tanzania, because only he and I will truly know what we went through.

It started on June 11th, 1987 at the airport at St. Catherines where a crowd of people had come to see us off. A few tears were shed saying good-by and I could see in the eyes of my relatives what was in my mind. Will we ever see each other again? I had no idea what challenges lay ahead. Having heard that others had perished attempting to do what we were about to do, I was aware that this might be that last time we would be together.

At our first stop in Moncton, New Brunswick, we were inspected and questioned by the authorities to make sure we had the necessary background and equipment to make the Atlantic crossing. (Our equipment included survival gear in case we had to ditch, but I'm happy to say it was never needed.) The following day we were off to Goose Bay, Labrador where we spent our last evening on Canadian soil.

Two days later, on June 13th, we started our leg of ocean crossing. During the first anxious hours of flight, when ice built up on the aircraft adding weight that caused us to lose altitude, I couldn't help looking over my shoulder to see that the life raft was close at hand. But, thankfully, at 7000 feet, we encountered warmer air that melted the ice enabling us to stable off. With Malcolm's excellent navigating, we made Greenland by early afternoon. We originally intended to spend the night there, but due to high costs and our limited funds, we decided to continue on to Iceland. While Malcolm was occupied in the flight planning office, I refuelled the aircraft and we were ready to go by 4:00 p.m. We hadn't eaten yet, so I made a mad dash to the only food establishment within reach without the use of a dog sled. Not being familiar with the language, I was only able to come away with a bunch of raw salmon sandwiches. Raw fish sandwiches + empty stomachs = serious gas - not good when sharing five hours in very close quarters!

By 3:00 a.m. we'd arrived in Iceland in a city I can't remember how to spell. At that time of the morning, no customs official was coherent enough to worry about who we were, so within a few minutes we were fast asleep in the nearest hotel.

On the morning of June 16th, we got an early start for our third and final leg of ocean from Iceland to Glasgow, Scotland. We were able to complete this stretch in just over five hours, so with the Atlantic crossing behind us, of course we had to find a pub to celebrate the fact that our survival gear was still in its original packing. The following day, with only a slight throbbing in our heads, we were able to reach Rotterdam in a short three and one half hours.

We stayed an extra day in Rotterdam to prepare the aircraft for the next part of our journey. The survival gear was shipped back to Canada and we bought aeronautical maps and sent telexes to advise the various countries on our route of the day and approximate time we'd be entering their air space.

On June 18th we landed at Grossetto, Italy, the halfway point of our trip. Not being able to find fuel there, we flew on to Naples where, supposedly, it was available. When we arrived in Naples, our fuel gauges registered "empty". But, we had been misled. There was no fuel for sale in Naples. It took us five hours of begging and good story-telling to convince a pilot to sell us some of his private stock. The few gallons we were able to purchase enabled us to reach Brindisi, Italy where we were able to fuel up.

On June 22nd, we left Italian airspace and flew toward Luxor, Egypt. We were advised to put down in Crete to refuel, but after several hours of flying and the island of Crete was in sight, we were advised that there was no fuel there, so we had to backtrack to Athens to refuel. This cost us a lot of time, so our ETA for landing in Luxor was several hours later than we'd anticipated. We now expected to be arriving there at 11:00 p.m. Close to 7:30 p.m. darkness descended so I hit the switch to light up the instrument panel. Nothing happened. Without being able to see the instruments it is impossible to know in which direction you're heading, or whether you're diving or gaining altitude. Malcolm grabbed our flashlight and held it for the next three hours, switching back and forth from the instrument panel to the navigational charts. We finally made it to Luxor with a three bounce landing before rolling to a complete stop. There we were met by a military "welcoming committee" who "entertained" us until one in the morning before letting us find a hotel to get a bit of sleep. By 6:00 a.m. we were back at the airport, where the same "welcoming committee" grilled us for another two hours.

Not long after taking off from Luxor, we ran into a sand storm that forced us to put down in Khartoum, Sudan. We had no problems leaving the airport there, but when we tried to re-enter the facility the next day, a "nice man with a machine gun" kept insisting that we produce airline tickets. It took some time before we could convince him that we had our own airplane and that we were the pilots. He kept saying, "Fine, but where are your tickets?" When he finally let us through and we were able to board our aircraft, we took off for Addis Ababa, Ethiopia. Not being able to reach the altitude requested of us to fly over the mountains, we had no choice but to fly visual. Soon after departing, thick clouds amassed and it began to rain. We could see neither the mountains in front of us nor how close we were to the ground. Neither Malcolm nor I admitted to the fear that each of us felt, but when we broke through the clouds, we had the mountains off both wings and a clear path ahead of us. God had seen us through!

The following morning, when we were ready to leave Ethiopia, we ran into the same problems we'd encountered in Khartoum. The doorman kept insisting that if we didn't have tickets we weren't going to get into the airport. Finally we persuaded him to let us board our plane to fly to Nairobi, our last stop before Tanzania. We entered Nairobi without further difficulties, but since we had no navigational charts to guide us from there to Dodoma, our final destination, we planned this stretch of our journey using a road map. Needless to say, when we did get to Tanzania we were two hours off-course to the west. We managed to get back on track, and, when we arrived in Dodoma, Bro was there to meet us and congratulate us on the completion of our Canada-Tanzania flight.

Well, that's about it in a nutshell, Father Nick.

Ciao until we meet again.

Ted

****

To our son, Dave:
Manyoni, Tanzania
July 2, 1987

Dear Dave,

These missionaries are holding nothing back. Before asking us to make a long-term commitment, they are leading us to experience Tanzania in all its dimensions.

We just returned from a short safari to rural Msemembo, where we, along with Bro, Malcolm, Ted and Brother Luis, tagged along with Fr. Tonino who was making a pastoral visit. Because there are few priests, laymen of character have been trained as catechists to teach the basics of the Christian faith and lead weekly prayer services in their home villages. A priest routinely travels to these remote communities to offer advice and guidance or just to keep in touch. Today it was Msemembo's turn for a visit where we were guests of the head catechist.

We elders were invited to ride in the cab of the Toyota double-cab pickup while Ted and Luis, the two youngest of our group, were forced to sit on the spare tires in the open Toyota pickup box where they were subjected to the heat, flies and dust of the African bush. Washouts had created huge cracks in the bush trail exposing sharp rocks that tore at the tires and impeded our progress. Our route took us through tobacco fields interspersed with fallow areas where grey spiny brush had retaken the land. The tobacco leaves had been harvested; only the brown crisp remnants were left. Here and there, in the midst of the sere fields, sat a few tobacco-drying houses built of sod.

When three nomadic Barabaig women walked out from the tobacco fields, Fr. Tonino stopped the vehicle to chat. The women were fascinating to look at. They were clothed in brown leather and, on each face, circlets of scars formed decorative patterns around the eyes. Tight coils of copper wire were wrapped around each dusky arm from elbow to wrist, and around their necks they wore wide copper collars that extended out over their shoulders. Their heads had been shaven and from their slit and distended earlobes hung small loops of copper wire. The only bit of colouring against the brown clothing, bronzed skins and copper ornamentation was provided by a huge red rooster that one lady carried in her arms. She was wearing the flared leather skirt that, according to Bro, is worn only by married women. A female god, so the Barabaig believe, taught women how to make the skirt that has a panel of sheepskin sewn in front to promote fertility. The government has tried to get them to give up the leather-panelled skirt in favour of printed cotton *kangas*, but there's no way they will give up what, to them, has become a sacred garment.

As we resumed our journey, Bro filled us in on the ways of the Barabaig tribe. "They refuse to settle in one place and won't send their children to school. They persist in living wild and free, even though many have been forced out of their traditional territory by the development of the Tanzania/Canada Wheat Project farms," he said.

"The Barabaig believe," he continued, "as do the Maasai that all the cattle in the world have been given to them by God. This, understandably, has caused bitter battles between the two tribes."

Fr. Tonino told us that the Barabaig are a fierce, tough people who expect a lot from their young men. One rule is that they must kill a lion before they are allowed to marry. In earlier times they were required to kill a man, but the law, thank God, has forced them to moderate this position!

A group of Bantu men and boys had come out of the bush and were standing by the side of the road. Because they were in the midst of an initiation rite, they wore only loincloths and their bodies were smeared with clay. We had done some reading about the local customs and learned from the writings of P. Van Pelt, in "*Bantu Customs in Mainland Tanzania*", that each tribe has its own way of initiation, but generally, this is the time when boys are subjected to endurance tests designed to cast off the last vestiges of childhood. They may, for example, be forced to dance around a central fire until they can dance no more. Even then, the older boys may prod them with a stick or firebrand into continuing the gruelling dance. Beatings and floggings without reason are endured, and the slightest disobedience is severely punished. At this time they are also taught a symbolic language in which they're given instructions on the traditions, institutions, rites and secrets of the tribe.

Circumcisions, too, are carried out as part of this "coming of age" ritual. In earlier times the local blacksmith performed the procedure, but now often a person from a nearby dispensary attends, so it's done in a more hygienic, and, hopefully, less painful way. If a boy tries to escape, he will be caught and punished. During this period of isolation the family brings food to the edge of the fenced-off area. And if a boy should die during this ordeal, Van Pelt reported, his body would be buried in the bush and there would be no official mourning.

When we arrived at our destination, boys were playing soccer on the hard-packed earth of the village square. They were barefoot, and the ball they were kicking around was no more than a bundle of rags tied together with twine. When our pickup rolled to a stop, the children stopped their play and ran toward us calling out, "*Wazungu, wazungu*", the Swahili word for "white folks". The head catechist came forward, shooed the children away with a verbal reprimand and walked with us to his mud-and-stick home. At the entrance, his wife Mariam, took me by the hand and led me into the tiny primitive structure. We ducked our heads to avoid bumping them on the low doorway and entered the dark, almost windowless dwelling. Mariam showed me to my place at the rough hewn table and then invited the men in. When everyone was settled, there were ten of us; nine men and me, the only woman, who were perched on the small stools that wobbled on the hard packed earth.

Mariam and her sister carried in two enormous platters of rice, two bowls of sauce and a bowl of chicken from the outdoor *jiko* (kitchen). Alongside the food, Fr. Tonino set out the thermoses of boiled and filtered drinking water that he had brought for our consumption. Then the hand washing ritual began. Our hostess handed a metal bowl of warm water to Bro who washed his hands and passed it on to the next person. When everyone had finished washing, Mariam poured the sauce over the rice, Fr. Tonino said grace and we began to eat. The women, as is the custom, did not join us at the table. Their role is to serve their men-folk and any guests regardless of sex. They and the children would be eating later.

Dad and I took our lessons in protocol from Ted. He passed each of us a spoon from the jar on the table and whispered, "Use only your right hand." There were no dinner plates; we spooned the rice directly into our mouths from the section of the tray in front of us. When the chicken was passed, Ted told us softly, "You can take the chicken in the left hand, but you must transfer it to your right for eating." At one point Dad forgot the right-hand rule so I had to remind him with a gentle nudge to the ribs.

We Europeans were the only ones who used the spoons. The Africans scooped up the rice directly with the fingers of their right hands. The meal finished with another round of hand washing and it was at this point that introductions were made.

(Isn't it interesting that in our culture we would introduce everyone first and then proceed with the meal, while here it is the other way around?)

As we filed out into the bright sunshine toward the big mango tree for a picture-taking session, Ted fell in beside us and gave us the reason for eating with the right hand only. "The left hand has, by many cultures, long been considered the "sinister" or unclean hand. In places like this," he continued, "where they have no tissues or even disposable rags, the left hand is used exclusively for those nasty clean-up jobs after using the toilet or blowing one's nose." No wonder it's considered unclean!

Our visit drew to a close after a short welcoming program of music and dancing in the cool adobe church. We elders were given places on the altar dais near the cross, a plain construction of two rustic branches tied together with twine, while everyone else sat on the narrow backless benches in the nave.

As we drove away, Bro reached into his tote bag, pulled out a shiny yellow soccer ball and tossed it out the window toward the children who had resumed their game. Shrieking with delight, they abandoned their ball of rags and gave chase after the new ball, a precious gift.

Our progress to and from the village had been onerous for Ted and Luis who had ridden in the pickup box, but time flew for us and we gloried in the day so crammed with new and unusual events.

Stay tuned - there'll undoubtedly be more adventures to come!

Love you,

Mom and Dad

****

To our friends:
Manyoni, Tanzania
July 4, 1987

Dear Bob and Loverna,

The kids tell us they've been forwarding our letters on to you, so we'll send this portion of the African saga your way. Please do keep them circulating as it saves my shoulders from the stress of writing the same news over and over.

A few days ago Father Domenic and Brother Tim came up from Dar es Salaam for a visit. We were so happy to see these friends and allies. They were as unenthusiastic as we about the accommodation we've been offered and agreed that it's not an acceptable residence for us. Father Domenic says it can surely be renovated and said that he'll push for this at the next meeting. Later, over glasses of brandy, we sat with Brother Tim in the darkening "bunker" and poured out our concerns. We talked about our feelings of isolation and the complexity of trying to work within three cultures and three languages. Brother Tim totally understood: "When I first came to Tanzania," he said, "I couldn't even say *jambo* (hello). I struggled to communicate in Swahili and by the end of the day, totally exhausted, I yearned for companionship. I needed to relax. I wanted someone to talk to me in my own language; someone to ask how my day was, how I was coping, did I need any help. But no one ever did. One day I climbed up Manyoni Mountain, where no one could hear me, and screamed at the empty sky, in complete and utter frustration."

"Many times," he continued, "I would sing to myself, 'No one can shake my inmost calm while to this rock I am clinging. My rock is Lord of heaven and earth. How can I keep from singing?' Sometimes I would sing this a hundred times a day."

It helped enormously to know we were not alone and that what we feel is but one facet of "culture shock".

One evening, while we were attending the rites of welcome for five Tanzanian women entering the Sisterhood, fires broke out on the rocky outcropping behind the convent. Through the chapel windows we could hear the crackling of the flames and see them licking at the scrub brush that was growing in the crevasses. Flaring up they'd consume a branch, die back down and then burst into flame on another offshoot. No one, except us, paid any attention to the fire as it swept toward us, accepting it as one of the most natural and unthreatening things in the world. They knew, as we did not, that the fire would burn itself out once it reached the base of the hill. The ceremonies continued against that dramatic backdrop until the culmination, the hanging of leis around the necks of the young women. This was accompanied by loud expressions of joy called "*vigelegele*", a shrill, high-pitched trilling the women make by moving the tongue rapidly against the roof of the mouth.

On another occasion, we were invited to dinner with the Area Commissioner and his wife in their large British-style home on a quiet street in downtown Manyoni. The walls of the aging white stucco bungalow are chipped and greying; security shutters sag from their hinges and shingles had fallen from the red roof. The garden was lovely, though, and the red earthen walk flanked by long-stemmed white lilies had been meticulously swept. Branches of a huge flowering lilac jacaranda tree hung over the vestibule, its fallen petals exuding the earthy smell of Africa.

Mrs. Nyagawa, in a green and white *kanga* and floral headscarf, greeted us and ushered us into the large sitting area. Crisply-ironed white embroidered cloths lay over the back of each upholstered chair and, although the garden was ablaze with flowers, artificial bouquets had been placed on every table. A naked light bulb suspended from the ceiling cast a pale yellow glow into the centre of the room. (The effect was rather charming, in a wistful sort of way.)

Mr. Nyagawa lifted his hefty frame from his seat and, with a toothy jovial smile, welcomed each of us in turn with the traditional African handshake. First, a regular hand clasp, then an encircling of thumbs followed by another regular clasp, all done in three quick movements. His ample belly sought to escape the confines of his blue safari jacket that stretched tightly across his middle. Indeed, the buttons straining against the cloth seemed about to give up and pop off at any moment.

Shortly after we arrived, the town's power system failed and we were drowned in darkness.

Manyoni is not on the national power grid, so the government has provided a diesel generator for the post office, government buildings and homes of political dignitaries. But, because of the high cost of diesel, the generator runs only intermittently. Power failures are the rule rather than the exception; accordingly, everyone is equipped with alternate lighting sources. Using flashlights, Bro and Dad assisted Mr. Nyagawa in locating and lighting a kerosene lantern.

To prepare for dinner, we lined up at the small sink in the corner of the dining room to wash our hands. Our hostess showed me to my place at the table first. (This very pleasant privilege of being seated first is one that Cyril says I'd better not become accustomed to.) Bro was shown to his place next and then everyone else was seated according to perceived rank or the dictates of African protocol. Mr. Nyagawa opened a bottle of local Dodoma white wine which proved to be an acrid brew, but we toasted one another with tiny glasses of it. After offering a prayer of thanksgiving for the food, our host signalled to us to begin eating our meal of locally grown rice, boiled meat, cooked plantain, papaya chunks and cabbage salad. The power never did come on again that evening, but we enjoyed our visit under the illumination of the amber light of the lantern that flickered and sent out small wisps of smoke blackening the glass. When time came to leave, our host walked us to the car, as Tanzanian etiquette demands.

After breakfast this morning, Bro surprised us with the promise of another adventure. "Throw something into an overnight bag," he said. "We're going down to the mission in Chibumagua. It's a 45-minute drive down into the Great Rift Valley where the Italian Sisters operate a dispensary and Ana is setting up her maternity clinic."

To reach "Chib," as it's called for short, we drove east toward the village of Kilimatinde perched on the edge of the Great Rift Valley. There is little left of Kilimatinde, but it has a most interesting history. During WW I, German General Von Lettow raised horses here that were used by the German cavalry in the battles against the British on the Tanganyika/ Kenya border. Bits of German influence remain. In earlier days, German Lutheran missionaries built a hospital and nurses' training school here and operated it until the Tanzanian government took it over. But now, saddled by a lack of financial resources and trained personnel, the government has found itself unable to cope and has invited the Lutherans to return.

The deeply rutted road that runs through Kilimatinde is flanked by piles of broken concrete from tumbledown buildings. Children playing on the rubble waved to us as we passed. Outside the decrepit shops scattered amid the debris, Arab owners in long dusty *kanzus* (robes) and round *kofia* (caps) sat in front of their merchandise: a conglomeration of hardware, toiletries, buckets, basins, matches, light bulbs, candles, insecticide spray and, incongruously, in one shop, delicate lace bras and panties dangling from nails above the toiletries shelves.

The road veered sharp left at the outskirts of the town and we began our descent into the Rift Valley. Bro stopped at the edge of the escarpment and put the Toyota into low gear before proceeding, because, at its steepest part, the curving, rocky track reaches a grade of 45°. Bro steered carefully, keeping the vehicle from high-centering on the more prominent boulders and avoiding the jagged rocks that threatened to puncture the tires. A shepherd boy was mounting the escarpment with his herd of cows and goats. Swinging his stick, he beat the backsides of the animals, ushering them off the track and into the dry, dusty shrubbery. His head was swathed in a turban, exactly as one would see in pictures of shepherds in the Bible. We had truly left the jet age and for the moment were back in Biblical times.

When our descent was complete, we were able to speed along the track that runs between the dry rice fields toward Chibumagua.

The mission house, situated amid whistling thorn bushes and flat-topped acacias, is truly an oasis in the desert. Light, bright and airy, it lies within view of the shallow lake. Attractive African-patterned curtains cover the louvered windows, and tasteful batiks decorate the walls. We sat under the comforting breeze of the ceiling fan and enjoyed a cool drink with the priest in charge, Father John, a handsome, soft-spoken man. We were attracted to him by the intelligence and sensitivity that shone through his soft brown eyes. And what a flare for fashion he has! What panache! Although he's situated down here in the Rift Valley among tribal people who could care less about such things, he dresses with considerable dash. His sharply pressed slacks were topped by a casual button down shirt open at the neck and sleeves rolled up halfway to the elbow. Completing his ensemble were Gucci shoes and Safari brand wraparound sunglasses that he pushed up into his receding hairline. Father John's class extends to his taste in art, literature and music, evidenced in his fine collection of books and classical tapes.

After a brief visit in his quarters, he walked with us in the blazing sun to the Sisters' dispensary and residence where we rested until suppertime. Sister Clarisa left her duties and showed us to a pleasant room where laughing doves rustled and cooed in the cooling shade of a white-blossomed bougainvillea bush that bloomed outside the window.

After supper, before settling down for the night, we strolled to the lake and observed the two resident hippos wallowing in the mud.

A windmill pumps water from the lake for the mission and dispensary. A long PVC pipe runs far into the lake and has been a target for the hippos which have, more than once, munched through the pipe, cutting off the water supply. Ted, never one to shrink from danger, was brave enough to wade out and dive under the water to make the necessary repairs. What a guy!

Tomorrow we are going on another safari; this time across the flatland to visit some remote villages. (Bro seems to know exactly what we need to lift our spirits.)

Expect further updates as our journey progresses.

Love to all.

Prayers, please.

Leona and Cyril

****

To our friends:
Manyoni, Tanzania
July 7, 1987

Dear George and Muriel,

Our latest safari deep into the Great Rift Valley was an experience we will never forget. Father John and Bro were our guides across the barren landscape that took us to the remote mission of Sanza. We left Chibumagwa in the early morning and headed south through grey scrubby terrain toward the village of Mpandagani where we crossed a dry sandy riverbed and stepped into the "stone age".

The long, low rectangular huts of the Wagogo tribe of this area are crudely constructed of vertical sticks and mud. Narrow openings in the walls near the roofline let in fresh air and a little light. Hollowed-out orange pumpkins and long green gourds that will one day be sturdy and strong enough to carry liquids, lay drying on the flat roofs. Grains and flours stored in roughly-fashioned barrels of dung and clay, and racks of maize cobs still in their brittle beige husks, had also been hoisted up onto the roofs where they would be safe from marauding animals.

Some of the dwellings are constructed in an L-shape forming two sides of a quadrangle. A tangled ring of thorn bushes completes the other two sides. This creates a *boma* (corral) for the cattle that are brought in each night for protection from hyenas, lions, leopards and thieves. We passed several compounds where the cattle stood on mounds of their own manure: mounds so thick the silhouettes of the cattle towered above the roofs.

Cattle represent great wealth for the Wagogo but they seldom sell any to buy goods to improve their living conditions. They prefer to accumulate them for their prestige value. We saw many herds of undernourished cows being urged along toward the nearest watering hole by raggedy boys who whacked them on their bony wasted backsides with long herding sticks.

The terrain became more interesting as we passed through a stand of enormous baobab trees. Baobabs are reputed to be among the oldest and strangest things on the planet. Most baobabs live up to 500 years, but a few are believed to be 5,000 years old. They seem to be growing upside down with their gnarled branches resembling roots sitting atop a huge smooth trunk. But, according to legend, baobabs weren't always like this. Once, it is said, they grew like other trees, but, in some way, in an ancient time, they offended God, who, in retaliation, ripped them up and stuck them back into the ground, root side up. Another legend says that poets and musicians are possessed by the devil and, if given a normal burial, would pollute the earth. Therefore, their bodies are placed into the hollow trunks of baobabs. So watch out, all you poets and musicians; you don't want to end up stuffed into the bowels of a baobab.

Fr. John stopped the pickup and hopped out to pick some of the ripe baobab fruit that is rich in protein and vitamin C. The furry ovals look like small coconuts but, unlike coconuts, are easy to break open. Father cracked one open and we tasted the chalky lemon-flavoured substance that clung to the fibres inside.

Women, bent from the waist with legs stiff and backsides in the air, were gathering reeds called *milala* that grew in small clumps among the baobabs. Beyond them we could see the shimmer of a lake where a dugout canoe had run aground and was resting on the shallow bottom.

The chill of the morning was soon burnt off and it grew hotter and hotter as we motored on through an area of extreme desolation where neither a blade of grass nor thorn bush could possibly survive. We were beginning to feel a little *wasi wasi* (apprehensive) and were grateful when Father stopped to pick up a native man who was striding across the pan. He climbed into the back of the pickup and turned out to be a welcome guide who directed us along the trackless plain toward our destination.

En route we came upon a salt recovery operation. Even in this wasteland, God has provided His people with industry. A group of women in dirty ragged *kangas* and brown canvas sarongs hovered over the procedures. Mounds of off-white coarse salt were piled here and there around the operation and a tangle of twisted firewood lay close by the open fire. Using traditional *jembes* (hoes) women were digging holes in the salt flat that immediately filled with ground water. Using empty Blue Bonnet margarine tins, others scooped up the water from the holes and poured it over earth scrapings in a container. In time, the water absorbed the salt from the dirt. This slurry was poured onto tin pans and heated over the fire. When the water evaporated, only the salt crystals remained. As we watched this operation, an elderly lady was watching Cyril very closely. Approaching shyly she made an inquiry of Fr. John. In response to his reply, she giggled and turned away, hiding her toothless smile behind her hand. Fr. John told us that, because Cyril was wearing a red shirt, she thought he was the Bishop. She was coming forward to receive his blessing.

When we arrived at Sanza we visited the early mission station that had been built by the White Fathers in the late 1800's. The beautiful red-brick church and mission that had once provided relief to this desolate landscape had fallen into disrepair. Several years ago the White Fathers left this area and turned it over to the local diocese. The two catechists stationed here are doing their best but fall short in resources to keep up the premises. However, all was not neglected. In an effort to save the refectory table made from precious *mninga* wood from being eaten by termites, the caretakers had immersed each leg into an old lard tin of diesel fuel. The catechists had prepared tea for us, and as we sat at the table sipping it from cracked mugs and eating *karanga* (peanuts), the smell of the raw diesel stung our nostrils.

A hand-drawn map circa 1905, stained and yellowed with age, hung on the dining room wall. On it, distances were marked in the number of hours needed to walk to neighbouring villages. One hour equalled three miles. The map was so precious it deserved to be placed in the mission archives.

While we studied the map, the catechists engaged in conversation in Swahili with Fr. John. (We think they were probably sorting out some theological problem.) Bro had gone outside, having finished his tea, and was scouting around trying to locate a meteorite that he knew had fallen close by. He found it laying a few hundred metres from the mission. We don't know why he felt he could take it but, aided by some of the village fellows, he loaded it into the back of the pickup truck. It's a most interesting specimen. Silver-grey in colour, it measures about four feet by two and, judging by the efforts the men put into lifting it, weighs well over 200 pounds. As we drove off, we wondered when the Tanzanian Department of Antiquities will catch up with Bro's antics and demand its return.

We needed a refreshing shower when we returned to Chibumagwa after our safari across the saltpan in 40° heat and choking dust. Then, after supper with Fr. John and Bro, we retired to our room at the Sisters' quarters where Cyril read aloud excerpts of P. Van Pelt's book on Bantu customs.

The climb back up the escarpment to Manyoni next morning was no less adventurous than the ride down. The vehicle, engine whining and tires biting into rock, made the ascent using the lowest gear and in four-wheel drive.

We never know what adventures each day will bring, but there are sure to be many more. Experiencing Tanzania is like peeling an onion; there's always one more layer to be discovered!

More news later.

Love,

Leona and Cyril

****

To our daughter Laura, son Greg and girlfriend Carolyn:
Manyoni, Tanzania
July 15, 1987

Dear Laura, Greg and Carolyn,

Our brains can scarcely hold the impact of all the discoveries that our escapades have revealed to us. Since our last letter home we've been to three new places and we squeezed them all in on a four-day safari.

Ted, Bro and Ana were our escorts for the first leg of the journey that took us to Itigi, where our mission is setting up a modern hospital. The road to Itigi passes through what is undoubtedly the most unappealing terrain on the planet. A tangled mass of coarse thorn bushes and stunted acacia trees grow on both sides of the sandy track. Giraffes, lions and hyenas inhabit this God-forsaken area, although, being hidden by the scrub, they're not often seen by passing motorists. Hacking and slashing through this brushwood surrounded by wildlife was surely a formidable challenge for the early explorers.

"I call this area the armpit of Tanzania," Ted chuckled, gripping the wheel against the pull of the deep sand.

Itigi is a collection of mud and concrete buildings, situated on a shade-less dusty pan. As we passed through the centre of the village, Ted veered off into the ditch to avoid a large broken-down bulldozer that was sitting across the roadway.

Dad was curious about this and asked if it had been there long. Bro replied, "Well, yes, several months, in fact. Spare parts are costly, so it'll take a long time for the village to get it running again. It seems to be abandoned but, in fact, a watchman is camped nearby to prevent theft of parts." Then he laughed, "Some years ago a front-end loader was left in a similar situation. Sitting so long, the tires had gone flat. When the parts finally came and the loader was fixed, the mechanics re-inflated the tires. As the air was pumped in, honey oozed out from the sides of the huge rims. The villagers were delighted at this unexpected gift and rushed home to fetch containers to gather a bit of the sweet treat." As an aside he added, "Those African bees will use any nook or cranny as their hives."

At the far side of Itigi is the mission hospital, a series of single-story buildings roofed in sturdy metal linked by covered walkways against a windbreak of eucalyptus trees. We visited the modern wards, the dispensary, the operating rooms, workshops and stores. Some areas are already up and running, while others are still under construction. Solar panels were being installed on the roofs and two windmills, pushed by the stiff wind, pumped water from the boreholes into the storage tanks to overflowing. In the course of our tour we met lithe, long-limbed Dr. Laura, the dynamic Italian surgeon, and the very large Italian nursing Sister in charge of the medical staff. I didn't catch her name, but everyone calls her "Mama Grande" when she's not within earshot.

We joined them for an espresso in Dr. Laura's office where the conversation centred on the hot topic of the use of imported medications marked with an expiry date. So called "expired" medicines not used in our developed world are often shipped to developing countries such as these. In fact, they are often the only medicines available to local hospitals and clinics. A few health professionals, mostly the newly arrived, are adamant that they not be used. But the prevailing wisdom among long-time health care workers in sub-Saharan Africa is that, with certain exceptions, many are perfectly safe and effective within given time frames, citing the expiry dates as merely a marketing decision.

Some politicians have "jumped on the bandwagon" accusing developed countries of dumping useless meds on their population while at the same time their officials are raiding clinics, scooping up the medications, selling them privately and pocketing the cash.

Who would guess that such games are being played with the health and well-being of the populace?

Dad, Ana and I spent the night in one of the houses for the hospital staff. No one had been staying in it for a while and hundreds of *wadudu* (bugs) had made their home in the cracks of the warped boards of the back door. Still, we'd be quite content to have such a house as this in Manyoni. It is so much brighter than "the bunker". Lots of windows let in the light. At the same time, the long roof overhangs keep out the direct sunlight. We were surprised to see that the floor was tiled with linoleum; so much easier to clean than concrete. There was even a small wood-burning heater to ward off the chill of winter days. Ana found three bottles of beer in the fridge and while drinking them we talked about the role of lay missionaries and the relationship we hope to establish between ourselves and the Priests, Sisters and Brothers. I felt much better after our talk and slept soundly that night, confident that any problems we were likely to face could be worked out.

The wind blows constantly in Itigi. There's a bleak feel to the flat, grey, dusty place. At night we could hear the wind whining around the house and rustling the tall dried "lion's tail" stalks that grow like weeds around the hospital compound. (We'd seen these "lion's tail" plants on an earlier trip to Kenya when they were in flower with balls of orange petals bursting along the long square stems.) The Fathers have planted rows of red lilies and hibiscus, but it will take some time before they grow large enough to transform this area from its desolation.

Next day, our safari continued west to the village of Mitundu, where Austrian nursing sisters operate a maternity clinic and dispensary. The sandy track wound through more of the same ugly landscape for several miles before the vista changed and the coarse scruff was replaced by gently rolling hills covered with tawny grasses and dotted with lacy flat-topped acacia trees.

In this pleasant veldt lay the mission compound. At the centre, a windmill was turning gently, pumping water for the clinic and dispensary. As we descended from the vehicle, Sister Carmen, white veil flying, burst from the house like a diminutive dynamo and welcomed each of us with a firm handshake. This lady is one of the most vibrant, fearless and energetic persons I've ever met.

The grey wall behind her was peppered with bullet holes where bandits had blasted it during last week's robbery. Sister filled us in on the heist. "We had just finished evening prayers when a commotion broke out in the yard. Car doors were slamming, men's voices were raised and our watchdog started barking frantically. I pulled back the curtain and looked out. Seeing men with machine guns moving toward the watchman's hut, I called out to him to take cover and to take the dog with him. I was afraid both might get shot. My shouting drew the attention of the bandits who wheeled around and fired directly at our front door. We kept ourselves below the level of the window and prayed for our own safety and that of the patients. By some miracle, the robbers ignored the hospital and our quarters and went directly into a container of goods that had just been delivered. They took only clothing, thank God, and left the medicines."

She concluded, "God is good."

Wherever a need for water is identified, Ted and Bro move in to provide well-drilling services and windmills. There is need for another well and windmill here, so Bro and Ted occupied themselves with inspecting the water system while Sister Carmen showed us around the dispensary and small cottage hospital.

Several moms had given birth and were recuperating on the hospital beds, cuddled closely to their newborns.

Because Tanzanian hospitals don't provide food, there's a shelter behind the clinic where family members can cook for patients for the duration of their confinement.

The Sisters have a sunflower seed press where village folk bring their crop for processing. Nothing is wasted. The nutritious oil is used for human consumption while the sunflower seed residue is pressed into cakes and used as animal feed.

Dad wanted to see the workshop, the centre for the maintenance for this incredibly well-run mission. He was impressed with the machinery and tools and with the young Austrian volunteer who keeps everything shipshape.

After dinner of wild game and vegetables, Sister showed us to our rooms in the two-storey Swiss-chalet style guest house where the windows look out across the expanse of African plains.

The next day we headed to Singida, the main town in this district where the Bishop of the Diocese lives.

The five of us packed into the double-cab Toyota for the three-hour trek. Heading north from Itigi, we passed through more of the same inhospitable terrain. But as we neared Singida, moonscape vistas interspersed with huge, rocky outcroppings and knolls provided relief from the monotonous thorn-infested pan. On our right lay a small lake where knock-kneed water birds waded in the shimmering shallows.

We drove directly to the Bishop's residence and Diocesan offices. The Bishop himself was away, but Fr. Oliver, an Irish priest, the Bishop's right-hand man, received us. We followed this rather unkempt, yet very intense, man along the wide and cavernous corridors to one of several parlours for a short visit before touring the offices and shops. There have been many thefts in recent days, and this has Fr. Oliver seething. Unable to keep abreast of all the activities, he seems fed up to the point of absolute frustration. At the workshops, he offered Dad a job on the spot. (Tempting as it is, I don't think Bro would take very kindly to us defecting to Fr. Oliver.)

After lunch with him and a charming, yet equally unkempt Spanish priest, Dad, Ana and I walked into town to see the sights, leaving the Fathers to conduct business with Bro and Ted.

A lanky Maasai warrior in crimson cloak was striding down the centre of the road near the market place. His spear and herding stick were slung over one bare shoulder and his large bony feet were strapped into oversized rubber-tire sandals. Multi-coloured beads and shiny metals discs adorned his ochred hair and hung from the flaps of his slit earlobes. Around his neck hung a multitude of necklaces, some snug as chokers, others dangling to his chest. As he swept past, a rush of wind picked up the edge of his red robe and flung it back revealing his buck-naked black body. Bystanders giggled, but he proudly strode on. He either was unaware of the government's request to tribesmen to please wear shorts while visiting the towns, or was choosing to ignore it.

A collection of small *dukas* (shops) and an assortment of mud-brick and cement-breeze block buildings, both large and small, ranged along the dusty, rutted streets. As in Itigi, the wind blows incessantly. Gusts had driven rubbish into the deep storm ditches where it lay trapped by the steep sides. Swirling dust devils whipped up the grey silt, stinging our eyes and sending grit into our teeth.

Under the gunny sack awnings of the market stalls, a few late shoppers were picking through the leftover produce or stopping at a kiosk to smell the freshness of the bars of homemade lye soap that reminded me of the ones my pioneer mom used to make. At the edge of the market, fishermen's wives shooed away droves of black flies that always returned to settle on the piles of silvery grey fish displayed on tarps on the ground.

To escape the heat, flies and dust, we went into one of the *dukas,* where I felt obliged to buy something. I chose a green *kitengi* with peacock design. (A *kitengi* is like a *kanga* but twice as long. A *kanga* is a length of cotton large enough to wrap around a lady's waist to form a skirt, but a *kitengi* is large enough to wrap both upper and lower torsos.) I haven't the faintest idea what I'll do with it, but it could make a couple of nice tablecloths.

We carried straight on back to Manyoni after supper and it was well after 11:00 p.m. before we hit the sack. Even the lumpy cots in the bunker felt good.

Bro, Ted and Ana left for Dar es Salaam this morning and everyone else was busy, so we were left to our own devices. I tried to iron, but found there was no power. It comes on and off at intervals and until today we'd not figured out why. There are two generators on the mission site, one at the workshop and one at the main mission. To conserve fuel, one or the other is fired up only during set hours. At the back of the bunker is an electrical box, and in the box is a switch. No one told us that for us to receive power, the switch should be in the "up" position when the mission generator is on and in the "down" position when the workshop generator is on. I've often noticed how Dad's mechanical mind works. If there's a button to push or a lever to pull, he'll figure out which does what. I noticed him mentally visualizing the electrical circuitry, putting it all together in his mind, pulling the right lever and "presto," another African mystery was solved.

The next "shocking" discovery came when we tried to change a made-in-China light bulb. We put a new one into the socket and turned on the switch. The bulb glowed brightly for a few seconds before the fragile filament burned out in a cloud of white smoke.

"Well, that was a dud," Dad said, and reached for another replacement. The same procedure followed with the same result. Now we had power but no light.

Seeking a solution to the light bulb failures, we went to see Fr. Tonino. When we explained what was happening, he laughed and said in his halting English, "You have to turn it on for only a little."

Well, I was puzzled by this explanation. How do you turn a light on for "only a little"? But Dad caught his meaning and back to the bunker we went and began the "Tanzanian light bulb shuffle". Dad screwed in yet a third bulb while I manned the switch. I flicked it on for a second, then off. Then I tried it for two seconds, then off. We dared to leave it on for longer and longer periods, until at last the filament was able to withstand the stress of full power. Weird, eh?

The other morning Dad woke up with an incredibly itchy rash on his neck. We weren't sure if he'd been bitten or was having an allergic reaction to something other than bug bites. The nursing Sister gave him some cortisone cream to apply, and we took the mattresses and pillows off the beds, soaked them with insecticide spray and left them in the hot sun to sterilize. He hasn't had the problem for a few days, so our treatments seem to have helped.

A very interesting guest arrived at the mission yesterday. Father Crema, originally from Italy, has been working as a missionary priest in Tanzania for many years. He's the only priest at the mission in the village of Heka, about 50 kilometers from here. But before coming to this area, he worked among the Wahehe tribe in the south, who, in the not too distant past, practiced cannibalism. Every few years he goes back to Italy, where he is a guest lecturer at the University of Bologna. He's authored many books on tribal customs and kept us spellbound well into the night with his stories about witchcraft and voodoo. (Such beliefs are deeply rooted in the African psyche; so much so that even the most educated Africans sometimes maintain strong beliefs in these practices, and that includes church and civic officials. Now that is something to really get your head around, isn't it?)

I'm not at all sure I can fit into this milieu. It is one thing to be a tourist enjoying a new cultural experience and yet another to be a prospective resident. My roller coaster of emotions continues on a rough and uncertain ride, and it will take time for them to rearrange themselves to accept or reject this assignment. Please pray that we will be led to make the right decision.

We watched some of *Out of Africa* on the VCR after dinner. We never fully appreciated some of the dialogue until we saw Africa for ourselves. There is one line that Karen speaks which really set us to thinking about the wisdom of our eagerness to serve on this continent: "When God wants to punish us," Karen said, "He answers our prayers." Is that what is happening to us?

Love to all. Till next time,

Mom and Dad

****

***To our son Kurt, daughter-in-law Carole and kids*:**
Manyoni, Tanzania
July 20, 1987

Dear Kurt, Carole and kids,

It's been cool and windy these past few days. The sky is grey and overcast, but not in the sense of impending rain. Indeed it will be many months before the rains. Scrub fires continue to break out on the rocky knolls, causing the seed pods to open and spread their seed in readiness for the new crops. At times a brief crackling flash of flame erupts in the thickets, devours a branch and then dies down.

The depressing greyness of the weather has surely affected our moods. Everyone seems to move about their chores with grim determination. A few terse words are spoken over meals then each one moves off to continue his task. We, having been given no task at all, have been trying to find something useful to do.

To lift my spirits, I volunteered to help with the "*pumba*-for-clothing" exchange last Saturday. Brother Luis had come up with a system that he felt would expedite the procedure and was anxious to try it out. His plan was simple. As each of the villagers came forward with a gunny sack of *pumba* (corn husks), Luis measured it out into four-gallon paraffin tins called *debes*. Then he gave each a scrap of paper entitling the bearer to a certain amount of credit which they brought to me, the clothing distributor. Luis ascribed a value to each type of garment and it was my job to square the amount of credit with the goods. I stood by the door of the large shipping container that held the shipment of used clothing and waited for my "customers" to arrive.

My first challenge was in trying to deal with a wily woman with two runny-nosed ragamuffins. Handing me her credit slip, she pushed past me into the container and began ransacking the piles of clothes. She chucked her choices out to the kids, who slipped on as many as they could over their brown rags. Pants, shirts, dresses and skirts galore, well in excess of the amount of her credit, went flying out the door propelled by her swift and determined arm. Other folks, who'd been patiently awaiting their turn moved closer and, taking advantage of my incompetence, grabbed up some of the items and ran off.

"*Hapana, hapana*!" I shouted. "No, no!" In the end I was no match for the villagers, and Luis had to rush over and shut the whole operation down for the day. The experience didn't do much for my self-esteem, but did provide a bit of levity over the dinner table.

Insects have bitten us during the night. Both of us are being tormented by an itchy rash of raised red welts stretching all around our middles. Someone suggested that bed bugs were the likely cause and someone else suggested fleas. As we did when Dad was last bitten, we took the mattresses off the beds, sprayed them with insecticide and put them out in the hot sun to sterilize. We hope this treatment destroys whatever bugs are the reason for this latest affliction.

Just being here these past few weeks has made us face some truths about our own needs and limitations. We realize, all too clearly, we're not cut out for the "monastic life" as practiced by the Fathers, Sisters and Brothers. We're certainly no strangers to prayer, sacrifice and hard work, but central to our lives is the warmth and companionship of family and friends. If we come back, we'll have to work very hard at building those relationships for our own emotional survival. (More thoughts to process as we try to make up our minds.)

I can't imagine what life is like here for Ted and Ana, who are each alone in their respective jobs. They have clear roles to play, but as lay people they are not part of the regular mission life of the priests and nuns. It's lonely on the outside; a good reason for us to create a cozy home where young people can drop in and relax.

Apart from the need for better accommodations, we'd really like to have a car. We never realized just how attached we, in the western world, are to the freedom and independence that "wheels" represent.

Fr. Dino, the priest in charge of all the C.PP.S. missions in Tanzania, just got back from Italy where he'd gone for medical attention. Going in to dinner today, we saw what a difference his arrival has made to the staff. The crumby gravy-spotted tablecloth that had lain on the table for weeks has been replaced by a crisp, freshly-laundered one and the accumulation of dead bugs and dust has been wiped from the windowsills. Loaves of freshly baked bread were laid out on the sideboard and two bottles of red wine had been uncorked. In the centre of the table a bouquet of bougainvillea and cosmos sat in an empty aluminum soup can, a make-do vase. Platters of crispy chicken, pasta and vegetables were toted in by the happy cooks and after grace in Swahili, we all tucked into the feast. All these efforts showed the reverence the staff have for this man who has been their benefactor and advocate in so many ways.

Fr. Dino is the man we've been waiting to see. He was one of the first of the Precious Blood Fathers to come to Tanzania some 25 years ago and knows the conditions and mentality of the population well. It is he we must speak to about our involvement here. This gentle, soft-spoken man seems to carry the heavy weight of his particular world on his shoulders. Given to shyness, he does not speak nor smile easily. It will not be easy to get to know this man. As he rose to leave after supper, he turned to us and said, "I'll meet with you soon." So stay tuned for the report on our meeting.

Earlier in the week, Sr. Carmen, the nursing sister from Mitundu, and her driver dropped in for a short break en route to Dar es Salaam. They had just come from the mission hospital in Itigi where they had taken a desperately ill patient, a pregnant woman who had been in hard labour for two days. When the village midwife realized she was not competent to deliver the baby, she sent the husband on his bicycle to the nursing station to fetch Sister Carmen. Sister told us that when she arrived at the mud hut, it took a moment for her eyes to adjust to the darkness. A fire burning on the clay floor was sending smoke into the small suffocating space. Through the blue haze she found the mother's delicate frame wrapped in a blood soaked *kanga* lying on a cowhide robe. The midwife was squatting at the pallet wiping away the mother's sweat and tears with the hem of her own *kanga.* Sister examined the woman and found that the baby was lying in an oblique position. She realized that the woman's only chance of survival was going to be by the performance of a C-section. Family members lifted the mother onto clean sheets in the back of Sister's Landcruiser and she was transported to the hospital. By some miracle, both mother and baby survived the two-hour drive and Dr. Laura, the skilled Italian surgeon, was able to save both.

Stories like these continue to motivate good people all over the world to assist in mission ventures. Without these clinics and hospitals, so many lives would be lost.

Well, dear ones, it's time to go. We must consolidate our thoughts for our upcoming meeting with Fr. Dino.

Love to all,

Mom and Dad

****

To our son Mark and daughter-in-law Christian:
Manyoni, Tanzania
July 21, 1987

Dear Mark and Chris,

This morning, on our last day in Manyoni, Fr. Dino finally invited us to talk with him about our possible participation here.

Many days had gone by without any encouragement from him and we were beginning to think that perhaps our services were not required after all. We'd spent hours observing at the workshop and training centre and had compiled a list of recommendations that we were anxious to share. We found that there has been no competent person tending the facility for more than ten years, and the neglect is obvious. Theft is rampant, yet the gentle Fathers forgive time after time.

At our meeting, Father listened quietly while we put forth our suggestions. We emphasized the need for: a preventive maintenance program, standardization of equipment, proper storage and inventory for parts and tools and the hiring of a qualified foreman. When we'd finished, Dad said to Father, "That is what I think we could do, but it's not our decision to make. What do YOU think should be done?" Father took it all in, but didn't speak for a moment. He was beginning to make us feel uncomfortable; as though we'd inadvertently stepped into areas that were none of our concern. We searched his impassive face for clues as to his thoughts, but his expression gave nothing away. Then, suddenly breaking the silence, he announced, "The Fathers will be discussing your proposals at our meeting next week, but as far as I'm concerned, you can do whatever you need to make the operation efficient."

How, we wonder, are we going to do what needs to be done? We'll need the full co-operation of all the Fathers, Bro and the organization in Italy to accomplish all those things. Many puzzling questions remain. What, for example, can we expect from the Fathers? What can we expect from the workshop employees? Can we expect co-operation from the government officials? Who will be in charge of the budget and where will the funding come from? How will we deal with the problem of corruption?

Father didn't have time to walk with us through the workshop areas, but he made a promise that he would do this before we left. He rose to leave, but I was not prepared to let him go. I was not going to wait another hour before discussing the question of our accommodation. If we were expected to return, I wanted a commitment from him for better quarters. So before he could get away, I blurted out my feelings about the "bunker". I babbled on and on about its shortcomings. When, at last, I finished my litany of woes, Father admitted that Bro had already talked to him about it, particularly about the lack of light. So, seeing how distressed I was, he postponed his next appointment and went with us to see what could be done to make the house liveable. Evening was drawing in and it was at its gloomiest. Grey sludge had backed up into the sink from the quarters next door and there was a fresh invasion of long snaky things from the shower drain. Father walked from room to room and considered the options. Finally he said, "I think we'd be better off building you a new house." A flood of relief coursed through me and at that moment, although I knew it would be an unseemly thing to do, I wanted to give that dear man a hug. Then we went for a stroll to an adjacent property to choose the location and Father asked us to draw up a plan of something we might like. Imagine that!

When we got back to the "bunker", I immediately began blissfully drawing sketches for the house, considering dimensions for the rooms and how the house should be positioned on the site to take advantage of the morning light, the evening sunsets and the view of Manyoni Mountain.

Fr. Dino has been very fragmented, forever dashing off to either Itigi or Chibumagwa as though he were putting out fires. Several times a day, his vehicle would roar past the bunker in a plume of dust. When he wasn't on the move, he was closeted in his office with a government official, a parish council member, an employee or one of the Sisters or Fathers. Consequently, he had very little time for us. But, late this afternoon, he freed himself from his other duties and together we walked through the workshop areas where we discussed possible physical changes to the layout. When we returned to the mission house, he broke out a bottle of brandy, and we drank a toast in a farewell gesture. I think we're gently being nudged toward coming back!

Tomorrow Ted will drive us into Dar es Salaam for a few days' R and R before we head home. Bro is not flying back to Canada with us. He's staying on in Dar es Salaam to attend the meeting of the mission hierarchy. Before we can make a decision on whether or not to return, we'll have to wait for this "summit" to be completed to find out what expectations would be placed on us.

Ted and the farm workers will be up before dawn butchering a pig to provide meat for the Italian and Canadian "brass" who'll be convening in Dar. (The load of freshly killed pork will be riding in the pick-up with us.)

Until tomorrow,

Love,

Mom and Dad

****

To our daughter Kim, son-in-law Blair and David:
Dar es Salaam, Tanzania
July 22, 1987

Dear Kim, Blair and David,

We're now back in Dar es Salaam at the retreat centre where we've settled into the same bright room we'd stayed in on our arrival. What a pleasant contrast to our accommodation in Manyoni!

Last night marked the end of our stay in that dreary "bunker" where we finished packing by the light of the kerosene lamp. It was late when we tumbled into our rustic beds, but neither of us slept well. We were disturbed by the sounds of distant drumming and haunted by troubling dreams and unsettling thoughts. It will soon be time for us to make a decision and we have no idea if we're up to the challenges that coming back to Tanzania would bring. We had hoped this visit would give us a sense of purpose, but we feel only confusion.

When we heard the sounds of men's voices and the wild squealing of a pig being butchered at 4:00 a.m., we were glad that our anxious night had come to an end. We got up and, using our flashlights, walked toward a crackling wood fire in the barnyard that was sending sparks into the dark morning. When we got there the pig had already been gutted. Ted and the farm workers were scooping boiling water from the steaming barrel on the fire and pouring it over the hide to soften it before scraping it with dull knives to remove the bristles. When that was done, they quartered the carcass with blunt axes, packed it into plastic crates and stowed the lot into the pickup box of Ted's Toyota.

There was no point trying to go back to bed. By dawn Ted was ready to go and so were we, so we grabbed our cases that we'd already slipped into protective black plastic bags, and set them in the pick-up box beside the fresh pork. We detoured down to Chibumagwa where we had a bit of breakfast with Ana and the Sisters. Clarisa, the littlest sister, was sick with malaria and didn't join us, but we popped into her room to say goodbye. Poor wee thing. She looked so small and vulnerable under her white sheet. She wanted to give me a hug and said she hoped we'd be back. After we'd left Sister's room, Ana asked, "Well, do you think you'll return?" I could only shrug and raise my eyebrows in the gesture of a question mark.

Ana had also met with Fr. Dino. "He's promised me my own house," she said, "and he spoke about you two coming back, said how pleased he was with Cyril's plans for the workshop." That was encouraging news.

When we reached Dodoma, Ted stopped at a seedy-looking food stand and bought a bag of 24 samosas. We must have looked dubious about the cleanliness of the place but Ted reassured us that he knew the family and promised they'd be the best samosas ever. He was right. They were so good in fact, that the three of us polished off the whole lot before we'd even left the dust bowl of Dodoma. Ted is good company, and as we cruised along the smooth pavement that stretches eastward to Dar the tensions of the previous night vanished. By noon we were in a chipper mood. Ted took us to a lovely lodge in Morogoro for lunch. We ordered beer, and hamburgers which were edible, except for my bun that had a cooked white worm in it. While I was examining the worm, a large flying insect dove into my beer and swam a few strokes before sinking to the bottom of the glass. Africa is not for the squeamish!

Coping with traffic in Tanzania is nightmarish, especially in the dark. The sun had already set by the time we came to the outskirts of Dar where the road is abominable. Some of the vehicles had only one headlight while others had none. Buses, transport trucks, pickups, passenger vehicles, donkey carts and bicycles fought for passage along the less hellish parts of the crumbling pavement. They weaved in and out of the ditches and across the road trying to avoid falling into the worst of the jagged potholes. There is surely no stretch of highway in the world more horrible than this. And, would you believe it, Ted chose that time to tell us that the Toyota pick-up we were riding in had no front brakes at all!

When it became obvious that we weren't going to get to the guest house in time for supper, Ted pulled off at a bar/café frequented by the locals. We were intrigued by the construction. It comprised a corrugated iron roof supported by tree trunks that sheltered the half-walls of ornamental brick. African rhythms thrummed over the noisy chatter of the diners. We found a spot at a metal table and lowered ourselves onto stools that rocked unevenly on the earthen floor. The café was out of samosas, but the waiter persuaded us to try the "ribs". They sounded delicious and I visualized tucking into a rack of golden succulent sweet and sour pork ribs but when he brought us a tin plate piled with steaming goat ribs floating in a grey watery broth, it was disappointing. Ted tried one first and gave his OK, so we dug in. When we'd finished eating the meat from the ribs, we did as the other folks did. We tossed the leftover bones to the curs that moved under the tables. It was like being in a medieval scene from the time of Henry VIII!

In two days time we'll be leaving Tanzania and be back home in "so called" civilization. We're told that we can expect "culture shock" in reverse so don't be surprised if these experiences have changed us.

We can't wait to see you all soon.

Hugs for wee David!

Love,

Mom and Dad

****

To our son Dave:
Dar es Salaam, Tanzania
July 23, 1987

Hi Dave,

Today was the last day of our exploratory visit to Tanzania. We really wanted to have a period of calm to rest up for the long flight home, but that was not to be. Like almost every other day since we arrived, it started with a bang. (One has to be ready to "hit the ground running" if one is going to stay abreast of all the demands that Africa dishes out!)

The day's problem surfaced just as we were beginning our breakfast. When Brother Tim came into the dining room there was a vague sense of uneasiness about him. "I need to have a look at your passports," he said. "There's flimflam going on at the airport." Wondering what could possibly be wrong, I got up and went to fetch the passports from our room. Tim flicked the documents open to the pages where immigration had inked our entry and exit stamps. "Cyril's is OK," he said, "but yours, Leona, needs a correction." We looked over his shoulder and saw that July 11 was marked as the date I was supposed to leave the country. "But that was 12 days ago," I squeaked.

"Yes," Tim said, "And we need to get it corrected before you go to the airport tomorrow or you could be in for trouble."

My voice was shaking as I asked, "What kind of trouble? Could they refuse to let me out of the country?" I'd heard of people being refused entry into a country but never the other way around.

"I don't suppose there'd be any point in keeping you," Tim said, "but they'd give you a hard time; probably accuse you of trying to deceive them. They're just after a bribe, but, don't worry, Ted and I will sort it out."

When a visitor enters the country, the immigration authorities stamp a permit, a type of visa, into the passport, showing the date of entry and the expected date of departure. Even though a high-ranking government official had taken our return tickets along with our other data to an immigration official, my passport was still stamped incorrectly. Tim and Ted conferred about it and agreed that Ted would take the document to the Bishop's office. Someone there would straighten it out with the authorities. We don't understand how it'll be done, but we've learned enough to know that Africa works in mysterious ways.

Ted dropped us off at the beach before he continued on into the city to confirm our flights and, more importantly, to have an adjustment made on my passport. For the rest of the day, confident that Ted would take care of our problem, we relaxed at the Kunduchi Beach Hotel, drinking in the incredible beauty of this spot. It was good to be alone in this haven of peace. We spent our time sitting under the graceful palms sipping Safari beer and munching on fresh roasted *karanga* (peanuts), wading in the warm surf at low tide, and watching the Arab dhows skimming by. We talked and talked, weighing the pros and cons of accepting this mission. One would think, with all that talking, that we would have come to some conclusions, but no, we can't yet reach a decision. When we get home, perhaps you folks can help us put things into proper perspective and make it easier for us to decide.

When Ted returned from the city to pick us up at the beach, he told us that the passport problem would be corrected, but we'd have to pick it up at the Bishop's office en route to the airport tomorrow. Thank God our flight doesn't leave until 9:30 p.m.

Ted was anxious to get back to the Procura, but we persuaded him to join us for lunch and private conversation in the hotel dining room. While we enjoyed our beef stroganoff at a sea-view table, Ted laid out his perceptions of the rewards and challenges of accepting this mission.

The first appealing yet intimidating prospect that we have to think about is whether or not we feel competent to take up Bro's offer to study in Italy for three months. He feels that, by giving us an introduction into Italian culture and language we'd be more comfortable with our Italian colleagues. (Both Ted and Ana have completed their Italian studies in the fascinating medieval town of Perugia.)

Also, every volunteer with our group who plans to work here must become familiar with Tanzanian culture and study Swahili, the language of the people. Ted has already finished his four months of training at the Maryknoll Language School at Musoma on Lake

Victoria and Ana will soon be following. These two are both in their twenties, so perhaps this is not daunting for them. But for Dad and me, in our late fifties, trying to learn two languages back to back would be a marathon. Still, we're drawn to the tremendous opportunity.

We encouraged Ted to talk about the trials we could expect in this situation where three languages and three cultures are merged. I particularly wondered about the loneliness. It's not likely this talented and resourceful young man, adventurous to the point of danger, would ever admit to feeling lonely.

"Although Ana and I want you to come back," Ted said, "you should know that you're likely to experience frustration such as you've never experienced before. Adapting to the differences in these three cultures is going to try your patience to the breaking point. But consider," he concluded, "if you can make a difference in even one person's life, it'll be worth it all."

We finished our lunch in silence and returned to the retreat centre for our last night in Tanzania. It's time for bed so I'll sign off now. I'll ask Tim to mail this before we go to the airport tomorrow, even though we'll likely be home before it arrives.

Love you guys.

See you soon,

Mom and Dad

(Continued)

Departure Lounge,
Dar es Salaam Airport

July 24, 1987

I intended to give this to Tim to mail before we went through into the "Passengers' Only" zone, but it went clean out of my mind. I probably forgot because I was apprehensive going through Customs and Immigration. Even though we'd picked up my passport from the Bishop's office and everything was in order, those humourless deadpan fellows rattled me. Customs officers always make me nervous! I even made a mistake filling in my Embarkation Card. I didn't realize I'd goofed until the immigration officer looked at Dad and asked, "How many months old is your wife?"

Dad replied, "I beg your pardon?"

The officer repeated, "How many months old is your wife?" He was grinning now!

"I beg your pardon?" Dad said again, still confused.

The officer then swung the card around so we could see what I had written. In the space for "Date of Birth" I had written 26 March, 1987 (three months ago), instead of the true year of my birth. Dad has a way of defusing tense situations with humour, so I wasn't surprised to hear him quip, "Oh, that," he said, "Well, you see, I like to get a new model every year!" Everyone within earshot burst into laughter! It was the first time I'd ever seen an immigration official of ANY nationality even so much as crack a smile.

Well, dear friends, they've just called our flight so I'm hoping that, if I attach a 200 shilling note, the young lady at the Duty Free will post this for me.

Goodbye again.

Love,

Mom and Dad

****

Interlude

We spent the next few weeks at home conferring with family and praying for discernment. Was this the role God meant for us? We had seen the need and felt the challenge. Could we rise to it? Slowly, day by day, our apprehension subsided and, as though compelled by some unseen force, we yielded to the intangible, almost magnetic draw of Africa and began to prepare for our mission.

We set about accumulating college course outlines, instructional materials, vehicle inspection forms, parts order forms, etc., which we could adapt for use in Tanzania. We signed up for Italian correspondence courses and began to study in earnest, viewing this interim as an excellent time to acquire knowledge of the structure of a romance language. I audited "English as a Second Language" lessons at the college and began to amass folders of pictures to use as teaching aids.

We ensured that our passports were up to date and our immunizations "topped-up". Our doctor wrote prescriptions for a year's supply of our regular medications, an emergency supply of broad-spectrum antibiotics as well as anti-malarial medication.

Our son Chris agreed to stay on in the house and look after domestic matters in our absence, and we waited for a clear invitation to return to Africa.

Bro's call was several weeks in coming. He had stayed on in Tanzania to oversee the needs of the Canadian contingent in managing the water project, setting up the maternity clinic and clearing the way for our return.

When he finally called in mid-November and asked us if we could begin Italian language training in Italy on January 7, we were almost ready. We had six weeks left to get the last bits and pieces together. We made lists of things we knew we'd need in Tanzania and proceeded to fill our two trunks with these precious items.

Cyril bought a small toolbox and filled it with hand tools and I bought a small electronic piano. Around these we packed personal items: family photo albums, flashlights, short-wave radio, scissors, pens, pencils, erasers, exercise books, novels, tapes, extra batteries, music books, key tags, pressure cooker and meat grinder (for tenderizing tough African beef), sink stoppers, Toni home perms, hair curlers, razor blades and a year's supply of insect repellent along with the instructional materials and a ten-inch globe. These we shipped off to Bro in Toronto, who directed them to Tanzania.

Our tickets from Whitehorse to Rome arrived and we waited out our time in Whitehorse by preparing for our last Christmas at home, attending farewell dinners and spending as much time as possible with our three grandchildren, who lived with their parents in a nearby cozy log cabin. The Yukon winter took on a special charm as we prepared to leave it behind. Sometimes we felt we wanted to cancel the whole thing and stay in the bosom of our family and friends. But we had gone too far down the road - we had passed the point of no return.

When the day came for our departure, everyone was at the airport to see us off. It was hard for all of us, especially for wee Dyana, our youngest granddaughter. With tears coursing down her chubby cheeks, she held her tiny hand over her heart and said, "Grandma, it hurts." I knelt down beside her and cradled her in my arms as she sobbed softly into my shoulder. When our flight was called, I released her into her Mom's arms and giving a final wave, we walked, with trepidation, through security.

En route, we spent a few days in Calgary with family and, when the time came to leave there was the same heart-rending send-off. Bro met us in Toronto and took us directly to the residence of the Precious Blood Fathers to meet Father Provincial Nick Areoli for cocktails. Then he whisked us out to the Gran Feste restaurant for an Italian dinner, where our son Greg and his fiancée, Carolyn, joined us. There was no time to think about the enormity of what we were doing.

We were treated to lunch next day by Andrew Salkheld of Canadian Executive Services Organization (CESO), with whom we'd previously corresponded concerning volunteer postings. Andrew had spent several years in Dar es Salaam as an executive with Brooke Bond, the "tea people". Picking up the tab, he offered this bit of wisdom: "You're going to love those Tanzanians," he said, "and from time to time, you're going to despair of them. I want you to know it's OK to do both."

On January 3, there was a special Mass at the mission chapel that was packed with well-wishers. Cyril and I each read a passage from the scriptures and we received our missionary crosses. On January 4, D-Day, Fr. Nick drove us to the airport. We will never forget his words as we stood together at the Alitalia counter, "Now you're going to see the human side of the church." With that he left us and we were on our way to continue our journey 'In a Sun Scorched Land'.

To our daughter Laura:
Perugia, Italy
January 13, 1988

Dear Laura,

It's been a week since Dad and I arrived in Perugia in the region of Umbria that Italians call the "green heart" of Italy. We'd love to find time and energy to explore this medieval town that's built on top of and between risings of a hill, but so far all we've seen is the part that lies along the half-mile walk from our apartment to the university. Our lessons are scheduled so we have to do the long walk twice daily. We're finding it tough trying to adapt to the culture and get into the swing of our Italian lessons. Both of us are tired beyond belief. In fact, it's taking every ounce of energy for my arm to push this pen along the paper. But, it's your birthday, so no effort is too great for me to write to you on this special day.

We were already exhausted when we arrived in Rome. Father Mario Dariozzi, one of the Precious Blood Fathers was there to meet us, holding a cardboard sign with "Lane" scribbled on it. We'd hoped for a layover in Rome but as we sped north it became clear that Father Mario was taking us directly to Perugia. He wound up his red Volkswagon and flew along the freeway as though escaping the very "hounds of hell".

Somewhere in the Italian drivers' manual, we're convinced, is a code that says, "*A series of dashes down the centre of the road means, 'tear along the dotted line'*", for this is precisely how Father drove. Whenever he passed a vehicle, rather than returning to the right-hand lane, he continued to tear along the centre line, moving over only when absolutely necessary to avoid a collision. He felt, apparently, that if he were to move over entirely, he would lose valuable time in his race to get us to Perugia before nightfall.

Father's English is quite good. Talking as rapidly as he drove, he lost no opportunity to practise on our tired and somewhat unwilling ears.

Dusk fell and the green hills of Umbria folded in on themselves as we climbed higher and higher, twisting and turning on the road leading to Perugia perched high on its mountain. On the outskirts we stopped and met Angelo, the owner of this apartment where we are staying. Driving in tandem, Angelo in his vehicle and we in ours, we zipped in and around the hills, past Etruscan and Roman ruins, until finally coming to rest at a modern apartment building so completely out of place in this medieval city.

But our day was not yet finished. We deposited our luggage in the large apartment and went with Father and Angelo to the supermarket around the corner. It was near closing time so we rushed along the aisles and tossed a few staple foods into our cart. Bread, butter, canned tuna, cheese, canned soup, cereal and milk would tide us over for next day's breakfast and lunch. When we got to the checkout, Father added a few special items: a bottle of fine wine (Orvietto Classico), a box of Perugino chocolates and a carton of *panetoni* (Italian Christmas cake). Then, back at our "digs", the men helped us bring in the groceries. They gave us their phone numbers, a map of Perugia, the address of the *Universita per Stranieri* (University for Foreigners) where we are studying and left us to our own devices.

We made ourselves tuna sandwiches and opened the bottle of wine, which sufficed as our supper, before flopping into bed.

Next day we studied the map of Perugia to orient ourselves. Because classes were to begin the following day, we planned a "dry run" to the university and trudged off, map in hand. Our modern apartment lies near the bottom of the sloping hill, but the university is at the top, close to the city centre. We made several errors and had to backtrack, but by hiking along a certain curving stone stairway bordered by ancient slate-roofed buildings, we eventually found our way through the maze of vaulted archways to the massive doors of the *Universita per Stranieri*. The building itself dates back to the 14th century. Who knows how long the university has been housed in it?

(Hiking in and around the hills of Perugia makes our morning walk up Grey Mountain in Whitehorse seem like a casual stroll in the park.)

There was mass confusion at the school next morning. People from several nations were milling around the registrar's office, all babbling in their native tongues. The computers were down, but the signs and announcements to that effect were only in Italian, so very few could understand what was happening. While we stood there looking baffled and mumbling to ourselves in English, a red-haired lady burst through the throng and introduced herself. "Hi," she said, "I'm Blanche Hinton. Are you two Canadians?" Blanche is from Toronto and is enrolled in the Advanced Italian Studies Program. She already has a working knowledge of the language, having lived in Italy some years ago. It's wonderful to have her help. She translates for us if we really get stuck, so, since that morning, we've been content to remain under her protective wing as she helps us sort out the intricacies of the "cultural divide".

Things continue to be confusing and frustrating in this mix of cultures and expectations. The learning situation is extremely difficult. People wander in and out of classrooms. People with no or very little knowledge of Italian, such as ourselves, are being lumped in with those who can strike up a conversation in Italian with the professor.

The style of one of our professors is to stand at the front of the class and read from the textbook. She's always in the huge hall, which we've labelled "Dickensian Hall". It's dark, damp and depressing. The pale lamps hanging from the vaulted ceiling are incapable of illuminating any area save what is directly below them. The room comprises tier upon tier of backless benches that rise to a dizzying height. On the first day the class was so crowded we sat with our coats on our knees, elbows crushed against our bodies, while trying to open our texts. (We counted no fewer than 80 students on the benches and another 20 seated on the floor and in the aisles). Dad is looking very grim, and I expect some action from him soon if things don't improve shortly.

After the first gruelling three-hour session, we left determined to find a way to deal with this appalling situation. We conferred with John, a distinguished English gentleman who is also in our class. Soon there was a knot of disgruntled students around us wanting to join in the effort. John and I were selected as "spokesmen" of the group, so we went to the English-speaking student advisor and pleaded our cause for the establishment of a truly beginners' class in a less crowded venue. She was very helpful and promised things will improve for us soon.

In the meantime Dad, in abject frustration, has vowed never to return to the class in "Dickensian Hall". He is going to study from tapes at home while I continue to attend classes. When the new class is set up and I find that it would be right for Dad, he'll probably come back. We called Father Mario, who was very supportive of our plan. He commiserated with us, citing his own problems in trying to learn another language.

I think Dad is already recovering, because he was back to his jocular self today when he left me at the door of "Dickensian Hall" and quipped, "You'd better get inside or six other students will get your seat." But the hall was not nearly as crowded as before. It seems there were many who opted out of this class. The same professor tore through three hours of irregular verbs while reading from the text. She allowed us only a five-minute break each hour. Never once did she use the blackboard or attempt a demonstration with actions or pictures. It's hard to follow the rapid Italian flying by. One Tunisian fellow shouted to the teacher, "Slow down. *Sono Vecchio*!" (I'm old!). And one blond young man got up mid-lecture, strode to the front, struck his name off the register and stormed out.

In spite of our dissatisfaction with the school, some interesting things have been happening that we hope will ameliorate our misery. Today, when the register was passed along, I noted that the young black woman across the aisle had signed in as Neema Nyerere. She's the niece of Tanzanian Past President Julius Nyerere. Neema is excited that we're going to Tanzania, and we've exchanged addresses and promises to get together soon.

Dad and I have both been suffering from bouts of stomach cramps, probably brought about by changes in the water and in our diet. Jet lag, coupled with loss of sleep and a big dose of culture shock, undoubtedly contribute to it as well.

However, the weekend is coming, and we're looking forward to a change of pace. We've been invited to explore the medieval streets and ancient buildings of the town with Blanche and her roommate, Sara.

Keep sharing these letters and continue praying for us, as we are for all of you.

Love,

Mom and Dad

****

To our friends:
Perugia, Italy
January 29, 1988

Dear Loverna and Bob,

Thanks for the phone calls, everyone. It was wonderful to hear from so many of you. Each call gave us encouragement and brightened our stay. We suspect it was the sad tone of our last letter that sparked the spate of calls.

It's been close to three weeks since we wrote. Since then our days have been filled with study and immersion into the new cultural milieu. I think that by speaking up about the horrors of Dickensian Hall, I can take some credit for our improved situation. A new class for true beginners has opened up, and it's been a joy, for the most part, to have two new professors who really know what they're doing. The class is relatively small, and we each have our own desk with padded seats, no less! Even Cyril has come back to the lectures, and we are both making headway.

From the windows of the top story of the University one can look out over the valley to the town of Assisi that lies beneath Mt. Subasio. It looks so calm and peaceful. We've promised ourselves a visit there next weekend to get away from the stresses of our studies.

Buses run between Perugia and Assisi so yesterday we went to the bus terminal to pick up a timetable to help us plan our trip. Getting to the depot located at the lower level of this hill town was an adventure in itself! Four very long flights of stairs led us down, but an escalator that runs partially underground through some fascinating Etruscan ruins was available to whisk us back up to the centre. By taking that pedestrian route we avoided the narrow roadways where mini cars, whining like angry hornets, careened up and down and around the tight curves, the drivers grimly gripping the steering wheel with one hand while resting the other on the stick shift, in readiness to grind into another gear.

Last weekend was glorious. It was beautiful and warm on Saturday as we walked with Blanche and her roommate, Sara, through the ancient streets to the topmost hill. The Umbrian Hills were magnificent. Partially obscured by gentle mists, they would have been a perfect backdrop to a renaissance painting.

In the evening we passed through the Corso Vannucci, the large central square, and mingled with the throngs of Perugians, who were dressed in their finest clothes. Strolling back and forth, they smiled and nodded to each other in the daily ritual of the "little walk"- the "*passeggiata*". A huge fountain blackened with age sits in the centre of the Corso. It being winter, no water is spouting from it now. Abutting the fountain is the cathedral, where paintings of the artist Pietro Vannucci, commonly called Perugino, are displayed. (So precious is Perugino, modern commerce has adopted his name for their famous chocolates.)

After our outing we went to Blanche and Sara's place for supper. They're sharing a crummy flat on Bontempi, a narrow side street off the Corso. Like most flats in the old city that are let to students, it's dark and dreary. The floral wallpaper is peeling and faded and the enamel on the window sills is flaking and yellowed with age. There is no kitchen; the girls do their cooking on a small hotplate in a corner of the main room where the wallpaper is splattered with grease from the preparation of bygone meals. There is no sink near the cooking space; they must draw water from the bathroom taps. Sara, in spite of these drawbacks, prepared a delicious meal of spaghetti *carbonara.*

Students at the Universita per Stranieri are here for various reasons. Our group is an eclectic mix. Blanche is here to brush up on her Italian for her job as tour guide. Sara has chucked over a career as a civil engineer to study Italian cooking. Neema is completing a Masters Degree in languages. John needs Italian for his work in Rome with the World Food Program, while Cyril and I have taken the option to familiarize ourselves with the Italian culture and language.

Even though we're getting out and about meeting new people and seeing new places, we're still under incredible stress. It's tough living in another culture. It's taken us a month just to figure out that the shops are closed for a long siesta at noon and don't open again until three or four; that one buys coffee at a "bar' and it costs more to drink it at a table than standing at the counter. The lessons are long and arduous and we're not sleeping well. In addition, we miss you guys like crazy.

Thank God for Blanche. Through her help we're managing to cope and to learn much about this beautiful country.

It's time to review all those irregular verbs, so that's it for this time. Keep praying.

Love,

Leona and Cyril

****

To our friends:
Perugia, Italy
February 28, 1988

Dear George and Muriel,

In a little over a month, we will have completed our Italian studies. The lessons continue to be heavy and the stress of functioning in another culture is beginning to take its toll. I caught a glimpse of myself in the mirror and saw, looking back at me, what seemed to be a raccoon, so black were the circles under my eyes.

But, we've learned a great deal about Italian culture, which should make life easier once we get to Tanzania and begin our work side by side with our Italian companions.

Our trip to Assisi became a reality last weekend. The bus took us down the curving mountain road away from Perugia and across the Tiber valley to the town where St. Francis preached his message of peace. The two towns are studies in contrasts. Perugia, the bustling capital of the region sits, true to its history, like an arrogant oppressor high atop a mountain while Assisi, the calm retreat, is snuggled in the valley. One place can easily be seen from the other, yet the differences in the atmosphere of each can be strikingly felt.

Perugians were a warlike tribe who gave rise to the Flagellants, medieval folks who used to whip themselves in a penitential rite, while the citizens of Assisi became the followers of the kindly St. Francis.

It was a tremendous experience to be in Assisi, a lovely and gentle retreat. There is tenderness in its ambiance. Flowers were cascading from window boxes and overflowing from ceramic pots that lined the winding stairways that rise along the softly sloping terraces. With guitars slung over their shoulders, laughing young monks robed in the brown habits of the Franciscan Order slipped through the streets, their sandaled feet slapping against the cobbles.

More legends are told about St. Francis than any other saint. His respect for all living creatures is probably the best known. To him, they were as Brothers and Sisters. He is said to have preached to the birds, referring to them as "Sisters" and to have calmed a ravaging wolf by making the sign of the cross and ordering it to come to him. "Brother Wolf" is said to have obeyed and lay down peacefully at St. Francis' feet.

There is a garden in Assisi where two doves play near the statue of the saint. Our guide told us that, curiously, there are always two doves, never more, never fewer.

Unfortunately the trip was flawed by the bus driver who blasted jarring "god-awful" music through loudspeakers while puffing on foul-smelling cigarettes that turned the air blue with noxious smoke. (The anti-smoking campaign doesn't seem to have reached Europe yet.)

Yesterday evening we spent more time exploring the centre of Perugia. As night fell, we came across a "*porta del mortuccio*" or "door of the dead." The bricked-in arched door, just big enough to allow the passage of a coffin, was situated beside the main doorway of an old shuttered building. The dead, the superstitious medieval people believed, should not leave from the same door as the living.

Sconces that had once held flaming torches flanked the ancient doorways along our walk. But now, the torches have been replaced by pale electric lamps that lighted the way back to our apartment.

I had two chances to practice my new-found Italian in situations where there was no translator. The first opportunity was during a three-hour stint at the hairdresser's where I got a perm; the next was when I returned to have the perm redone. (It had completely washed out after the first shampoo.) The hairdresser was very kind to me in my efforts to speak her language, but I was exhausted after those episodes.

Now I see that the second perm is also beginning to wash out. Am I going to have to go back for yet another three hours of tension? Just the thought of it is making me anxious. I think I'm becoming unglued!

There's a magnificent 14th century hall in Perugia where Romanesque arches span overhead and brilliant frescoes depicting legends, fables and Biblical stories decorate the walls. It's called the Sala dei Notari. Classical concerts are often held in this stunning venue and we were privileged to attend a most unforgettable performance by the fabulous Beaux Arts Trio from New York. Never before have we had such a moving musical experience. Indeed, the entire audience was so moved that after the last notes faded we sat for a moment in utter silence, overwhelmed by the sheer beauty of the peerless performance. Then we burst into applause. The trio came back for three curtain calls but still we would not let them go. Not a single person moved from his seat; we all just sat there applauding and applauding, unwilling to let the experience end. We did not stop until they finally favoured us with an encore.

Two more special people have joined our circle: Asami, a Japanese girl and Fr. Larry Hemmelgarn, an American priest from the same order of priests we'll be with in Tanzania.

Last week we hosted a potluck party at our bright and spacious apartment. We were a veritable United Nations, our guests hailing from such diverse places as: the USA, Japan, Australia, South Africa, New Zealand, Tanzania and Canada.

One weekend we, together with Blanche and Asami, rented a small Fiat and went to Florence. Blanche was our driver/guide. She knows Europe well and is confident driving here. For the most part it was a great trip. Blanche drove the Fiat right up to the door of the small hotel where her family has been going for years. From there it was an easy walk to the centre of the city. In fact we could see *Il Duomo* (the Cathedral) from our window. Cyril and I attended Sunday Mass there and found a pew where we could glance up and admire Brunelleschi's dome. We'd heard of the urbanity and sophistication of the Florentines so it was no surprise to see the congregation dressed in their finest. The men, particularly, looked as though they'd stepped out of the latest Haute Mode magazine. Impeccably groomed and wearing what seemed to be Armani camel hair coats and Gucci shoes, they'd genuflect deeply and devoutly before moving into a pew. But, a few moments into the service, many would slip outside and stand around smoking and gossiping on the cathedral steps until after the sermon. Then, they'd slide back into the pews just in time for the Consecration and Communion.

It was off-season, so we were easily able to take in many of the highlights of that marvellous city of art. Imagine walking straight into the Uffizi Art Gallery or the Academy to see the works of Michelangelo, Da Vinci, Botticelli and other great Renaissance artists without having to queue for hours as one would have to do in the tourist season, when the whole world seems to flock to Florence. Blanche knows her way around this city and, with us in tow, breezed into the most fascinating places. It was in the church of Santissima Annunziata where we saw and could actually touch Andrea del Sarto's fresco, "Birth of the Virgin".

But alongside all the beauty of Florence was a spot of ugliness. There had been threats of vandalism at a Synagogue and we were distressed to see that it was necessary for armed guards to patrol the property. I'm very much afraid that strains of anti-

Semitism are alive in the cities of Europe. Has humanity learned nothing since the Holocaust?

On the way back to Perugia we had a brief stop at San Gimignano where 15 of 72 stone towers still stand. In Renaissance times pro-pope and pro-emperor factions often fought against each other, using the towers as battlements for pouring boiling oil on attackers! Subsequent republican governments tried to make them tear down the towers, but, fortunately for we culture seekers, a few remain.

Before we could return the car to the rental agency we needed to top up the tank. Blanche pulled our Fiat up to an unmanned service station where there were two pumps. One was labelled "*Gasoleo*", the other "*Benzina*".

"Which one is the gasoline?" Blanche asked.

"Don't YOU know?" Cyril asked

"No," she replied, "I've never had to fuel up before. I usually travel by train."

We sat pondering for a while before Cyril said, "Well, I'm not sure, but I think it must be the "*Gasoleo*". It has the word, "Gas" in it."

There was no attendant to confirm or deny, so we thought we'd go for the "*Gasoleo*". Blanche fed a bank note into the machine and the automatic pump came to life. She stuck the hose into the tank and filled it up.

Moments after we pulled away the engine began to knock. Then it started to cough and sputter. We were at the base of Perugia's hill and looming ahead of us was the circuitous road that we would have to take, climbing higher and higher to the city centre. Blanche was alarmed, "What's the matter with it?" she asked.

"Oh, oh," said Cyril, "I made a mistake. "*Gasoleo*" must be diesel."

"Well, thanks a lot," Blanche said sarcastically.

The vehicle began to lurch and the gentle knocking of the engine had become a hammering.

"It's going to stall!" Blanche said, gripping the wheel as we rounded a steep curve. She was panicking at this stage.

"No, no," Cyril said, "Don't let it stall! Keep it revved up! It'll be alright. Keep going!"

Blanche kept the vehicle revved up and by some miracle it did not stall. We were relieved when she dropped us off at our apartment.

"What shall I tell the rental agency?" Blanche asked keeping the engine running.

Cyril replied, "Tell them absolutely nothing."

Last night, during a violent thunderstorm, all the lights went off in the apartment. I was cooking supper on the hot plate at the time, and the electric base heater had been on. Cyril suspected we'd blown a fuse or tripped the multi-breaker, because ours was the only apartment affected. We had no idea where to find the electrical box so, with the help of the English/Italian dictionary and the flashlight I wrote out my message of distress and dialled Angelo's number. He answered with, "*Pronto*?" and I launched into my spiel in fractured Italian.

"*Ciao, Angelo. Sono Signora Lane. Abbiamo Problema. Tutti le lucci sono spenti!*" which means, roughly, "All the lights are out." Angelo understood and replied in rapid Italian. As it flew by, I caught the most important word, which was "*scala*", meaning "stairs." Cyril took the flashlight and looking under the hall stairs found the electric box, flipped the switch and "*Allora*" our "*problema*" was solved.

We've not seen any of our neighbours in the apartment block but we know there's a reluctant, recalcitrant kid living directly above us. We know this because every weekday morning his mother screams and shouts in Italian for the blighter to, "Get up and get your lazy so and so backside out of bed and off to *la scuola*!" She storms about on clunky shoes and sometimes we think she'll go too far when we hear things being crashed around.

A cheeky brat lives across the hall, but he's had his "come-uppance". One evening we heard a loud "whump" on the door. We looked out. No one was there but we could see dusty footprints left on the door where the culprit had leapt up and slammed his feet against it. Cyril closed the door and waited for another "whump". I was thinking how delicious it would be if Cyril were to open the door at the precise moment the jumper's feet landed. I was not disappointed! The next "whump" came within seconds. Cyril yanked the door open and a guilty ashen-faced pre-teen skidded into the room. Cyril's timing was perfect! The lad regained his balance and wheeling abruptly sprinted out the door. Cyril gave chase. Down the stairs and out into the street they flew, boy and man. Boy, going like the wind but man, even though close to 60, closing the gap. Boy scooted down and around the labyrinth of short winding streets and was lost to man. Later, way into the night we heard a woman crying "Mario, Mario!" over and over again. Guess the brat was afraid to come home!

I think Angelo is feeling pity for us, because he came by and took us out for a weekend to the ancient 11th century abbey, Abbazia di S. Felice, now a retreat house. We would have frozen had plumbing and heating not been added to the bedrooms, kitchen and dining room. In the unheated areas, such as the chapel where we attended Mass, we shivered as we knelt next to the tombs of ancient monks that rested under the medieval arches.

Last week we had another reprieve from school. Fr. Mario called telling us to skip classes and go to Rome. Bro and a group of young Canadians were there on a stop-over from Tanzania. They were going touring and wanted us to join them. We were like kids playing hooky and, let me tell you, it felt good to escape the tedium of our studies. We took an early morning train to Rome and then travelled on the underground to the white marble residence of the Precious Blood Fathers that lies, surrounded by manicured gardens, on the outskirts of the city.

It was great to see Bro again and to meet the young mission-minded folks. They'd been waiting for us and we lost no time in setting out on our tour. Ten of us squeezed into a mini van and, with Fr. Mario Dariozzi at the wheel, zipped through the towns of the "Green Heart of Umbria" toward Assisi. Fr. Mario is one mad driver and had we not been packed together like sardines, we would have been flung around like so many rag dolls. We'd been to Assisi before, but this time had the opportunity to see things we'd missed on our last trip. Fr. Mario took it upon himself to show us the frescoes of Giotto in the Church of San Francesco, but got us into trouble when he bypassed the custodian, the Franciscan monk, who was the official guide.

Somewhat abashed, we slunk out of the church and away from Assisi. Jouncing against each other, we continued our journey; tearing along the road toward the city of Grosseto. A company there provides the vanes and gears for the mission's windmills in Tanzania and we'd been invited to have dinner with the CEO's. Our hosts had prepared an enormous feast featuring five courses: *antipasto*, (prosciutto), *primo piatto* (pasta), *secondo piatto* (chicken) *insalata* (salad), *dolce* (tiramisu) plus liberal draughts of red wine. Hours later we finished our meal, "rolled out" of the restaurant and packed into the van for the long drive back to Rome. The vehicle heater wasn't working and Bro stuffed his gloves into the air vent in a vain attempt to keep out the frigid air. It was a cold, long, miserable ride. When we arrived, frozen and stiff, back at the Fathers' house, it was well past 2:00 a.m.

But, in spite of our discomfort, the trip was a great diversion from our studies.

Thanks for all the letters and phone calls, and keep us in your thoughts and prayers.

Love,

Leona and Cyril

****

To our son Mark, daughter-in-law Christian and family:
Rome, Italy
April 8, 1988

Dear Mark, Chris and family,

Our formal Italian studies are behind us. We've survived the rigours of the last three months and are now staying in Rome at the Fathers' pristine marble residence for a few days' R and R before flying on to Tanzania.

The last few weeks of classes were especially onerous and we sought out new diversions to help our brains and bodies fight off the burden of fatigue. We were helped enormously by Blanche who suggested a weekend in Venice. It was just the tonic we needed! We loved the carnival atmosphere and uniqueness of the city where every roadway is a water course. Stepping off the train and onto the water taxi that bore us along the waterways, we felt we had left Italy behind and entered an exotic eastern republic. Boats of every description were plying the canals, whipping the water into wavelets that shimmered and glinted golden in the evening sun. *Vaporetti* (water buses), postal service boats, ambulance boats, fire patrol boats and police boats all shared the water courses with barges that carried fresh vegetables, fruit and flowers to the dock at the Rialto Bridge. In the narrower canals gondoliers in boater hats and striped shirts poled their black enamelled gondolas beside pastel Byzantine palaces that line the water's edge. A gondolier would occasionally break into a snippet of song much to the amusement of his passengers, young romantic couples who sat cuddled closely together in the prow.

We spent our first day wandering the cobbled lanes shopping for carnival masks. We crossed over the Bridge of Sighs that connected the interrogation room of Doge's palace to a prison cell, admired the gilded frescoes that cover the walls of St. Mark's Basilica and sauntered up and down the Riva Schiavoni where street artists and souvenir sellers plied their trade.

On our second day, we hopped onto the "*vaporetto*" that regularly works its way between Venice and the island of Murano, famous for its glass works. But we bought nothing - we were disappointed with the garish goblets and tacky glass-blown trinkets tailored to the tourist trade that were for sale in every shop.

On the way between Murano and Venice is San Michelle, the cemetery island. On our way back to Venice we met a black waterborne hearse transporting a coffin that was piled high with banks of flowers. In the rear of the boat, behind the coffin, a black curtained compartment afforded privacy to the mourners. The pilot of our "*vaporetto*" slowed respectfully and allowed the floating floral bier to pass smoothly across our bow and into the dock.

It was my birthday that weekend and I was surprised to find a dozen red roses had been delivered to our room in our tiny hotel on a sliver of a street just off the Grand Canal. They'd been ordered by Fr. Larry Hemmelgarn, the young priest we'd met at language school in Perugia. His Mom's birthday is the same day as mine, and since she's at home in the States, Fr. Larry chose me as his surrogate Mom for the day. (It seems we have an adopted son.)

Venice was so enjoyable we decided to stay over another day and skip Monday's classes. We didn't realize that by doing so, we were invalidating our return train tickets. We'd not read the fine print on the back stipulating that they were to be used within three days of purchase. The conductor threatened to throw us off the train if we didn't pay up again. We begged and pleaded with him but he was unsympathetic and gave us the choice of being put off at the next stop or buying new tickets. We paid up! Still, Venice was worth the hassle.

When we returned to Perugia we received an urgent message from Fr. Mario. He told us to have five passport-size photos taken and to rush them to Angelo at his workplace at a local bank before closing that very day. Angelo would direct the photos to Milan, where they'd be given to a person who was leaving for Tanzania. We found a machine that produced acceptable photos and hand-delivered them to Angelo before the deadline. These photos are required by the Tanzanian government for our residence permits, which we'll need before we can enter the country. Someone, somewhere, either in Canada, Italy or Tanzania, had lost the photos we'd given Bro before we left Canada. It will be interesting to see if we'll get the permits before we leave for Tanzania, but we'll try not to think about these things now.

Now that we're here once again in Rome, we're not missing any opportunity to further immerse ourselves in the Italian culture.

So far we toured the Vatican, went on a jaunt to the ancient ruins of Ostia Antica and revisited the Fountain of Trevi, where 34 years ago we'd tossed our coins into the fountain. (This little ritual, according to legend, is said to assure your return to Rome. We've been back three times since then, so the legend must be true, eh?)

Monsignor John Knight, the fellow who put us in touch with Bro and is responsible for starting us on this path, is here in Rome. It was wonderful to see him again. He invited us to join him for a pizza that we ate sitting in a small cafe at the base of the Spanish Steps.

We've spent some time visiting with one of the young Italian Precious Blood Fathers, Father Vincenzo, who's staying here at the Fathers' residence while taking advanced theological studies. He's been working in Tanzania for many years and will be returning to Manyoni once his studies are completed. Father took his seminary training in Tanzania, is fluent in Swahili and is as familiar with the culture as a native. We hope we'll see more of this dedicated and highly intelligent man when we meet again in Tanzania.

One evening we set out for a walk with him through the old parts of the city. As evening fell, artistically placed lights came on illuminating the ancient archways, columns and ruins. The Romans use light as a painter uses a palette; it was breathtaking to see the Eternal City by night.

The next letter you receive will be from Africa. Soon we leave for Dar es Salaam.

Before being sent off to Musoma for our Swahili studies we have four months to spend in the missions, dividing our stay between Dar es Salaam and Manyoni. We'll use the time preparing to take control of the workshop and training centre and letting our poor brains recover from the battering they received at Italian school.

Is there any room left in our tired old craniums to absorb another language? (We must be MAD! MAD! MAD!)

Love to all,

Mom and Dad

****

***To our son Kurt, daughter-in-law Carole and family*:**
Dar es Salaam, Tanzania
April 18, 1988

Dear Kurt, Carole, Brittany and Benje,

As you can see by the address, we've left Italy (*arrivederci Roma*) and are back in Tanzania at the retreat centre in Dar es Salaam. We've been here for a week waiting for a ride up-country to Manyoni. This is the period of the "long rains" and if we don't get through soon, the road will become impassable. We could be stranded here for the duration.

We've noticed a pattern to these tropical rains. Every morning, clouds begin building up and, by midday, when they've become so heavy with moisture they can't hold any more, they let loose and pummel the earth, turning it into rivers of red. Then the sky clears, the sun comes out, and we're bathed in a sauna-like atmosphere only to have the cycle repeated next day. The mission garden looks even lovelier than it did in the dry season. The red coral pathways, having been washed clean, look so much brighter, and droplets of water shimmer on the blossoms of the white frangipani and fill the wells of the yellow trumpet flowers. But, despite the beauty of the place, the heat and dampness are becoming insufferable. In fact, this air-letter is so limp with moisture it's difficult for my pen to lay down ink without tearing the paper.

We were confused when we arrived at the airport in Dar es Salaam. Our residency permits hadn't arrived before we left Rome and we didn't know which immigration line to get into. Should we be in the visitors' line or the residents' line? We wondered why we'd been sent along to Tanzania without the proper documentation and were concerned that we might be refused entry. But, when we saw Ted's blonde head towering above the sea of black figures in the immigration hall, we relaxed. Ted spotted us and moving toward us burst through the crowd with our residency permits in hand. He had come directly from the Immigration Office. It wasn't until that very morning that our photos were affixed to the documents and our status approved. Talk about split-second timing!

Ted was planning to fly us up to Manyoni, but has come down with malaria. He is not hospitalized but is receiving excellent treatment from the nursing Sisters next door.

The highest risk for malaria is now, during the rainy season, when mosquitoes breed in the stagnant water that accumulates in the discarded tins, tires and vessels of all sorts that lie in the garbage-strewn streets.

The malaria parasite is carried by the female anopheles mosquito. She bites between dusk and dawn so we take special precautions to avoid being bitten during that time. Long pants and long-sleeved shirts are the order of the day if we're going out in the evening or, if it's too hot for that, we dab on a bit of DEET. Tight screens on the windows keep most of the biting blighters out of our room but if any do manage to get in, we've protected ourselves by moving our beds under the whirling ceiling fan. These anopheles mosquitoes are so tiny and light they find it hard to land against the stiff breeze.

We take our anti-malarial meds every day and always carry medicine for treatment if malaria still strikes. The medical people here know exactly what to do, so don't worry about us; we're in good hands. A Japanese aid organization has started a program of mosquito eradication, but it'll be a Herculean task.

There's been some rotation of personnel since our last visit. Tim, the American Brother, has gone back to the States to study for the priesthood. We're going to miss his support and quiet enthusiasm. But we're happy that Fr. Domenic, our friend and supporter, is still here. He's been ever so helpful and has loaned us his car to go into the city to do some errands.

Our first errand was to deliver a package to Neema Nyerere's Mom. (Neema is the young Tanzanian lady that we met at language school in Perugia.) Neema's instructions were to go to the First National Bank of Tanzania, her Mom's workplace, and ask for "Mama Lulu". Mothers in Tanzania, Neema told us, are referred to by associating them with their firstborn. The title "Mama Lulu" indicates that this lady is named for Neema's sister Lulu, who is her eldest sibling. "Everyone will know who you mean," she said.

So off we went to the bank and asked for "Mama Lulu". The receptionist was not at all confused. She went directly into the Loan's Office and within minutes came back with Neema's mother. Mrs. Nyerere was overjoyed to meet someone who knew Neema and peppered us with questions about her daughter's well-being. Before we left she invited us to dinner at her home the next time we're in town. Something to look forward to! It's great to have an invitation to socialize with the local people.

We dropped off copies of our passports, residency permits and other important data at the Canadian High Commission offices. If there should happen to be an emergency at home and you couldn't contact us, the High Commission people would know how and where to find us.

It's been nine months since we were promised our new house, but reports from up-country say that it has advanced only as far as the foundation. In fact, Ted told us, it wasn't until Bro and the young Canadians were here six weeks ago that any work was done on it at all. It was they who dug the trenches for the footings. God knows how long it will be before it'll be built. In the interim, we'll be staying in that miserable bunker. (Oh joy!)

Records show that our trunks left Canada on February 2, but the ship carrying them has not yet arrived in port. It seems that, not only will we not be in our new home; we won't have our special things either.

Whenever we show the slightest impatience with these delays, one of the Africans will try to calm us by saying "*pole, pole*". (Pronounced "poley, poley" it's a Swahili phrase that means "slowly, slowly".) We're hearing this mantra over and over again, bringing us to accept the fact that, in Africa, nothing ever moves quickly.

Wow! Father Domenic just popped his head into our room and handed us the telegram containing the wonderful news that baby Patrick has arrived. So we are grandparents once again! You've been in our thoughts as the time for his birth drew close. We've been praying for a safe delivery and are relieved that everything went well. Thank God. We're feeling a twinge of guilt at being so far from you, but you know that if ever we're needed at home you've only to call.

We'll write once again as soon as we're in Manyoni. Lots of hugs for everyone, especially wee Patrick!

Love,

Mom and Dad

****

To our son Greg and his girl friend Carolyn:
Manyoni, Tanzania
May 18, 1988

Dear Greg and Carolyn,

After many days of waiting in Dar es Salaam, we finally got a ride up-country with the Chibumagwa Nursing Sisters. Their powerful Toyota Landcruiser had no trouble passing through the slick deeply-rutted road that runs between Dodoma and Manyoni. Other motorists were not so lucky. Here and there we passed by abandoned vehicles that had bogged down because their bald tires had been unable to gain traction in the mud.

The Sisters' driver took us to the main mission house in Manyoni where we dropped off our bags before heading directly to the site where our house is under construction. The young East Indian contractor was there supervising the laying of the cement blocks that will form the walls. He walked toward us and introduced himself. "You can call me Girish," he said. We liked him immediately. Darkly handsome, he resembles Omar Sharif in every feature, from the square jaw, soft brown eyes and black wavy hair to the dapper moustache. His skin, the colour of café au lait, was accented by the white shirt he had on. The sleeves were rolled up just below the elbows and on his left wrist he wore a steel bangle. He carried a clipboard which, astonishingly, had the foolscap sketch I'd made on our preliminary visit fastened to it. Since I am neither architect nor draughtsman, I had expected someone would have taken my rough draft and drawn up proper blueprints. But no, here was Girish, constructing our house using only my simple diagram and his experience.

It wasn't immediately apparent but, after we stood talking for a while, we noticed that the foundation had been laid the wrong way round; rather than being positioned to catch the morning sun in the kitchen and the setting sun in the living room, it was reversed. Too late for changes! Never mind, we're going to enjoy it, no matter what.

Girish left his crew and came to help us carry our bags to the bunker. When we got there, we were touched to see that Ted had repainted the interior white in anticipation of our return. It's made a tremendous difference to the light level. It's still on the gloomy side, but what an improvement from the purple, blue and emerald green walls.

We're not sure when Girish's family first came to Tanzania, but Indian traders have been coming to East Africa since the days when they followed the routes of the Arabs. There was a large influx in the 1800's when they were brought in by the white settlers to build the Uganda - Kenya railroad. Many stayed on to work as administrators, clerks and *dukawallas* (traders). (This is why the small roadside shops are called *dukas*.)

Girish had learned the building craft from his father who ran a small construction company in Singida. After his father's death, Girish took over as chief provider for the family. He and two of his brothers, Menoj and Gitu, operate a number of businesses. As well as contracting in building construction, they run a flour mill and a small *duka* where they sell imported items.

At first we thought that Girish was a Sikh because of the steel bangle that he wore. (It's one of "the five K's" (or *Kakkari* symbols) that all Sikh men are enjoined to wear.) But no, Girish just likes the bangle. It certainly has no religious significance to him at all since all we've ever seen him do with it is open beer bottles!

Girish's family is Hindu. His mother, Girish says, is devoutly religious and tends to the Temple that is attached to the family home in Singida. In conformance with her religion, she is a total vegan. But the boys, not being as reverent as their mom, will on occasion eat meat - much to her disgust.

If one is Hindu, Girish told us, you can tell what caste a family belongs to by their surname. Girish's last name is Vishani, which means that his family is of the third caste of merchants, traders, farmers and craftsmen: specifically - the sub-caste of "barber".

Girish stays in a small apartment next to the Sisters' station while he's working here. Like us, he doesn't have much to do evenings and weekends so we've come to rely on each other for companionship. We've already spent many happy hours at his place drinking hot sweet Indian tea - and an occasional cold beer - while getting a first hand education in Tanzanian life and culture.

I've already begun to teach English to the girls at the Sisters' well-managed Home Craft School. There was no gentle transition into the job. When I went to observe, the male Tanzanian teacher stopped mid-sentence, handed me the text and said, "Here, teach this." Then he went and sat down at the back of the room. The girls love to sing so we take the last few minutes of every English lesson to do that. I've already taught them a few lines of Schubert's "Ave Maria". They caught on to the classical tonality and style in a flash.

I've also begun teaching the young men at the workshop/training centre. But I have to confine the lessons to the first hour of the day before the workshop opens and the quiet is shattered by the start-up of the vibrating power plant. The meagre facilities consist of eight double-desks and a slab of pitted grey cement trowelled onto the wall. Writing on this makeshift blackboard is next to impossible. The poor quality Chinese chalk scuffs across the surface leaving gaps where it refuses to lay down chalk. A bundle of rags serves as a blackboard eraser. There are no text books or maps or any other type of teaching aid.

Conditions are far from ideal, as you can tell, but I DO enjoy the teaching. In a country where education is so highly prized, there are few discipline problems. Competition is stiff and once a student has secured a spot he tries to do his best knowing that, should he fail, there are others who would eagerly take his place.

When I'm not teaching, I'm helping Dad get a handle on things at the workshop. We've begun tool and parts inventories, set up personnel and vehicle files, drafted parts order forms, etc., etc., but there is much, much more to do and to discover. If we can get some of our questions answered, we hope to have a preliminary report for Bro and Father Dino before we leave for Swahili classes in Musoma.

Ted has moved the mission plane from Dodoma to a small airstrip here in Manyoni so he's able to fly the mission personnel around. Last week he flew us to Dodoma to get our Tanzanian driver's licenses. The flight there went smoothly and without incident, but the return trip was something else! Just as Ted was about to put the Cessna 206 down, a brush cutter swinging a *panga* stepped out onto the runway. Ted, cursing under his breath, pulled up the flaps and circled the airstrip. The man, seeing the plane, stepped off into the bushes, which allowed Ted to come in for a second attempt. But just as he was about to land, a gaggle of kids emerged from the bush and stood laughing and waving at us directly under the flight path. Ted mumbled something in anger (I think it was in Dutch), pulled up and circled around once more. In a few moments the children left the runway and we were able to land. Ted was furious! He stepped out of the cockpit and strode toward the wrinkled old guard who sat unconcernedly in his tiny tin shelter. Ted blasted him in Swahili demanding to know why he had not secured the area. The old man, genuinely puzzled by Ted's verbal assault, told Ted that he didn't think he could possibly land because, and I quote, "*Hewa mbaya*" (the air is bad).

It took us 30 minutes to fly from Dodoma and 15 minutes to land in Manyoni!

We never miss an opportunity for a diversion, so when we were invited to a wedding in the village of Chibumagua down in the Rift Valley we were eager to attend. Father John conducted the Christian (Catholic) ceremony, but incorporated into it were some aspects of the tribal ways of the Wagogo, the principle tribe in this area.

We arrived punctually and seated ourselves near the back of the village church. As the appointed hour for the ceremony came and went, local folk, unencumbered by the constraints of clocks, drifted in. The open-sided breeze-block church designed to encourage cross ventilation failed in its promise to deliver a fresh breeze; we felt no air moving at all. As we sat waiting for the ceremony to begin it grew hotter and hotter and the tin roof sent out pinging sounds as it expanded in the midmorning sun. A few doves cooed from the coolness of the one and only acacia tree in the church yard and minute mosquitoes floated by in the still air. We amused ourselves by trying to follow their flight paths. They're not at all like Yukon mosquitoes that can be seen and swatted once they alight on their prey. These tiny, but deadly, African insects suddenly loom into view, then, even as your eyes are on them, they disappear as though vaporized by some unseen force. The only time you can get at them is when they've already bitten someone and are sluggish and heavy with blood.

We were tiring of this game when at last Ted's white Toyota pickup, the wedding limo, rolled up to the church doors and the bride and groom stepped out. The groom, grinning from ear to ear, was glorious in a western style dark suit and flashy red tie. But the bride, who, by tribal custom, is expected to be grieving at leaving her family, is not permitted to smile. While everyone else looked happy, she kept a sorrowful face throughout the whole affair keeping her big brown eyes cast down and holding her white veil across her beautiful face like a shroud of sadness. After the wedding vows were exchanged, several elders moved toward the altar, and each in turn gave a stern lecture to the couple on their rights and obligations. It went on and on in the stifling heat.

Many Wagogo adults have a defining spot in the centre of the forehead. It is permanent, having been branded there at the time of the "coming of age" rituals. Both the bride and groom and many of the wedding guests were so marked.

The Fathers and Sisters keep wedding dresses and veils on hand that they lend out to brides if they want to have a European style wedding. Father Ernesto told us about a funny experience he had a few years ago. When he was preparing a couple for marriage, he offered the bride the loan of a wedding dress but, not knowing her size, gave her two to try. On the wedding day, as he waited at the altar to begin the ceremony, he was surprised to see both bride and groom walking up the aisle, similarly veiled and gowned in white. Somewhat puzzled, he looked from one to the other and asked, "And which one of you is the bride?"

Our lives are being changed by these peeks into different cultural practices. And, at night, when we hear hyenas prowling around the yard trying to get at the mission dogs, we realize how close we are to nature. There have been reports that elephants have been marauding in the *shambas* (fields) of the villagers, and we were told that a Barabaig tribesman killed a lion with a spear very close to the town.

Hivyo, ndivyo, vilivyo, (that's the way it is) in beautiful central Tanzania.

Love you guys. Continue to pray for us as we do for you, and keep these letters on the move.

Mom and Dad

****

To our son Chris, daughter Kelly, son-in-law Don and family:
Manyoni, Tanzania
June 23, 1988

Dear Chris, Kelly, Don, Vanessa, Dyana and Nicholas,

Before I fill you in on the news of the last few weeks, I have to tell you about a most chilling event that we witnessed today. So forgive me for forging ahead without the usual pleasantries.

It happened this morning at the Sisters' house. We were quietly having coffee with Mama Angelina, when suddenly the high-pitched screams of women's voices punctuated by the rhythmic sounds of bare feet pelting on earth, jolted us from our chairs. The shrieks were so filled with terror that we rushed to the door and looked out. A group of girls from the home craft school were streaking toward us along the path from the cassava field where they'd been hoeing. Behind them, propelling itself along at an astonishing speed was a very long olive-coloured snake. Girish had also heard the commotion and rushed out of his apartment carrying a shotgun. "It's a *mamba*!" he shouted. "Stand back!" The girls, still screaming, leapt to safety on the Sisters' porch where we stood pressed up against the wall. Girish edged closer to the snake that had come to rest against a stone wall and raised his gun. In rapid response the snake reared up and arched its coffin-shaped head. Moving its sinuous body back and forth, it spread its cobra-like neck flaps and, opening its fanged jaws, revealed the sinister black interior of its mouth. Fixing its eyes, stony and hard as chips of coal, on Girish's form, it hissed a final warning. Girish replied by releasing a blast of shotgun pellets that found their mark. The girls stopped their screaming and all was quiet as we watched the *mamba* writhing in its death throes; its body making taut loops off the ground before subsiding limply onto the grass. I didn't stay to see what Girish did with the snake's body. I stepped back into the Sisters' dining room and fought back the waves of nausea that accompanied my revulsion.

Later, at supper time, when we sat discussing the incident, Fr. Dino assured us that *mambas* are extremely shy and it was unlikely that it was in pursuit of the girls. It just happened to be on the same path. But, he cautioned, it will strike if cornered, not once but repeatedly, each strike injecting lethal neurotoxins that kill in minutes. He excused himself from the table and came back with a small plastic case that held a piece of black slate-like material - a "black stone". The instructions read, "The black stone is used against blood poisoning caused by the bite of snakes, scorpions and other venomous insects. The bite must be made to bleed and the stone applied. It sticks to the wound and cannot be detached until all the poison has been absorbed. Then, put it in warm water for 30 minutes and, when the bubbling ceases, the stone is to be put into milk for two hours, rinsed and dried in the open air. The stone can then be used again."

"Does it work?" you may ask. We're not sure. No one here has tried it or knows of anyone who has. But you can be sure we'll be mighty careful never to put ourselves into a situation where it might be necessary.

Now, having got that horror story out of the way, let's move on to more pleasant things. It was fantastic to hear your voices on the phone last week. The line was surprisingly clear. The kids sounded exactly as they do in person, bright as buttons.

Getting a call through to Canada from this part of Africa can be very difficult, but we were lucky on our first try. There is no system of direct dialling here. The telephone system still uses operators just as we used to in "the olden days". You have to crank the handle to reach the local operator and then ask her for "International". When the international operator comes on, you give the phone number of the party you want and stand by. At times they can get right through, but most often you're asked to hang up and wait. When the connection is made the operator calls you back. It can take anywhere from a few minutes up to several days to complete the process.

There's only one telephone at the Fathers' house. It's tucked away in a dark corner where there are always hordes of mosquitoes; they seem to appreciate the cooler temperature and darkness there. And the location guarantees that no one will linger long in idle conversation.

Last month was the holy month of Ramadhan, when, Muslims believe, Allah revealed verses of the Qu'ran to the Prophet Muhammad. Muslims fast from daybreak to sunset during this time. The beginning of Ramadhan, which comes every ninth lunar month, is determined by the sighting of the new moon. The end is marked by the celebration of *Eid-el-Fitr* (Feast of the Fast-Breaking). This year the Mullahs couldn't agree on which of two days the silver sliver of the new moon appeared, so we had both days off. Problem solved the Tanzanian way!

There are several Muslims on the mission staff, and they're given a few hours off every Friday to attend mosque. It's very refreshing to see all segments of Tanzanian society being honoured or, if not honoured, at least tolerated. These folks have no problem respecting Christmas, Easter, Ramadhan, Diwali, etc., as well as all the government holidays. Any excuse for a party and a day off work, eh?

Tanzania is a one-party socialist state. The "Party," called *Chama Cha Mapunduzi*, or CCM for short, is getting ready to celebrate *Saba Saba* Day. They're sending agents out to the villages to collect a tax for the big bash. *Saba* is the number seven in Swahili, so *Saba Saba* signifies the seventh day of the seventh month, i.e., July 7, marking the day and month the country gained its independence from Britain. The celebrations for this district will be held in Singida, 130 kilometres from here. That's a long way by car and even longer for a peasant who may decide to walk there to see how his taxes are being spent. Obviously, not too many peasants are going to make it to Singida to take in the festivities, so they arrange to be busy in their fields far from home when "the tax man cometh". And who can blame them? Loyalty to the Party is expected. In fact the law requires every school, even the two mission schools, to teach one lesson per week of *Siasa* (political education). This compulsory class is always announced by the striking of a gong.

But, let me get back to domestic matters. Our trunks have finally arrived. It took them three months to get from Toronto to Dar es Salaam and two months to get out of port and up to Manyoni. Go figure! One of the locks had been tampered with and we found that our powerful Eddie Bauer flashlight and my good pair of scissors were missing, but we were relieved to see that Dad's precious toolbox, all our books and my electronic piano were intact. Thank God. To get by without them would have been quite a deprivation for us.

All work on our house has come to a halt. The walls are up, the ditches are dug for the water and sewer pipes, but the roof, ordered from Italy, has yet to arrive. If we're in by Christmas, I'll be surprised. Girish has gone back to his home in Singida and won't return to Manyoni until he can resume his work. We sure miss him.

Weekends and evenings drag on and on. The *pumba* crowd still gathers at 4:30 a.m. outside the "bunker" every Saturday in the hopes of exchanging maize husks for clothing. Sometimes there's an exchange and sometimes not. Ever since I messed up so royally trying to help when we were here earlier, I've not volunteered again. To escape the noise and babble, we often go to the workshop on weekends where we work quietly on our reorganization plans.

Bro is expected to leave Toronto soon for his semi-annual visit over here. We're wondering if you could call Greg to make up a care package and get it over to his office ASAP. We'd really like to have some more paperbacks (spy thrillers and historical novels), classical tapes and movies. (We can play movies in VHS on the VCR over at the Fathers' house.) That would help to pass the long, tedious evenings. Send only a few things so Bro can fit them comfortably into his suitcase. Otherwise they'd have to come by ship and that takes months. Oh, and please have him bring a supply of good Canadian chalk to replace the awful Chinese stuff we're using.

We're really quite lonely here. We don't see much of Ted. When he's not out in the villages drilling water wells or erecting windmills, he works long and hard in his workshop, fabricating parts for the windmill stands. Often, after everyone has gone to bed, the generator behind his shop is still powering away while he grinds and welds until the early hours.

We don't see Ana much, either. She doesn't have a car and the only time she can come up out of the "Rift" is if she gets a lift from one of the Sisters. She's been putting pressure on Bro to fulfill his promise to get her a vehicle of her own. He says he's ordered two Isuzu Troopers from Japan which we can expect to be delivered mid-August. Ana is to have one of them and we'll have the other. Freedom is on its way! These four-door, five-passenger models are complete with A/C and tape decks. We'll have room for three friends or family members when you lovely folks come for a visit.

Dad has been spending many hours working on Ted's old German-made drill rig and truck. Yesterday he was chased away by a swarm of African bees when thousands of them swirled above the rig. They formed a black-dotted funnel intent on crawling en masse into a hollow support pipe. The steady dull droning alerted Dad and he wormed his body out from under the rig without exciting them. He wasn't stung, thank God! The only way to deal with bees is to leave them alone. When they have settled for the night into whatever nook or cranny they have chosen, they become sluggish and can be eliminated with insecticide or diesel fuel. A whole hive of them hunkered down in the electrical switch box behind our house and that's how we dealt with them.

We're still working 'flat out' on our workshop/training centre recommendations. We have put Elly Peter, a very intelligent and trustworthy fellow, in charge of parts and tools. He has become our "trustee" in the tool room and is proving to be the ally we need. Elly is Pentecostal and appears to totally live by the tenets of his faith. (Would that there were more workers like him!)

Fr. John has moved up from his previous post at Chibumagua in the Rift Valley and has been assigned to work with us on the workshop/training centre project. Education is a priority with him, so we're hoping we'll have a supporter in developing a really fine trade school.

Life is getting more interesting as we're now meeting some of the local folks. When Baldwin, the night *mlinzi* (guard) asked us if he could escort us on a tour of the town, we jumped at the chance. He came to collect us on Sunday afternoon still dressed in his church clothes: tapered trousers, white shoes and sparkling white shirt that fit perfectly over his broad black shoulders. We walked for at least two hours in the midday heat enjoying Baldwin and his stories. His English is excellent, due to the fact that he attended a seminary for several years. In the unlikely event Manyoni were ever to make it onto the "tourist circuit", Baldwin would make a superb professional guide.

The first half-mile along the dusty road took us through town past a collection of small *dukas* (shops) that ply their trade on both sides of the road. Parallel to them run deep drainage ditches that have become a repository for all manner of garbage such as maize cobs stripped of their kernels, browning corn husks, rotting banana peels, mango pits, bits of rag and cast off flip-flops with broken straps. Blue plastic garbage bags fluttered about in the streets. Occasionally a stiff breeze would pick one up and send it sailing up against the side of a building. Outside the mosque, at the side of the road, there's an abandoned rear axle housing and an old engine block. All the useful parts were stripped away long ago. Baldwin said they've been there for years. What's left is of no use to anyone, and no one minds them staying there forever, so there they sit.

Whenever we met children on our walk, they would shyly turn their heads and mumble something very softly, which sounded like *schik*. Baldwin told us they were saying *shikomuu* (pronounced *shikamo*), a greeting that is used by children when addressing their elders. The origin of this custom goes back to the days when slaves used the term when acknowledging their masters.

The full phrase used to be *nashika miguu yako*, meaning "I hold your feet." Baldwin told us to respond with *marahaba*, the Arabic equivalent for "you're welcome."

A group of dirty, ragged children were being plagued by bush flies. The insects were crawling on the youngster's faces, and kneading their feelers into the corners of their eyes and into their snotty noses. The kids weren't bothered by the flies and made no attempt to brush them away. Because bush flies breed in animal and human feces and spread eye diseases, Baldwin was concerned about the children's health. He stooped down and spoke to the eldest of the lot encouraging him to clean up and go to the Sisters' clinic for treatment of his red irritated eyes. The lad momentarily stopped his play and looked at Baldwin blankly. Then, ignoring his advice, he turned back to playing with his hoop, a rusty bicycle rim that he pushed along with a stick.

Baldwin, who has the classic broad nose and full lips of the Bantu, and is as black as boot polish, pointed out a cluster of fairer-skinned and finer-featured youngsters who were playing all by themselves. "There," he said, nodding in their direction with a knowing grin, "go the 'electric kids'."

These mocha-coloured six and seven-year olds are the result of liaisons between African women and Yugoslavian electrical workers who were here during the construction of the high voltage power line that runs through the area. Everyone is aware that these youngsters are different and the cry goes up whenever they're seen, "There go the 'electric kids'!"

A passenger train was sitting at the train station idling softly, so we ambled over to see what the problem was. A dozen rusting carriages ranged along the curving track, first, second and third classes all equally grungy. The train hadn't turned a wheel since it ground to a halt late last night, stranding hundreds of passengers. No one was shouting or in a temper because of the delay. A few children were crying, but on the whole, everyone sat or lay patiently on the grassy slope under the mango trees lulled by the steady thrumming of the diesel locomotive. A few farmers took advantage of the captive customers and were weaving among the crowd selling papayas, mangoes and oranges. A strong odour of urine overwhelmed the place. The few toilets in the station were either out of order or unable to handle the needs of so many at one time, so folks simply relieved themselves wherever they could. We never did find out why the train was stopped so long. Some told Baldwin there were bandits ahead; others claimed there were elephants on the track; while others were of the opinion there was a derailment somewhere down the line. Whatever the cause, the train didn't move off until later that evening.

Baldwin's white shoes were covered with dust and my heels and the tops of my toes were blistered, yet we pressed on with "the tour".

A small rustic motel built around a cool courtyard was our next stop. Above the door of one of the units was a faded wooden hand-painted sign saying, "Mwalimu Nyerere slept here." Mwalimu, which means teacher, is the revered title given to the illustrious Past President, Julius Nyerere, deemed the "Father of the Nation".

Baldwin is something of an historian and, as we stood in the courtyard, he gave us a lesson on Tanzania's move to independence. "Mwalimu," Baldwin enlightened us, "was the first President to try and make education and health care available to the rural people. It was difficult to provide clinics and schools for a population scattered throughout the country, so the new government started a scheme they called 'villagisation.' Being a Socialist, Nyerere encouraged rural folks to move together to form collective villages, which he called "*Ujamaa*" (Family hood) villages."

Baldwin then admitted, "There was some success, but he made his big mistake in 1975 by trying to forcibly resettle those who resisted his plan. In some villages there wasn't enough water for the larger numbers. Also, people resented being moved from the tribal areas they called home, so *Ujamaa* was doomed to fail."

One good thing resulted from the collective idea, though. President Nyerere, Baldwin told us, insisted that Swahili become the national language. This succeeded in unifying the nation. There are over 120 tribes in Tanzania. Each group has its own language that's spoken at home, but once the kids start school all lessons are taught in Swahili. Later on, in the higher grades, English is taught and has become the medium of higher education and commerce.

The wonderful result of having common languages is that Tanzania is one of the most peaceful countries in Africa.

I was hobbling along painfully nursing my blisters as the tour came to an end, but Baldwin never became impatient with my slowness. Even though he lives on the other end of town and it was far out of his way, Baldwin courteously escorted us all the way back to the "bunker".

Ted is going to fly us to Dar es Salaam soon, where we'll stay for a few weeks. We're going to visit other trades training centres to find out about required course content, prerequisites, apprenticeship programs, etc., so our training will mesh with theirs.

Then, of course, we'll need to know what supplies, parts and tools are available locally and what will need to be imported. So much to learn, so much to do: our heads are spinning!

Canada Day is coming soon. There's always a big bash for expatriates at the Canadian High Commission. It would be fun to attend this year. If we're lucky enough to get an invitation we'll be there, wrapped up in the good ol' Maple Leaf flag.

Well, dear folks, it's time to wrap this up. Chris, if you still want to come and see us in January, we would be so happy. The locals tell us that the short rains should be over in this area so, if our vehicle is delivered on time, we'd be able to take in some of the game parks. It would be wonderful to do that. But, don't make any firm plans until we see if our car arrives.

Love to everyone,

Mom and Dad

****

To our son Dave:
Dar es Salaam Tanzania,
July 26, 1988

Dear Dave,

We're nearing the end of our time in Dar es Salaam where, for the last few weeks, we've been helping out at the Procura and accumulating information relating to our work. Ted flew us down here in the Cessna 206. The flight was excellent and from our smooth comfortable perches we could look down on the vehicles, tiny as Tonka toys enveloped in dust, lurching along the rocky roadway. As we passed over Morogoro, Ted took the aircraft up to 11,500 feet and veering slightly north moved away from the "no-fly zone" where the liberation movement of South Africa, the ANC (African National Congress), has set up military training camps. "Don't want to get shot down now, do we?" he said through his headset.

We had the use of a Volkswagen Beetle while in Dar. Vintage transportation, but it handled well. The left-hand drive made for a bit of confusion but it was great fun being back in that energetic city.

A Canadian medical student is staying at the retreat centre waiting for a ride up-country to the mission hospital in Itigi, where he'll be doing a facet of his medical studies. Joseph Tham, who was born in Hong Kong but is now a Canadian citizen, is a bright, happy chap and we've been delighted to take him along on our escapades.

Together we took in the Canada Day celebrations at "Canada Village" where many of the High Commission employees live. The village is located at Oyster Bay north of Dar es Salaam beside the beautiful coastal road that parallels the palm-peppered beaches of the Indian Ocean.

A fluttering Canadian flag marked the entrance to the venue, a high-walled gated community secured by uniformed guards. Once admitted inside the compound we found spots at one of the white-draped tables that had been set up around the swimming pool. In the centre of each table sat a miniature replica of our flag.

Many of the High Commission staff and their families were on hand to welcome us "expats". In fact, High Commissioner David Rose and his wife began the festivities by presiding at the singing of "O Canada" while we all stood around the central flag.

We're not sure who paid for it, but we think it was probably you generous Canadian taxpayers who should be thanked for the traditional picnic fare: chilli, hotdogs and beer.

A surprising number of Canadians working on projects in rural Tanzania had come into Dar for the celebrations. One group at the Canadian/Tanzanian Wheat Project that's located close to us has invited us to come for a visit. How lovely that will be! Why, we are practically neighbours.

Bro arrived from Toronto on July 2. It was good to see him. He'd brought special treats from home in preparation for the multiple celebrations that fall within a day of each other: The Feast of the Precious Blood (marking the founding of this Order of Catholic Priests, Brothers and Sisters), American Independence Day (because Bro is an American), Canada Day and our wedding anniversary. It was a wonderful weekend. Pius, the cook, had obviously been briefed because, using many of the imported ingredients that Bro had brought, he outdid himself with every meal. For example, on the day of our anniversary, Pius served caviar on toast for breakfast and followed that up by preparing roast duck, trimmings and fine wine for dinner.

Word was out that Bro was "in town" and many local people dropped in to the centre to see him. One of the visitors was Cardinal Rugambwa's nephew Renatus and another was Godfrey, Mwalimu Nyerere's son. Bro obviously knows "who's who" in Tanzania's top society.

Mama Lulu Nyerere, our friend Neema's mom, had us out to her place for a visit. Her husband Joseph, the brother of Past President Mwalimu Julius Nyerere, looks exactly like him. For a moment we thought it was "The Founder of the Nation" himself. Our conversation was far-ranging and included politics and political systems. Tanzania, being a socialist country, has close ties to Russia, Cuba and China; in fact, there was a picture of the Nyereres with Chairman Mao on the mantle.

On another day, friends of Bro, Colonel and Mrs. Komba, took us to the Kunduchi Hotel for dinner. We sat outside under the southern sky and watched the fishermen on the beach "firing" their boats by smearing tar over them and setting them alight. The Colonel explained that this is done regularly to kill off insects that can destroy the wooden hulls.

We'd finished our report outlining our recommendations for upgrading the workshop/training centre and gave Bro a copy. He was very thoughtful about the suggestions, so we're hopeful we'll be given the green light for at least some of the ideas. But, the decision is not solely his to make; the Fathers also will have to agree.

The retreat centre was a revolving door of visitors and workers from Italy. Supporters of the mission hospital and relatives of the Fathers and Sisters had come for short visits and to travel the "safari circuit". Other Italian guests were engineers and builders who'd come to begin construction on a new seminary in Dodoma. With all the dialects swirling around us, we found our Italian almost useless. It was as though we'd never had an Italian lesson in our lives!

With all the guests, Pius had his work cut out for him. He took us with him on a shopping trip to the huge covered market they call Kariakoo. Before we left, he cautioned, "No jewellery, Mama. Many thieves at Kariakoo!" So I took off the only three pieces I was wearing: my two rings and my watch. Dad always stashes his valuables in the secret pocket of his Tilley's trousers and keeps a ratty old wallet containing a few shillings in the regular pocket as a decoy. Then, if he's accosted, he's prepared to give up that wallet.

Kariakoo is not a place you'd want to go by yourself. Tight narrow streets, teeming with people both night and day, run between rows of grimy apartment blocks where laundry flutters out over the balconies. When we arrived, a tangled jumble of vehicles parked every which way filled the area around the market. Some were stationed crosswise and a few had even been left facing each other, bumper to bumper. After Pius found a place to park, we followed him to the lower level, where we were jostled by the crowds that milled around the stalls of fresh vegetables and fruit.

Under cover, in the bowels of the marketplace, the air was muggy and reeking of rotting vegetation. Bits of lettuce, cabbage and all manner of vegetable matter had fallen to the floor and been trampled into a slick green mess, making it treacherous to walk. We felt hot and claustrophobic and could hardly wait for Pius to finish his selections and take us to the upper level to shop for herbs and spices.

Bro's 30-day stay in Tanzania stretched to 33 when he missed his flight. It was rather amusing! A chap from the State Department had come to take Bro to the airport and usher him through the VIP lounge. But, just before they were to leave, he asked to look at Bro's ticket and exclaimed, "You've missed your flight! You're exactly 24 hours late." At first Bro was in denial and began to argue that it was not so, but eventually had to accept it as fact. Next morning he drove into town and brazened it out with the Air Ethiopia people, persuading them to honour his ticket for their next flight. (That's what they'd call "chutzpah!") Unfortunately for Bro, the next scheduled flight wasn't due to depart for another three days so he was left to "cool his heels" around the guest house.

Our social calendar, believe it or not, was not yet full. Dad and I were also were invited to a wedding reception for two CIDA (Canadian International Development Agency) employees. The reception was at the Canadian High Commission beach house north of Dar off an unpaved rural road. There'd been a burst of heavy rain in the morning that had turned the road into a quagmire, but our trusty little Volkswagen Beetle saw us through.

As well as providing all the food and drinks, the couple had hired a boatman who was offering rides in a small, but authentic, Arab dhow. We took advantage of the offer and hopped into the roughly-hewn dugout vessel. Stabilized by an outrigger and propelled by a grey canvas triangular (lanteen) sail, it skimmed, light as a feather, across the warm bay.

And, I may have got our group on the Canadian High Commissioner's Christmas list! While we stood in line for the food, we chatted with four delightful Catholic nuns who were most interested in our mission. When it came out in conversation that, through Bro, we'd met a number of highly-placed Tanzanians, one of the nuns turned to Mrs. Rose, the High Commissioner's wife and said, "These people travel in top Tanzanian society. Why, through Brother Anthony, they've already had tea with the Cardinal!" Whereupon Mrs. Rose asked, "Who *is* this Brother Anthony, anyway? I really must update my guest list."

Life in Dar is sure different from life in Manyoni, especially if you tag along with Bro!

We even had a job offer from one of the nuns. "Listen," she said, "if things don't work out for you up-country, you have a job with us here in Dar." We're greatly tempted, but we'd feel like absolute heels to desert Bro when he's already invested so much confidence in us.

In case you think it was all fun and games, let us reassure you that, in between the social events, we did get a lot accomplished. We now have specifics relating to the trades: courses, exams, regulations, etc., and have located suppliers and automotive dealers. We've also inventoried all the items in the warehouse, which they call a "*godown*" (an Indian term).

There's a good news/bad news story about our house. The good news is the roofing panels have arrived. The bad news is they forgot to ship the steel roofing beams for the panels to rest on. God knows when we'll get into the house. It seems it won't be ready for Christmas, after all. However, our "wheels" in the form of an Isuzu Trooper will be delivered soon, so we'll have more freedom to come and go as we please.

We'll be returning to Manyoni in a few days to prepare ourselves for the flight to Musoma where we'll begin our Swahili classes. We expect it'll be gruelling, but are going to give it our best shot.

Please continue to share all these letters and remember to pray for us.

Love,

Mom and Dad

****

To our daughter Kim, son-in-law Blair and family:
Manyoni, Tanzania
August 3, 1988

Dear Kim and Blair, David and baby Robert,

Fantastic! Another grandson has arrived safely and right on the button. As we say in Swahili, *kumshukuru Mungu* (thank God). The phone connection was clear as a bell. We could hear the relief and excitement in Blair's voice. Letters are great, but there's nothing as intimate as hearing a person's voice. Every time we hear of one of these "blessed events" we ache with self-reproach at being so far from you and we wonder at the wisdom of our choice.

Thanks for taking time to write and phone as often as you do. You've no idea how much all the photos and news from home brightens our often-dreary days. We can get the BBC on short-wave radio late at night, but that's about it for international news. There is an English language newspaper, the *Tanzanian Daily News*, but we don't have a subscription yet.

When we were in Dar es Salaam we had many great experiences, but here in Manyoni, we're burdened by the tedium of village life. We're fine during working hours; it's the long evenings and weekends that are so onerous. Apart from mealtimes, there is little social contact with our mission confreres. Everyone seems to be rushed off their feet and none of them has offered to show us around. With Girish away, Baldwin, the Tanzanian mission guard, continues to be our only guide and mentor. He often pops in at the bunker for a chat in the evening before reporting for the night shift. He's as curious about our lifestyle as we are about his. There is much about Canadian living that he can't relate to, but when we described Kelly and Don's log cabin in the woods where moose, wolves and bears wander though the property, there was a real spark of interest as he compared it to an African peasant's existence close to the land surrounded by hyenas, wildebeests and lions. Baldwin talks freely about many African traditions but, no matter how much we prod, he steadfastly refuses to give us any information about tribal initiation rites. That's when the shutters descend on his dark eyes and we're denied entrance into his culture. This area is simply too sensitive to talk to *wazungu* (foreigners) about. All we can do is try to respect their ways as we expect them to respect ours. We value Baldwin's friendship and feel badly that, because we have no kitchen, we can't invite him for any refreshments.

Before arriving here, I had a romantic view of mission activity, but that has been shattered by the realization that much of the work is just plain old-fashioned drudgery.

For example, last Saturday I spent the afternoon in the large walk-in steel shipping container that we call the "Mission Mini Mart". A new shipment of food items had arrived and it was my job to sort through the stock and rearrange it so the cooks would use up the old inventory first. There were boxes of pasta holding a variety of shapes: flat lasagne noodles, spaghetti, penne and elbow macaroni plus cases of tuna, canned tomatoes, tomato paste, artichokes and olives. In short, everything needed for a tasty Italian supper. It was obvious that the old pasta stock had been there for a very long time, because floury dust sifted out from the bottoms of the boxes as I shifted them from the back to the front. I opened several of them and found the contents writhing with weevils. I reported this to Fr. Dino who asked me to salvage as much of the pasta as I could, so my helper, a village lad, and I, ran it through our fingers separating the worst worm-eaten bits from those with only a few holes. It was insufferably hot in there and after several hours of this, I was getting grumpy. I'd had enough when I found more weevils than product in the last box. "Take it and give it the pigs," I told my helper. Well, the way he looked at me you'd think I'd committed a mortal sin! In the end I'm not convinced that he gave it to the pigs at all but rather took it home to his mom where they continued picking out the bits of edible pasta.

Our departure to Musoma has been delayed because I had an accident. I fell, either getting in or out of the shower. Dad said he heard moaning sounds coming from the bathroom. And, when I didn't respond to his calls, he broke down the door and found me lying unconscious and bleeding profusely from a gash above my left eye. I obviously suffered from a concussion because I don't remember anything for a seven or eight-hour period. Dad tells me he first took me to the local hospital but when he was told I'd need stitches, he took one look at the primitive facilities and beat a hasty retreat to the Sisters' dispensary where Sister Delphina, the nursing sister, took over my treatment. She gave me a shot of penicillin, cleaned me up and, in lieu of stitches, put a butterfly bandage on the wound. She told Dad he did well to remove me from the local hospital.

When I woke up at the Sisters' dispensary, I was surprised to see Baldwin sitting beside Dad near my cot. He had come to support Dad. (There is something touchingly loyal about African friends.) Both of them kept asking me the same questions over and over again until I finally gave some coherent answers. The Sisters kindly let me stay at their place until I was stable. The left side of my face is still swollen and blue and my eye has turned a gorgeous purple, but I am healing well.

I'm feeling well enough to travel, so tomorrow we're leaving for Dar es Salaam to catch our plane to Musoma. (There are some American doctors and nurses there so don't worry about me - I'll be well cared for.)

Must wrap this up and get some rest for the gruelling, yet exciting, days ahead. Kim and the baby should be home from the hospital by the time we get to Musoma. If the phone system is reliable we'll call as soon as we're settled. In any event, the post functions relatively well so we can look forward to getting lots of pictures of baby Robert.

Stay well.

Love,

Mom and Dad

****

To our daughter Laura:
Dar es Salaam, Tanzania
August 10, 1988

Dear Laura,

We have our tickets for tomorrow's flight to Musoma where, once again, we'll be back in the classroom. It would have been better for us to have done these language studies years ago before our brains were hardwired. We found that, being older, it takes us twice the effort to accomplish half as much. I think we're entering what modern jargon calls a "steep learning curve".

Whatever were we thinking? At our age, we really should know better. Perhaps, when you get that degree in abnormal psychology, we should volunteer to be your first clients. Do you think you would DARE to analyze us?

Father Dino lent us a small Landrover for the trip down from Manyoni. Because my fall was so recent and my body felt battered by every bump in the road, we took an extra day to get to Dar es Salaam. First we detoured down into the Rift Valley to Chibumagua to see Ana. It was good to see her so happy now that the maternity clinic is up and running. It was a long haul for her to get the clinic built and furnished and supplied with medicines and medical equipment.

It takes a very long time to get things done here. There's always a shortage of supplies locally, so many items have to be sent from abroad. Take our house, for example: we waited three months for the roofing panels and now, because someone forgot to ship the beams to set them on, we must wait another three months. (There's an expression that we *wazungu* (white folks) say to one another when things go wrong: "A.W.A.," a code for "Africa Wins Again.")

From Ana's place, there's a shortcut back to the main road that precludes having to go back up the rugged escarpment. Ana pointed the way and we were off following one of the numerous tracks that run through and around the tiny primitive villages. We were making good progress until we came to a spot where a herd of cattle had crossed. There were only hoof prints as far as we could see; the track was all but obliterated. We stopped and took stock of the situation. We were thinking it would not be good to be lost in this sere and barren place. Other tracks twisted and turned through the scrub brush; any of which could have been the correct one. We knew that if we were to keep to the escarpment on our left we would eventually come to the main road, so we tried one track after another. But we were unsuccessful. Some tracks "petered out" at a collection of huts, while others lead us farther into the desolate expanse away from the escarpment. There were few people about and our apprehension was growing. Finally, a small boy in a dusty tattered shirt and shorts emerged from the bush. Dad stopped the Landrover, rolled down the window and called out to him. The lad came up to the vehicle and mouthed the traditional greeting of youngsters to elders, *shikamuu*. We responded with *marahaba*, and then, through gestures, conveyed our dilemma. A broad grin crept over his face as he hopped onto the running board and directed us toward the nearest hut no more than 100 yards away. There, immediately in front of us, lay the track. We gave the lad a 100 shilling note in appreciation for his help which was a huge sum to him. As he ran chuckling into the hut, we imagined him telling his mom about the crazy *wazunguu* who couldn't find their way out of his tiny village.

We were in need of nourishment when we arrived in Dodoma, so Dad pulled up and parked the Landover between two large concrete blocks that lay parallel to a small snack shop. (Only God and the Public Works Department know why they were there.) The obstacles were too low to be seen from inside the car and it seemed Dad had forgotten about them because, when we came out of the shop after lunch, he blithely started the engine, put the vehicle into gear and surged up onto the block in front of us. There we sat in embarrassment while the front end hung in midair; the wheels spinning lazily round and round. We didn't even have to ask for help; immediately, a hoard of laughing young men surrounded us, picked up the vehicle and lifted it off the block.

It was late by the time we got to the lush mountain area at Morogoro so we stopped for the night. We found a room at the lovely "Bushtrecker Lodge" where we had our supper and relaxed with a few beers while contemplating the contrasts of this land. In just one day, we had passed through the desolation of the Rift Valley to the magnificent Uluguru Mountains.

Well dear daughter, now that we're again revving up our mental engines for the next phase of learning, please keep us in your prayers as we move toward a new phase in our lives.

Dad and I have always maintained that "life is for living" and hold that one should never shrink from the possibility of adventure. Always follow your dreams. Remember "*The Road Not Taken*" by Robert Frost:

I shall be telling this with a sigh
Somewhere ages and ages hence:
Two roads diverged in a wood, and I —
I took the one less traveled by,
And that has made all the difference.

Love,

Mom and Dad

****

To our friends:
Maryknoll Language School
Musoma, Tanzania
August 13, 1988

Dear Loverna and Bob,

It's six years ago today since our beautiful daughter Kathy died. Please take some wildflowers to her grave. (You probably have already done so.) Thank you for that. We often think of her generosity and know she would approve of the work we're doing here in Tanzania. She would have loved this place and these people.

We're now in the town of Musoma situated on the shores of Lake Victoria. This spot is so lovely! Here at the Maryknoll Language School, we relish a view of the beautiful lake and the warmth of companionship. What a contrast from the drab loneliness of Manyoni! We'd love to move our mission here, but since that's not possible, we keep reminding ourselves that Manyoni has the greatest need and that's where our commitment has to be.

We flew here from Dar es Salaam via Air Tanzania on a Fokker 27, a compact 44-passenger turboprop capable of landing on these smaller runways. A staffer from the school met us and drove us along the lakeshore to the site where we'll be studying for the next four months. The school was set up in 1964 by American Maryknoll Missionaries. In the beginning the missionaries offered a variety of courses in East African studies, but after Tanzania gained its independence and Swahili became the official language they concentrated on the teaching of the Swahili language and culture.

The institute sits on grassland dotted with acacia trees atop a rise overlooking the lake. Central to the complex is the blue and white chapel. From there, building extension blocks fan out to house the offices, kitchen, dining hall, library, language lab, classrooms and student accommodation. Fronting the veranda are trellises covered with masses of white and red bougainvillea.

Our room is bright and sunny. African print curtains hang on either side of the large window, framing our view of the lake as if it were a gorgeous painting. I know I will be happy here. (Our only complaint is the depth of the mattresses that are so thin we can feel the hard wooden slats of the bed frame dig into our hip bones every time we turn over.)

The student body has started to arrive from such diverse places as Colombia, Mexico, India, U.S.A, Ireland, Britain, Norway and Canada. There are Catholic priests and brothers, Lutheran and Mennonite couples with children, one young Englishman who is a professional aid worker and us. We're the oldest of the lot. There will be 22 of us in all, and everyone will be serving either in Kenya or Tanzania.

Classes started on Monday and we expect we'll be in for a rough four months. The Swahili language has no fewer than eight noun classes, and every adjective has to agree. (We think English is hard, yet we have only three classes: masculine, feminine and neuter.)

The philosophy of the school emphasizes a balanced approach to study and relaxation so the administration has provided lots of diversions for after class and weekends. The selection in the library is excellent. There are racquetball and volleyball courts and the recreation room is well stocked with games, cards and videos. In one corner of it, there's a fridge where we can help ourselves to beer or soda pop. (We sign for whatever we take and pay for it at the end of the week.) Our food is prepared and served for us, our laundry is done and our rooms are cleaned daily, so we can devote full time to our studies.

Although I've recovered from my fall, I still look as though I've been beaten; the area around my left eye has turned bluish black with splotches of yellow, orange and green where the healing has begun. That side of my face is still numb and so swollen I look like a lopsided chipmunk. I feel fine, though, and ready to take up the new challenge.

We'll need all the encouragement we can get from you folks back home, so do write and phone as often as you can and please send lots of photos.

Love,

Leona and Cyril

****

To our son Mark and daughter-in-law Christian:
Musoma, Tanzania
September 5, 1988

Dear Mark and Chris,

Your telegram just came letting us know that our new grandson arrived on August 25. We really like the name you've chosen. Stephen Alexander has such a nice ring to it. At 9 lbs. 4 oz., he's a big fellow, isn't he? Congratulations! (Or "*hongera,*" as we'd say in Swahili.) You're going to be overwhelmed with the demands of this little boy, but trust us when we say you'll soon adapt.

Now that all three new grandsons have been safely delivered, we can relax knowing that all's well on the home front.

Our Swahili studies are progressing as well as could be expected given our somewhat advanced age plus the fact that we'd recently weathered three months of Italian instruction. Swahili is a very strange language. It's not at all like English or German or any of the romance languages that I've studied. It has very old roots (Bantu and Arabic) and was originally written in Arabic script. The first dictionary was compiled, using the Latin alphabet, by Christian missionaries who added words that crept into the language by the influence of the arrival of the English, Portuguese and Germans. What with all the prefixes, infixes and suffixes that indicate class, person, number and tense, some words are so long they're sentences in themselves!

For the first two weeks we had no textbooks; the emphasis was on training the ear. We listened over and over again to simple sentences and then tried repeating them. The teachers use lots of pictures, actions and visual aids; otherwise we'd be totally lost. (We feel so sorry for the Norwegians who had to learn English before Swahili, as all the translations go from English to Swahili and back.)

This school has some wise policies. Husbands and wives are never put in the same class because, generally, women are more are adept at languages than men. (Okay guys, settle down. It's only a generality.) Given the extra stress put on everyone by the studies, it's probably saved a few marriages!

The intense concentration that we pour into our solid seven hours of instruction each day leaves us exhausted. We're 'wiped" after a session and often fall asleep during our lunch break and at the end of the afternoon's lessons.

There are no more than four students in each class and there is a different teacher for each aspect of the course so there is opportunity for individual instruction. All the teachers are Tanzanian and have a good background in English.

I've developed a personal friendship with my favourite teacher, Magdalena. She's bright and chipper and loads of fun. Every few days she comes bouncing into class sporting a new hair-do. Sometimes it's just a cap of curls; other times it's done up in tight corn rows or spikes tied up with tiny red ribbons. One day she was wearing it braided in small loops that formed a tiara on the crown of her head.

"Shall I braid your hair?" Magdalena asked when I commented on how tidy she looked.

"Thanks, Magdalena," I replied, "but I don't think it would work."

Her neatness made me aware of my own shaggy mane and I vowed to do something about it. (The perm I'd had in Italy had long ago grown out.) So next day I set about giving myself a Toni home perm. When we were living on the Alaska Highway, we young moms often gave each other perms from a kit, but I found that rolling up my own hair was not so simple. When I finished, my arms were aching with the effort of holding them above my head. The curls were bunched up and uneven but I applied the waving solution anyway confident I was going to make an improvement. I waited the required 45 minutes for the solution to do its work and tried a test curl.

Ah, perfect! I thought. It was time to rinse.

Sticking my head in the bathroom sink, I turned on the tap and let the cool water pour over my head. (Rinsing stops the curling action and is a most important step.) Moments later the water pump cut out and the tap went dry. My head was only partially rinsed and I was aware that the solution would still be cooking away at my curls. It was a good half hour before the pump surged back to life, the water started flowing again and I could complete the process.

I re-rinsed, applied the neutralizer, rinsed again and unwound the curlers.

"Maybe it won't be so bad," I said to myself. But it WAS bad! Very bad indeed! Curls that had been properly rinsed fell nicely into soft waves but others, where the lotion had worked long past the curling time, stood up crisp and crinkly. I threw myself on the bed and howled in abject frustration, wishing I'd taken up Magdalena's offer to braid my hair. (Since then I've been covering my head with a scarf. I'll be wearing it until I can get to Dar es Salaam and find a beautician who knows how to handle European hair!)

We have found another friend in Fr. Bill Fryda MD, an energetic American doctor/priest who is here to brush up on his Swahili. Bill has been here before. Following his medical internship at the Mayo clinic he came to Africa as a volunteer doctor and was hooked! After serving at a mission hospital for a while he returned to New York and studied for the priesthood and now is back in Tanzania to do double duty as priest and doctor. At his insistence, everyone simply calls him "Bill". Others with similar qualifications might insist on being called Doctor or Father or Reverend, but this charismatic man, the son of a humble South Dakota farmer, has no such insecurities. He's a born leader, and, as our elected social convener, is shepherding the lot of us around. He's organized sports events, picnics, sing-a-longs, birthday parties and video screenings.

We always attend daily prayers with Bill who celebrates Mass in the warm soft evenings. Most mission stations begin the day the other way around. They offer Mass at dawn, but Bill says he never could go in for those cold early morning devotions that he calls "toothpaste" Masses. "What better time is there to give praise and thanks than when the day's work is done?" he asks. We couldn't agree more.

I hesitate to tell you this, but I've, once again, been "in the wars". That's right. I fell for a second time. This time it was on the concrete racquetball court where dirt and grit ground into the palm of my right hand. Within twelve hours, red streaks were running up my arm and I knew I was in danger of getting blood poisoning. I went to see Bill who cleaned it up and gave me antibiotics to ward off the infection. It seems I've become a first-class klutz. (Dad is feeling badly because people seem to be looking at him in a curious way, as though he were a "wife beater". He thinks he has to explain to everyone why his wife is walking around with a black eye and bandaged hand.)

We often stroll down to the lake and try out our Swahili on the fishermen. Yesterday we witnessed, what was for us, an unusual phenomenon. We saw, rising from the lake, a curious black cloud. It was quite eerie as there was no indication of rain. Actually, apart from that darkening mass, the sky was perfectly clear. As we stood on the edge of the lake, the cloud moved toward us growing bigger and blacker and soon tiny flies dropped from it and began circling around us. A fisherman clearing his nets sensed we might have trouble coping with this event and shouted a warning, "Go indoors *Mzee na* Mama. Lake flies coming! Lake flies get in ears, eyes and noses." Heeding his advise we walked quickly back to the safety of the school before the whole area was enveloped by billions of swarming gnat-like insects. We were told that these tiny flies incubate as larvae on the lake bottom where they feed on plankton. At this stage they're called "glass worms" because of their transparent bodies. When they form pupae, they rise to the surface of the lake and burst from their cases. Their movements seem to be governed by the waxing and waning of the moon since they swarm only once a month, at the time when the first crescent appears. They're generally harmless, but a few individuals do suffer allergic reactions to them if they're inhaled, and there have been reports of babies being suffocated.

The flies are edible. Indeed, folks who live along the lakeshore often catch them in nets or on woven sisal mats that they hang in the trees. When the invasion passes, they shake the flies out of the nets and mats, compress them into cakes and dry them in the sun.

We don't think the cooks here at the school have served us these delicacies yet, but we found a recipe in the library, so we know they know how to prepare them. They are very high in protein and calcium and have six times the iron content of liver so if ever you should want to give lake flies a try, here's the recipe:

1 cake lake fly
1 tomato, chopped
1 onion, chopped
1 cup peanuts, chopped
Salt
Boil lake fly gently; then add other ingredients and fry in a little oil. Serve over rice.

Yummy, I'm sure. Fly cakes, anyone?

We went to downtown Musoma the other day and wandered around the streets to do some people-watching. At the fish market, ladies were walking with huge Nile perch draped across their heads, the tails and heads of the fish bouncing in rhythm with every step.

These sights are becoming more and more unremarkable to me. For example, when Dad pointed to a lady carrying the bloody head of an ox on a platter on her head and exclaimed, "Wow, do you see that?" and I thought nothing unusual of it, I knew I'd become truly "Africanized".

Well, dear ones, it's time for us to get back to our books. We know you'll be frantically busy with the new baby, so if you don't have time to write, we totally understand.

God bless and keep you. Give a special cuddle to our new grandson!

Love,

Mom and Dad

****

***To our son Greg and his girlfriend, Carolyn*:**
Musoma, Tanzania
September 27, 1988

Dear Greg and Carolyn,

So, you've set your wedding date! New Year's Eve in Calgary sounds super. Our course finishes here on December 8, so the timing is good for us. We're going to try our best to get there. We've missed the birth of three new grandsons since we left home, and we sure don't want to miss your wedding as well. We're going to Dar es Salaam next week for our mid-term break and will try to find a good agent there who can book our flights home.

And, we have another reason to be happy. Ted called telling us that our new vehicle has arrived from Japan. It's been serviced and is ready for us to pick up in Dar es Salaam. We're going to drive it back here to Musoma after our break. We're so excited! It's been many months since we've enjoyed the freedom that wheels provide.

Most evenings, after our exhausted brains will hold no more, we join a group of other students on the front veranda of the school. From this vantage point, we can look across the lake to a sheltered cove formed by a rocky spit of land that juts out into the water. On moonless nights, we often see rows of lights bobbing and winking off the ripples of black water: this is the lantern-fishing fleet. A kerosene lamp that rides on the prow of each vessel casts dancing lights onto the water drawing the silvery sardines toward the boats. The fishermen propel their boats closer and closer together in an ever-tightening arc and scoop the witless fish into their waiting nets. Then, in the morning, they spread their catch on the shore to dry before it's taken to market. Often we see fish-eagles, egrets and hammerkopfs (birds with hammer-shaped heads) hovering over the lake, doing some fishing of their own.

We've found another diversion in the antics of a family of mongooses that regularly patrol the school grounds. These furry ferret-like animals have a reputation as snake-killers and we feel better just seeing them on their daily rounds. They've taken a dislike to the school's mascots, two battle-scarred dachshunds that are owned by Father Joe, the principal. The dogs are kind of cute, but not at all bright. In fact it's their sheer stupidity that has provided us with more than a few laughs. We didn't understand why their butts were so terribly scarred until we watched them sparring with the mongooses.

Working as a team, thé mongooses seemed to delight in setting up the dachshunds for shaming. "Hey," we could imagine one impishly saying to the others, "why don't we have a bit of fun with these mutts?" Then they'd move into action. Luring the dogs into battle, one mongoose would make a mock charge toward the dogs, then, when he'd got their attention, he'd scuttle away and up onto a little mound. From there he'd stand upright and taunt them by making shrill chittering noises. Inevitably, one of the dogs, unable to resist the challenge, would lunge at the cheeky rodent. But none of them could ever connect with the mongoose who'd zip to safety faster than a striking cobra. As the bewildered dog stood yapping in frustration, another mongoose would flash in from behind and take a nip out of his backside. This went on and on until the dachshunds gave up and, cringing in humiliation, slinked off to the safety of Fr. Joe's room.

Spike Milligan, the British comic, is said to be responsible for this little gem of a mongoose story that I think you'll enjoy:

> Letter from one zoo curator to another:
>
> *Dear Sir,*
>
> *Would you be so kind as to send me a pair of mongoose for my collection? No, sorry, that must be a pair of mongooses or is it a pair of mongeese? I tell you what. Please send me one mongoose, and then send me another.*
>
> *Yours thankfully,*
>
> *Zoo Curator*

Last week Dad was feeling poorly and excused himself from class. When we broke for lunch, I went to our room and found him lying on the bed suffering from muscle pains, a splitting headache and the classic fever and chills of malaria. I called Bill, who put him on chloroquine at once. Dad recovered well, but suffered a horrible reaction to the medication. All night long he lay wide awake, every nerve and muscle so tense that he jumped at the slightest sound. He told me he thought his brain had finally snapped from the stress of the studies. When he felt better and was able to return to class, he mentioned this to his teacher, who said, "Oh, that's common. I have the same reaction myself." Thus reassured that Dad was not, in fact, totally going out of his mind, we relaxed and went back to our studies. (I say "totally" because, by simply being here, we're not too sure about our sanity in the first place.)

Now, don't you be worrying about us. We're in very good hands here. As well as Bill, there are several nursing Sisters on staff who've lived in Africa for years and know well how to treat these tropical diseases.

Must go now and practice more vocabulary for tomorrow's lessons. We'll definitely call you from Dar es Salaam to let you know if we can make it home for the wedding. Here's hoping! Stay well and God bless.

Love,

Mom and Dad

****

To our daughter Kim, son-in-law Blair and family:
Musoma, Tanzania
November 5, 1988

Dear Kim, Blair, David and Baby Robert,

We're definitely coming home for Greg and Carolyn's wedding. We got the last two seats on a KLM flight that will bring us into Calgary on Christmas Eve. Lucky us! Greg has our flight number and arrival time, so we expect a huge welcoming committee at the airport.

It will be so wonderful to see you all again and meet our three new grandsons. We'd love to get up to Whitehorse for a brief visit after the wedding. Would you be so kind as to check out flights? There should be some great specials on. We don't think there'll be a rush to get up to the Yukon in January, do you?

Our week-long break from school was fabulous. We flew to Dar es Salaam and were collected by one of the mission staff who drove us to the guest house where our vehicle was parked. We rushed over to see it and, like kids examining a new toy, ran our hands along the shiny green fenders of the new Isuzu Trooper. Then we climbed in and just sat there on the comfy bucket seats smelling the newness of it. After lunch we took it on its first outing, and, after many months of depending on others for transportation, tasted the liberty of being able to go and come as we pleased. It was one of the happiest days of my life. How very spoiled we have become in our affluence, yet I felt no guilt in enjoying it. Is that terribly selfish of me?

For a while we were able to put aside the stress of our studies. We lounged at the beach, ate in fancy restaurants and checked out a wonderfully innovative venture in downtown Dar es Salaam called Nyumba ya Sanaa — House of Art. The brainchild of an American Maryknoll nun, it's a combination restaurant, art gallery, and textile printing and sewing centre where local artists have an outlet for their work. Designed in the style of an African hut, it opens onto a lily pad pool surrounded by tables holding batiks, ebony carvings, basketry and bolts of textiles. A wooden bead curtain separates the gallery from the cozy restaurant where we had chicken escalope and chips, the specialty of the house.

And, in the Kilimanjaro Hotel, I found a hairdresser who trimmed and repaired my hair that I'd so badly mangled when trying to give myself a home perm.

The drive back to Musoma through the Serengeti National Park was both magnificent and horrendous. We were grateful that Geoff Hayes, one of our friends from language school, rode along with us sharing the responsibility of the long and somewhat dangerous drive.

We were familiar with the road until we reached Dodoma, but then, as we left the pavement and swung north we entered new territory. It took us over 14 hours to complete our first day's journey to Lake Manyara Lodge, a distance of 350 km. The road, full of jagged potholes and huge imbedded rock projections was dreadful. That, coupled with the fact that we missed the sagging faded sign to the lodge brought us into our night's lodging well after dark.

The lodge, perched on the edge of the Rift Valley, overlooks Lake Manyara. Next morning, as we stood on the rim of the Rift escarpment, we could see hundreds of flamingos feeding in the shallows of the soda lake.

Next day we passed through lush forests climbing to an altitude of over 7,000 feet. The air was refreshingly cool where we stopped at a pullout and looked down into the Ngorongoro Crater, the famous caldera that is one of the natural wonders of the world.

All too soon we left the coolness of the higher altitude and were back into a world of heat and dust. The terrain changed from heavily forested to a wilderness of scruff. The road had turned to washboard, but once Dad hit just the right speed, the Trooper skimmed over the corduroy ridges, making for a smoother and faster ride. As the day wore on, the heat became insufferable. Our air conditioner had "packed it in" on our first day out, so we had the choice of either keeping the windows closed and suffocating from the heat or choking in the dust that roiled up from behind and was sucked in through the open windows. Some choice!

Geoff had travelled this route before and directed us to an idyllic spot to stop for lunch. The soil and dust turned red where we swung off the main road and followed the sign to Gibbs Farm that is a coffee plantation and guest lodge - a most exquisite place.

On a rise in the land overlooking acres of coffee bushes, a central fish pond sits surrounded by velvety green lawns and flower beds. From there, a cobbled pathway leads to the stone reception area and dining room which was once the plantation house. Spread out from either side, thatched guest cottages lie tucked under fan palms. In the distance, at the far edge of the plantation, we could see rows of flowering lilac jacaranda trees bordering the trails that separate the coffee fields. We ate our smorgasbord lunch while sitting on lawn chairs around the pond.

But all too soon our respite ended, and we were off again into the heat and swirling dust.

There's a bush lodge near the Serengeti gates that Geoff was game to try. So before leaving Gibbs, he asked the manager to contact Ndutu Camp on the two-way radio and book us in for the night. Retracing our path to the farm junction, we left behind the fertile red soil and rejoined the main roadway of grey ridges and dust-filled potholes that stretched relentlessly ahead. Trundling past the turnoff to Olduvai Gorge, the archaeological site where Dr. Louis and Mrs. Mary Leakey discovered evidence of early hominids, the landscape took on an eerie, desolate quality. A short distance later, we came upon the weathered sign pointing to the track that would take us to Ndutu Camp far off the beaten path.

Apart from one Masaai moran and his herd of cattle, the only other living thing we saw on the 24-km stretch was a baby hyena that trotted forlornly along the track ahead of us. Serving mainly as a base for camping safaris, Ndutu, situated among giant flat-topped acacia trees, is so rustic that there were no barriers to the genet cats that wandered in from the bush and scampered along the wooden overhead beams, their long, fluffy ringed tails trailing behind them.

Next morning we entered the Serengeti, the most famous game reserve in all of Africa. It spread before us, a vast golden plain punctuated by rolling hills, granite *kopjes* (outcroppings) and acacia trees. A rainstorm had passed during the night dampening the dust so we could drive with our windows down and enjoy the antelope population: wildebeest (gnu), Thomson's and Grant's gazelles, impala, topi, hartebeest and eland that grazed and cavorted across the plain. At one point we had to stop and give way to 50 or 60 wildebeest that tumbled single file across the road.

But the best (and worst) of our safari was yet to come. Bill had spoken of a wilderness track that cut across the Serengeti. "Take the lower trail at Seronera Lodge," he'd said, "It'll be just you and the animals." Buoyed by such a recommendation, we drove onto the track straddling the growth of long grasses that had sprung up between the ruts.

Patches of flat-topped acacias are numerous in this part of the Serengeti, but not so numerous as to obscure the movements of the vast numbers of animals. It was as Bill said it would be. Not only were antelope ranging there in astonishing numbers, but also buffalo, zebras, giraffes, wild dogs, hyenas, jackals and warthogs. And then there were the birds! Beautiful lilac-breasted rollers, superb starlings, finches and larks flitted from branch to branch and raptors swooped from treetop to treetop. It was as though Paradise itself had opened up for us.

We had driven for maybe half an hour revelling in these sights, when our idyllic circumstances changed. The rain that had passed through had changed the black cotton soil into a quagmire. Dad put the Trooper into four-wheel drive, and we pressed on around mud hole after mud hole. From time to time, Geoff or I would get out and walk around a particular patch, testing the soil for firmness before we ventured past. (This was a dangerous thing to do. The presence of antelope would certainly draw lions and leopards to this place.)

Black clouds were amassing on the horizon ahead of us, and after an hour of anxiety, during which we met no other vehicle, we decided to turn back. Circling an acacia tree we came within six feet of a single buffalo. Startled by the sudden appearance of our "green machine" that he may have mistaken for some new species of animal, he flinched. Dad, startled also, sped forward. Geoff and I twisted around in our seats to keep the buffalo in view. Mud flew up from our tires and struck the beast in the face. In retaliation he swung his massive horns from side to side and lunged toward us.

"Tramp on it!" Geoff screamed. Dad's grip tightened on the wheel, he pressed the pedal down and a brief but terrifying chase was on.

A lone buffalo can be the most savage of all African animals capable of reaching a charging speed of up to 55 kilometres an hour. We don't know why he lost interest after pursuing us for only a few yards but thank God he did. Perhaps it was because he had us on the run and that was satisfaction enough for him.

The area was teeming with game as we retraced our tracks to Seronera, but we were too apprehensive to enjoy it. We had used up two precious hours of travel time, and our diesel was running low. There are no service stations in the Serengeti. There are fuel supplies at Park Headquarters, but they sell it only if they have enough for their own vehicles. We were relieved that the attendant understood our plight, but he could only spare 20 litres. He put on quite a performance transferring the diesel from the underground tank to our car. The regular pumps were broken down, so, using a hand pump, he drew up the diesel into a bucket, poured it into a jerry can and finally into our fuel tank. (Now we had the added concern of the possibility of contaminated fuel.)

We struck off then and found the upper track to Musoma, our apprehension eased by the fact that this route took us through several villages. We knew that, should we get stuck, scores of young Tanzanian men would rush from the huts and lift our vehicle out. As before, the road was very bad. Straddling a pile of rock, we heard the crunch of metal from the undercarriage, yet, even when the rocky roadway turned into a muddy track that swerved around swamps, we pushed on. We were immensely relieved when we came to the main paved road and eventually to Musoma. (We were told that we were wise to leave the lower track when we did. The west of the Serengeti had endured three days of solid rain and was still impassable.)

Here's a question posed by Mark Twain that every adventurer must ask himself at one time or another. "Why is it that when I'm sitting in my easy chair, I wish I were having an adventure, and when I'm having an adventure, I wish I were sitting in my easy chair?"

We have no answer for Mr. Twain, but that is certainly something we've asked ourselves a dozen times since arriving in Africa.

Well, dear folks, it's time to get back to our grammar texts.

God bless everyone, especially the three new grandsons.

Love,

Mom and Dad

****

Brother Anthony Canterucci (Bro) with AIDS orphan

Manyoni Mission Workshop
Laurenti, Leona, Cyril, Georgie, Kimome

Cross on Manyoni Mountain

Ted and Baldwin with the Queen of Heaven

Bro and Ted by abandoned well

Bus Depot Manyoni

Mosque Downtown Manyoni

Old man reading the Koran
Zanzibar

Beverly, Jim, Anna, and Linda Lamb

Mama Vishani cooking dinner

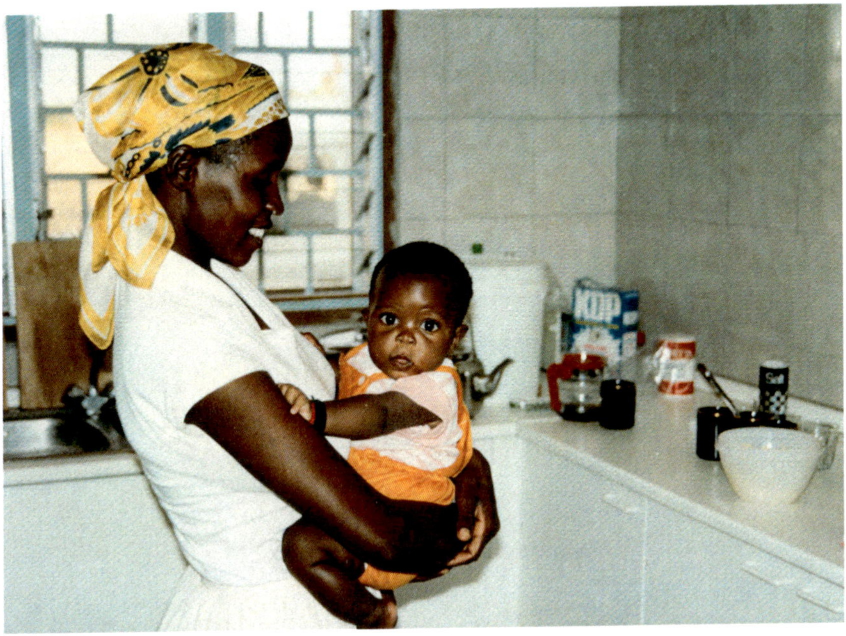

Gemma, our cook with baby Patrick

Ted Van der Zalm

Girish Vishani

Elephant in the Ngorongoro Crater

Giraffes in the Serengeti

Hyenas in the Ngorongoro Crater

Lions in the Ngorongoro Crater

Kunduchi Beach Dar es Salaam

Dhows -Kunduchi Beach

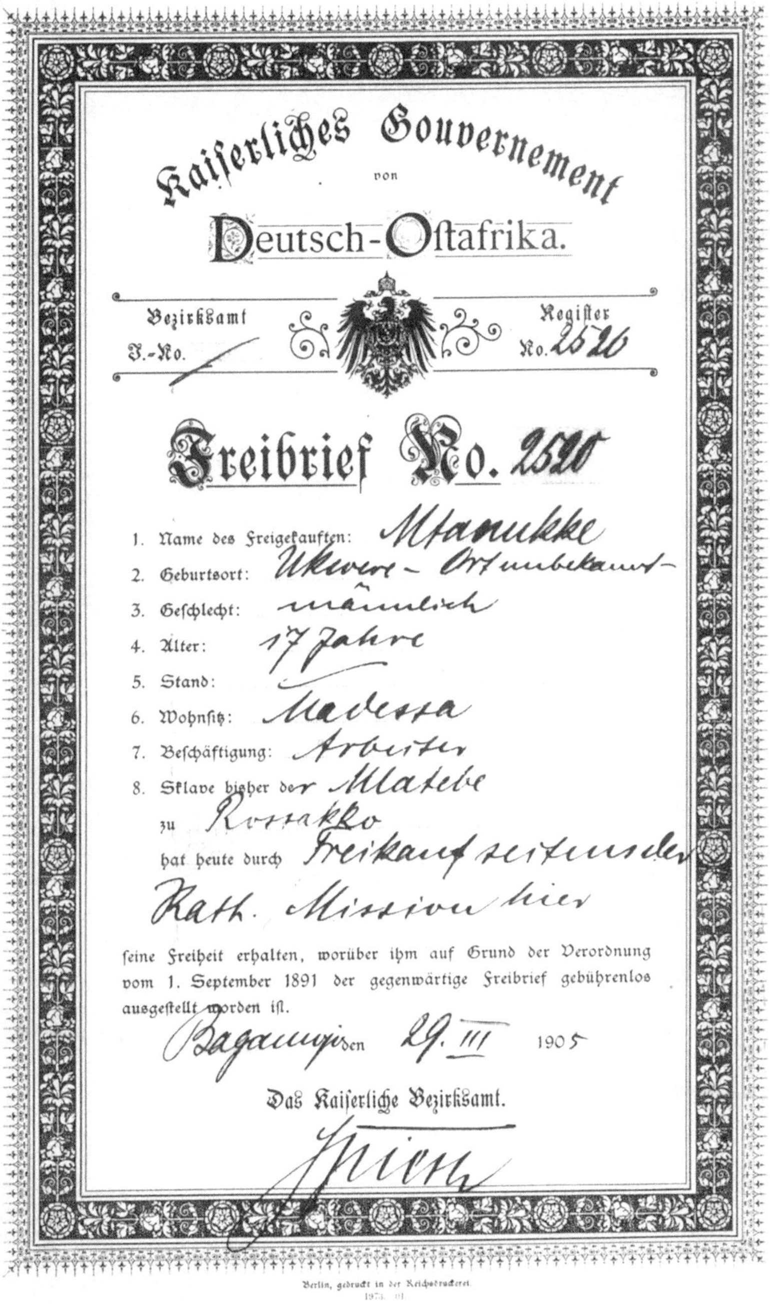

Kaiserliches Gouvernement
von
Deutsch-Ostafrika.

Bezirksamt J.-No. /

Register No. 2520

Freibrief No. 2520

1. Name des Freigekauften: Mtamukke
2. Geburtsort: Ukwere – Ort unbekannt –
3. Geschlecht: männlich
4. Alter: 17 Jahre
5. Stand: —
6. Wohnsitz: Madessa
7. Beschäftigung: Arbeiter
8. Sklave bisher der Mlatebe

zu Rossakko

hat heute durch Freikauf seitens der

Kath. Mission hier

seine Freiheit erhalten, worüber ihm auf Grund der Verordnung vom 1. September 1891 der gegenwärtige Freibrief gebührenlos ausgestellt worden ist.

Bagamoyo, den 29. III 1905

Das Kaiserliche Bezirksamt.

[signature]

Berlin, gedruckt in der Reichsdruckerei.

Certificate of Freedom
Bagamoyo Museum

To our son Dave:
Musoma, Tanzania
December 5, 1988

Dear Dave,

In exactly 19 days we'll be on our way home for Greg and Carolyn's wedding. It will be almost one year to the day since we've seen any of you. We can hardly wait!

Soon we'll be finished our Swahili studies and will be heading back to Manyoni where we'll stay for a few days before going on to Dar es Salaam to catch our flight. We'll not be driving through the Serengeti again; there was altogether too much anxiety on the last trip. This time we're going to travel a safer, more populated route.

It's been a full month since we wrote anyone, and we apologize for that. Our time has been so filled with study and activities that there's little energy left at the end of the day.

Every Friday afternoon, we have lectures on Tanzanian tribal customs where we're given a glimpse inside traditions surrounding the central events of cultural life: pregnancy and birth, the naming of children, initiation into adulthood, marriage and inheritance, traditional healing, death, mourning and burial, the belief in ancestral and non-ancestral spirits, and among some sectors, the belief and practice of witchcraft.

The African teachers show each of us such warm hospitality. They are used to foreign students and are always prepared to stop and speak with us. Emmanuel, one of our teachers, asked us to drop by his home to meet his wife and new baby girl. When we arrived at his home, according to protocol, we called out "*hodi*" and waited. Within seconds, Emmanuel, who was expecting us, scuttled to the door carrying two rickety stools that he set down on the hard packed earth. We perched there chatting with him in English until his wife came out to join us carrying their new baby. From then on, because his wife knows no English, our entire conversation was in Swahili. She placed the baby girl in my arms and I rocked her by simply moving my body back and forth on the wobbly stool. Until the baby is baptized, Emmanuel told us, she's called simply *tano*, Swahili for "fifth", she being the fifth child born to the family. At baptism she will be given the name Esther. Greetings are very important in this culture and we'd been well schooled in how to ask after the health and welfare of each and every family member along with the state of their livestock. We must have made a few gaffs but, if so, our hosts were too polite to notice.

Through these classes and associations we're becoming aware of the differences in the Bantu view of the world vis-à-vis the Western perspective. The Africans seem to perceive that "life is for living" rather than rushing headlong into racking up accomplishments. (A famous South African author summed it all up in one quote, "The European *does* while the African *is*.")

Because we're the only students with a vehicle, we've been taking groups of friends from school on outings. We had a wonderful picnic out in the Serengeti with Bill, Father Charles, an American priest, and Geoff last Sunday. Bill brought the samosas, Fr. Charles, the beer and Geoff, the soft drinks. The school's cook, Jumapili, prepared meat loaf sandwiches for us and our contribution was the vehicle. Rain had been intermittent throughout the week, and the tracks in the park were very muddy. No cars had been through for several days, but the game warden told us we could go in a short distance for our picnic. When we got stuck, which was often, the men took off their shoes and squishing barefooted in the mud, pushed the car along until we settled on a patch of high ground. We lounged there under a spreading acacia tree on picnic blankets reading, eating, and watching the wildlife through binoculars. Gazelles grazed and ostriches strutted by. A mother warthog with her seven squealing youngsters trotted past in single file with tiny tails held high, and on a dry mound a group of rodents raised dust as they burrowed into the ground.

We kept a sharp eye out for predators, and left the car doors open in case we needed to make a quick scramble to safety. Vultures perched on a nearby acacia and kept careful watch over us hoping for a spicy bit of human should one of us fall victim to a lion. (Seriously, they were most likely only interested in our meat loaf sandwiches!)

At the end of the afternoon, our faces and arms were sunburned. Dad received a burn on his bald spot that was so badly blistered, medication was needed to cool the fire on top of his head. None of us realized, lying there under the acacia tree, that the sun filtering through the lacy-leaved branches could be so strong.

Some evenings we drive with Fr. Finbarra, my Irish classmate, and Fr. Charles to the Musoma Railway Hotel for a change of scene. (No railroad runs here, but nonetheless the corporation operates a hotel.) It's a little tacky, but it sits right on the lakeshore where the view is breathtaking. Even at night, when the lake is just a black wash, we sit outside drinking safari beer, eating *karanga* (peanuts), and watching the fireflies flit about. At times like those, there's no more glorious place on earth to be.

Geoff, Dad and I went exploring the spit of land that runs out into the lake. Walking along the narrow trail among the rock and scrub, we came upon a mottled gold, brown and grey rock python that slithered across our path. We stopped in our tracks and watched the loathsome thing move off and disappear into the high yellow grass. Of course, no one stopped to measure it, but it was at least six inches in diameter and twelve feet long! After the python passed, Geoff and Dad continued on, but I, repelled by the sight of it, retreated to the safety of the car. Dozens of rock hyraxes and brightly coloured lizards were scampering on the rocks and, once I got over the shock of meeting the python, I quite enjoyed watching them play.

As we were driving back to the school we caught up to a funeral cortège moving slowly along the road. The body, wrapped in a brown canvas shroud, was lying on a stretcher that was being carried along like a litter by four men wheeling bicycles; each corner of the litter was supported by the crossbars. We stayed behind so as not to disturb the mourners who were walking quietly alongside the bier.

Terrific thunderstorms have been breaking over and around us all week. Dark clouds gather on every horizon and fork lightning shatters the sky from the dome above to the edge of the earth. This display continues hour after hour until, at last, the clouds burst and rain pours down like a cascade. Last night two men of the village were struck by lightning; one had been adjusting the dial on his radio; the other had been riding his bicycle.

Another massive lake fly invasion swept through our area at the time of the new moon. When we woke up in the morning we found the corners of our room covered by a carpet of miniature gnat-like flies that had come straight through the window screens. The janitors had a busy time of it sweeping the halls, and, with long cloth-covered poles, clearing away the billions that had clustered under the eaves. (We imagined that, when the flies began to arrive, traditional village folks living along the lakeshore had said to one another, "Here comes dinner!" and rushed about putting out mats and nets to catch the edible insects.)

It was Dad's 60th birthday and American Thanksgiving last week, and Bill arranged a big celebration for all the students and the staff members. The cooks prepared roast goose with all the trimmings and a cake. We were like one big happy family.

We're going to miss every one of this fantastic crew, but most of all we'll miss Bill. He's one of those dynamic people who lights up a room. An aura surrounds him. When he's away, the earth loses its flavour; our mood goes flat, and we sink into a mini-depression. Then, as soon as he returns the word goes out, "Bill's back!" and suddenly the room seems brighter. This is no ordinary man. We predict that, one day, he will accomplish extraordinary things. Whoever has him for priest and doctor will be very blessed.

There are several American Maryknoll Sisters working in the area who've adopted us. We're often invited to their place for tea, homemade goodies and interesting stories. Three years ago, they told us, they were held hostage for hours in their own home by a gang of armed men who robbed them of everything that could be carried away. The bandits were never caught - there is speculation that the police were in on the plot.

A few weeks ago an odd thing happened to one of our classmates. A zealous CID (Criminal Investigation Division) policeman arrested José, a student from Mexico, who'd been bird watching down by the lake through his binoculars. Accusing José of being a Russian spy, he seized the binoculars, slung them around his neck and put them up to his eyes the wrong way. Squinting through them, he zeroed onto a flight of birds and exclaimed, "Oh, they look so small and far away!" Then he whisked José off to jail where he "grilled" him for several hours. The CID man eventually released José, but kept the binoculars. It wasn't until Fr. Joe, the principal, went to the police to plead José's innocence that the item was returned. (The whole thing is rather curious because Tanzania, being a socialist country, has good relations with Russia.)

Well, what can we say? It's a different world!

We'll be having the graduation ceremony tomorrow, and it will be bittersweet; in three days we leave Musoma and prepare for our visit home.

See you soon!

Mom and Dad

P.S. We left our parkas in Calgary. Please remember to bring them to the airport when you come to pick us up on Christmas Eve.

****

***To our son Chris*:**
Manyoni, Tanzania
February 16, 1989

Dear Chris,

You have no idea how very precious it was for us to spend Christmas at home and to attend Greg and Carolyn's wedding. When we saw you all standing there at the KLM arrivals gate in Calgary, we were almost moved to tears. We'll never forget the thrill of meeting, for the first time, our three new grandsons cuddled in their moms' arms. Even the -40 degree temperatures couldn't chill the warmth of the welcome home.

Now that we're back in Africa that sense of belonging has gone and we are once again on the outside of cultures we're only beginning to understand.

When we landed in Dar es Salaam we found the earth drenched and the roads awash from the long rains that had begun. We were told that the dirt road past Dodoma, the section we would have to travel to reach Manyoni, was in terrible shape. We waited for a few days for drier weather, but when the rains did not let up, we became impatient and decided to go for it, planning to drive at least as far as the point where the pavement ended.

The Uluguru Mountains near Morogoro were blanketed in mist and intermittently, along the five-hour drive, the rain fell so heavily it rebounded off the hardtop in giant sprays. The wipers and defoggers labouring at full force kept the windshield clear however, so we had no difficulty driving to our destination.

We checked in at the Dodoma Railway Hotel, the only reasonable inn in town, and then dropped off some supplies to Antonio, the builder who's supervising the construction of the new mission seminary. A harried Fr. Ernesto had just arrived there in his Landrover after two unsuccessful attempts to shepherd his load of oxygen bottles and other medical supplies to the hospital in Itigi. "I'm afraid we'll be stuck in Dodoma for a while," he said. "There's no traffic moving through."

Antonio's wife, Patricia, invited us to stay with them, but since we'd already checked in at the hotel, we decided to go back there after supper. Unhappily for us, it was disco night. The clerk put us into a room as far away as possible from the action, but there was no escaping the heavy African beat that throbbed relentlessly through the paper-thin walls from late evening until the wee hours. By 6:00 a.m. all the guests in the hotel seemed to be up and about. A radio was playing next door, broadcasting the same pulsing beat of the disco band. My nerves, now frayed and raw, got the better of me. I threw on my robe, stormed out into the hall, hammered on the door and shouted, "*Acha kelele, watu wanataka kulala*!" (Stop the noise! People want to sleep!) The radio was muted instantly, but only for a moment; then the volume crept up to a level even louder than before. We gave up, and still groggy from lack of sleep, escaped from the hotel and returned to Antonio and Patricia's house, where we were given a place to flop down in blessed silence.

We stayed in Dodoma another day before attempting to traverse the route to Manyoni with Fr. Ernesto, he in his vehicle, and Dad and I in ours. From there Fr. Ernesto would try to reach Itigi. There'd been an urgent call from the hospital, asking him to try once again to get through to deliver his precious cargo. So off we drove, armed with ropes and chains. We'd travelled no farther than 25 km. when we met a lone 4x4 vehicle heading back to Dodoma. "The road is impassable," the driver told us. "There's a truck stuck up to the axles blocking the road, and his trailer is lying on its side. Dozens more heading both east and west are lined up, unable to go past or turn around. It's going to be weeks before things will start to move again."

We did the only thing we could do, return to Dodoma and reconsolidate our plans. Fr. Ernesto decided to try to get to Itigi by taking a long circuitous route, a distance of 800 km. (In the dry season such a drive takes approximately 27 hours and much longer in these conditions.)

Dad and I opted to get to Manyoni by train. It was impossible for us to get tickets at the last moment, but one of our Tanzanian mission staff managed to get two in third class for the next day's train. The agent told him that if we paid extra once we got on, we'd be accommodated in first class. Next morning we repacked our cases, cramming only essentials into two small carry-ons, and went to the train station. Hundreds of people were milling around, but we strode through the throngs, confident that we'd soon be comfortably seated. A surly agent in a shabby blue uniform and conductor's cap with a frayed peak accepted our tickets along with the cash for the promised upgrade. Then, hoisting us into a car marked "second class" he ushered us to a spot in the corridor adjacent to the toilets and told us, "Stand here. All the compartments are full."

"But," I protested, "we were promised seats in first class." Whereupon, pocketing the extra shillings, he told us, "This *is* first class!" Then turning on his heel he exited down the stairs.

The car, which had once been a posh British coach, had fallen into a state of advanced decay. The odour of stale urine penetrated our nostrils, and a glimpse into the nearest compartment revealed ripped and tattered upholstery, the stuffing completely gone. Blue blankets had been thrown over the bare boards in an attempt to cover the carnage. A few passengers tried to pass from one car to the next, but stopped short when they saw that the protective plates normally covering the links between the carriages were gone.

The lock on the carriage door was broken and had been replaced by a bent nail and a piece of twisted wire, and plywood was inserted where a pane of glass should be.

Our companion in the corridor was a businessman who held a battered briefcase close to his side. Never once did he set it down. "It's full of cash," he confided. "In these parts of Tanzania, traveller's cheques are not commonly accepted. My customers insist on dealing in cash." Dad asked him if it wasn't dangerous to travel about with so much money. "Yes, very dangerous!" he replied and I edged farther away from him not wanting to be in the line of danger should someone try to snatch his briefcase.

Women carrying babies on their backs, bundles on their heads and chickens under their arms pushed past us in the corridor as they tried to find the correct car. Those with chickens were ushered into another car and one lady who was carrying a baby goat was denied entrance to the train.

It was some time before people stopped shoving and jostling past us and the conductor shouted, "All aboard!"

Dad had been suffering from an upset stomach and headache since early morning. I suspected he was coming down with malaria and sensed how uncomfortable the trip was going to be. I whispered to him, "It's still not too late to bolt."

"It'll be OK," he replied soothingly.

The train lurched forward and the die was cast. Leaning out of the open windows, we were rewarded by a fresh breeze. The countryside, usually burnt brown, was now a lush green, and we saw many women working ankle deep in their muddy *shambas* (fields). The train moved along at a good clip, and my apprehension was beginning to evaporate.

It's quite amazing the sights one sees in a different culture. At one point, a pair of arms emerged from the compartment ahead holding a bare-bottomed baby out into the corridor and he was encouraged to do his “job” right then and there! Dutifully, he emitted a tiny trickle of urine that snaked along the aisle toward us. Another time, a white-clad waiter walked through the car tinkling a little bell to summon would-be diners to the dining car. We declined, not wanting to risk stepping across the wide gap between the carriages, although the waiter had obviously done so.

As the trip wore on, Dad felt sicker and sicker and sat down on our hard-sided case, holding his head in his hands. One of a group of Muslim men in the nearest compartment noticed this and invited us to squeeze in beside them. “*Karibu, karibu.*” (Welcome, welcome), he said. It was a little hard on the blue-blanketed boards but we were grateful for that small comfort. En route, we noticed the remnants of wrecked, rusting carriages lying bent and twisted by the rail side, reminders of less successful journeys.

At the village of Saranda, our last stop before Manyoni, townsfolk selling foodstuffs were lined along the tracks. A few passengers alighted to make their purchases, but most reached into their bags and withdrew tin plates. They handed these out through the windows and shouted out their orders. The sellers on the platform filled the plates with rice, vegetables and meat or fish and passed them back up through the window. Shillings were passed down and change passed up. Everyone who was preparing to eat took a jug of water and poured some over his right hand. Even the mother who’d encouraged her baby to relieve himself in the corridor took the tyke over to the window, extended his tiny right hand out the window and washed it meticulously.

We were relieved when the train finally pulled into Manyoni station. Dad was not at all well and needed to get started on anti-malarial medication. We fumbled with the wire and nail, opened the door, and, because our car didn’t align adjacent to the platform, stepped down three feet to the ground. Dad had to rest twice on the walk to the mission, but two of our students saw us and came running to take our cases and helped Dad into the bunker. Even this small kindness took on significance and made us feel that someone at least valued our return.

As we neared the mission, we heard the comforting sound of Ted's plane overhead. Later we learned that he was returning from Dodoma, where he had gone to fetch us. How ironic is that?

Fr. John brought a telescope from Italy, and on clear moonless nights, we often follow him out into the black African night. Dancing in the blue velvet canopy of the sky, the stars in the southern hemisphere appear more numerous than those in the north. On one particular night Pleiades was lying just above the horizon. "The Bantu," said Fr. John, "see Pleiades as a plough and use its position to tell them when the time is right for planting." I think this is very common in other cultures as well, because an early Greek scholar wrote:

Pleiades rising in the dawning sky
Harvest is nigh
Pleiades setting in the waning light
Ploughing is right.

We never cease to marvel at the perfect order of the Universe which is surely the handiwork of God. On moonlit nights such as this, I often look up and think, that's the same moon that watches over everyone, and I feel very insignificant yet more closely connected to home.

We'll write again soon and tell you all about our re-entry into Manyoni.

Love to all,

Mom and Dad

****

To our friends:
Manyoni, Tanzania
March 28, 1989

Dear George and Muriel,

Receiving your phone call last week telling us that you're planning to come for a visit has us "over the moon" with excitement! But, hold off for a while. We won't be able to receive you until our new house is ready. If there aren't too many setbacks, such as happened yesterday when the water tanks came crashing down, it should be ready for occupancy in a few months. (The weight of the tanks, when filled with water, was too much for the stands to bear. Luckily, no workers were underneath when the tanks crumbled and came apart at the seams.)

Work on the house is progressing more quickly now that Bro has arrived from Canada and kicked a few butts: Bro himself brought more window glass and plumbing fixtures. Girish, the Indian contractor, is back on the job; the roof is finally on, the security bars are in place and the carpenters at the workshop are building the doors and window frames.

Two large wooden boxes containing cooking pots, dishes and linens have arrived for us, and Ted told us that our furniture is among the items of cargo on a ship that just docked in Dar es Salaam. Our moving day is getting closer, thank God, because living in this place has become almost intolerable.

The only bit of brightness for us today was in seeing the last rays of the sun filtering through the narrow window, illuminating a magically fragrant bouquet of jasmine and a bottle of Napoleon brandy that the Italian missionaries gave me for my birthday. Darkness is closing in, and as I sit at my desk writing this, it's hard for me to see. But, the power plant will soon be started and the light bulb that hangs from the ceiling will cast a pale yellow glow onto the page and scuttle the shadows into the corners of the room.

Our difficulties with this place are not confined to the interior. Outside, hundreds of swallows have taken up residence under the eaves that hang over the walkway to the door. We hear their annoying chatter as they leave every morning and now, at sunset, we hear them fluttering back to their nests. We've hired youngsters to chase them away, but the birds always return in angry determination. We even had the lads string up chicken wire under the eaves as a deterrent, but it's no use. So every morning we must skirt around the deep accumulation of droppings that cover the area, even though we'd cleaned up the mess the previous day.

As well as being beleaguered by the birds, we have a problem with bats that have attached themselves to the stucco. When the swallows leave in the morning, the bats return to their hanging place above our doorway and unload a stinking pile of guano on our doorstep. While the youngsters have had no luck deterring the birds, they've been successful in getting rid of two of the bats. With incredible accuracy, they dispatched them with slingshots for the sum of 100 shillings each. (We do know that both these species are most useful in that they eat thousands of mosquitoes every day, but we fervently wish they would live elsewhere.)

The workshop/training centre has been officially turned over to us and we are up to our "*ying yang*" in work. As the "management team", our responsibilities are huge. We're expected to look after the repair and maintenance of the mission's equipment, conduct trades training in mechanics and carpentry (theory as well as practical), order and organize tools, parts and supplies, oversee the electrical systems, and operate a carpentry workshop where we fill orders for custom built furniture. All this, while administering the whole lot! Then we have the job of responding to the technical needs of outlying missions. And to top it off, this is the only workshop between two major centres along the road to Rwanda and Burundi, so we're often called upon to repair government and commercial vehicles. Help!

We're trying to bring a new look to the training centre. We got tired of seeing our students come to class in shirts with the elbows out and pants ripped at the knees and decided they should have uniforms of some type. We checked the workshop's bank balance and found that, with careful budgeting, we should be able to provide each with a pair of coveralls. As far as we know, no shop anywhere in Tanzania stocks them, so the only way to turn this into a reality was to buy material and have them sewn. We chose a bolt of blue denim cloth from an Indian shop, measured up the lads and took our order to the local tailor who plies his trade on a treadle machine in front of his *duka* (shop). We settled on a price for the labour and left, confident that he'd do a good job for us.

When the order was complete and the 30 pairs of coveralls were delivered, we were appalled. Sleeve and leg lengths varied by as much as two inches on the same pair, seams gaped open where the stitching had missed the cloth, collars were crooked and button holes puckered and frayed. We were furious with our own lack of foresight. Why didn't we have him sew one pair first before committing ourselves to 30? Anyway, we were stuck with them and had to make the most of it. We called the students in one by one and had them try on pair after pair until they found an approximate fit. Actually, from a distance they didn't look too bad. The boys didn't seem as perturbed as we were by the result, and, in fact, put on prideful swaggers as they strode to class in their new garments. Well, if they were happy, we were happy! (That is, until after the first laundering.) The first young man to complain came to the office and stood before me looking, for all the world, like a skinny scarecrow. It was impossible for him to stand with his arms at his side. The blue garment was so tight across the back and around the armpits it seemed as if he were stuffed into it. None of the buttons could be fastened; the cloth was simply too shrunken to meet in the middle. The pant legs were uneven and so short his bony ankles were exposed above his run-over-at-the-heels, laceless boots. "Please, Mama," he pleaded. "Do I have to wear this?" "No, Samweli," I said with a sigh, "you don't. You can go home and change." At this point Bro stopped in at the office and, seeing the pathetic situation, said, "Let me call Canada today and order some coveralls. There's a container due to leave shortly. I'll see there are enough pairs in it for everyone at the workshop."

We're happy that Fr. John is now our liaison with the Italian Fathers. He's a real "eager beaver" when it comes to education and is moving full speed ahead with plans to build the new trade school. He has already drafted the plans for it, and the concrete construction bricks are being pressed as fast as the single brick mold will allow. We can hardly wait! At the moment, the allotted space for teaching is still in the storage area behind the generator room where teaching time is limited to the first hour of each school day before the power plant is started. In the chill of the morning, mosquitoes emerge from the piles of lumber stacked at the back of the room to torment us. They float by lazily, but before we have a chance to swat them, they disappear before our eyes. Yesterday, a rainstorm broke while I was in the middle of class and in a deafening roar pummelled the leaky corrugated-tin roof. Within minutes the area was flooded. The students leapt up and tried to shuffle their desks to drier areas, but it was futile and the lesson had to be abandoned.

Today is Easter Sunday and the Holy Week services have come to a close. On each feast day, the church community took part in worship ceremonies. There was nothing unusual or distinctively African about any of them with the exception of the one on Good Friday. On this day there were three "mini - processions" inside the church. Each one required the worshippers to move from the pews and out into the aisles for the walk to the altar. As usual there was no order to the comings and goings; folks behaved spontaneously moving back and forth from their places whenever they felt inclined, even if it meant pushing and stumbling past others still seated. First, they went to deposit their offerings in the straw collection basket, later they paid homage to the cross in front of the altar, and finally they walked up to take communion. All this took the better part of three hours.

But most memorable was the "Stations of the Cross", a long procession that took place outside. Fourteen small shrines had been set up along the path that began at the church door and wended its way through the village to the summit of Manyoni Mountain. Each one contained statues or other art objects that depicted a scene in the final hours of Jesus' life on earth. The journey started with Jesus being condemned to death and ended with Him being laid in the tomb. Father Dino, two altar boys and a strong young man carrying a large wooden cross led the way. The procession stopped at each shrine where Father recited prayers in commemoration of the event. Most people stood at each station, but a few elderly ladies knelt, their knees separated from the rocky ground by only the thin cloth of their sun bleached *kangas*.

At the base of the mountain the most infirm could go no further; but others, young and old, pregnant women and women with infants on their backs, scrambled to the mountaintop in an impressive gesture of faith. We've participated in this devotion many times, but never was it as dramatic as this!

Today, at Mass, the choir performed Handel's *Hallelujah Chorus*. Our choir director at home would kill to have strong basses like these. Unfortunately, the sopranos weren't up to the calibre of the basses, so the sound was very uneven. Kudos to the director for giving it a try; it was a brave effort to tackle a piece of western music so alien to African culture.

After work tomorrow we're going to head down to the field to watch the final game for the regional soccer league championship. It should be fun. The Singida team has brought its own witch doctor. Yesterday, he sprinted out onto the field at half-time when the match between our home team and Singida was tied one to one. He sprinkled *dawa* (medicinal powder) on his team's goalposts and on the Manyoni players' entrance. The Manyoni team, rather than going through the entrance, vaulted over the fence in an effort to avoid the consequences of the curse. They had several shots on Singida's goal but not one went in, while Singida managed to rack up another two points. The result of the game was a three to one win for Singida, so there just might be something to this witchcraft business!

Well, dear friends, much as we want you here with us ASAP, do wait until you hear that we're in the new place. After your visit, you'll never be the same!

Do share all this news with the kids and other friends.

Love you guys,

Leona and Cyril

****

To our son Kurt, daughter-in-law Carole and family:
Manyoni, Tanzania
May 17, 1989

Dear Kurt, Carole, Brittany, Ben and Patrick,

It's hard to believe that Patrick has already had his first birthday. That little "roly-poly" will have learned so much in his short life. Your photos and letters are the most important links to the warmth and love of family and friends. Please, everyone, keep them coming.

We've been exposed to much in this past year, but, unlike that new grandson whose young brain soaks up every sight and sound, our hardwired old brains just don't want to absorb the new realities swirling around us. Our eyes seem to say, "We're not seeing this," and our ears, "We're not hearing this!"

We go to work every day intending to speak Swahili, but when the sheer volume of work overwhelms us, we look for an English-speaking staff member to translate.

Our expectations of our roles were not at all realistic. We knew we'd be involved in maintaining the mission equipment and overseeing the trades training, but we were unprepared for the responsibility of running a commercial enterprise. Transport trucks come limping into the workshop in various states of disrepair. Springs and shocks are the greatest casualties of the horrendous road conditions, so what to do? There is an expression here, "making *maarifa,*" which means doing a temporary patch-up job. The Tanzanians are quite good at it, and it does get the trucker on his way, but the *maarifa* tends to be more or less permanent.

The other day a beat-up truck trundled in through the workshop gate, listing precariously to the left. The cracked rear leaf springs on that side had been bound together by strips of rubber inner tube wrapped tightly around. This *maarifa* had held all the way from Dodoma, but now the leafs had shifted, and the spring needed to be welded and rewrapped. Believe it or not, this trucker was on his way to Mwanza, a distance of roughly 400 km. on rough, unpaved road.

For the most part, Dad has learned to turn a blind eye to these *maarifa* jobs. But one was just too dangerous to ignore.

Coming back from lunch break one day, we noticed some of our crew wheeling the arc welder away from a leaking fuel tanker. Alarm bells went off in Dad's head but he remained cool as he asked, "What were you doing with the welder?"

They replied innocently, "We were welding the tanker." That's when Dad "lost it" and shouted, "You were doing what? You were welding? You were welding on that thing? Unbelievable! Don't you realize you could have blown the whole mission to kingdom come?" The bewildered workers, oblivious to the risks they had taken, stood staring at him as he launched into a heated lecture on the hazards of what they'd just done. Then turning to the uncomprehending Somali truck driver, Dad issued a warning. "Get that thing out of here and into Dar es Salaam where it can be properly fixed and don't come back until it is."

The saga didn't end there, though. Two weeks later, guess who came back? Yep, the Somali driver with his leaking gas tanker. Dad showed him the gate and we've not seen him or his tanker since!

We've finally finished taking inventory of all the mission vehicles and stationary engines and have set up a maintenance schedule for each piece. Now, if we can persuade everyone to bring their vehicles in on schedule, major problems could be averted. We discovered that we're responsible for the repair and maintenance of 14 different makes of vehicles and 17 different models. Most have arrived in Africa without repair manuals or other technical information. (We found a manual for only one of the trucks, and it's in Italian!) Vehicles have come from Italy, Japan, France, Great Britain, South Africa and Canada. Can you imagine the job of trying to stock spare parts in the middle of Africa for such a diverse lot of equipment?

Most spares have to be ordered from abroad. If our orders get through to the suppliers, and we're not always certain that they do, it takes months for the parts to arrive. Still, equipment is often run until it breaks down and then it's brought limping into the shop with a demand that it be repaired forthwith.

Recently, a Peugeot sedan was brought in from Itigi with the rear differential housing cracked like an egg. (For those not mechanically in the know, that's the bell-shaped hump in the centre of the rear axle.) In all of Dad's 40 years of experience in the mechanical field, he'd never before seen anything like it. The driver had taken the vehicle in the bush hunting *dik-dik* (tiny antelope), if you please. He claimed he was just creeping along ever so slowly when all of a sudden it broke. *A likely story!*

There were problems at the carpentry shop too. We found that lumber stocks were all but depleted. Orders for custom-built chairs, tables and cupboards taken months ago, before we arrived, were waiting to be filled. When Mzee Peter, the carpentry foreman, came to us to report that irate customers were coming to him demanding their furniture, we had no idea where to find seasoned lumber. There's not an Irly Bird or Home Hardware store anywhere in the country. Timber, Mzee Peter told us, has to be ordered directly from the woodcutters. We did that, and the rough timbers have finally been delivered, but now they have to be ripped into boards and seasoned before they can be fashioned into furniture. It will be weeks before we can satisfy our customers.

Our North American mentality demands results, but in light of the new reality, we've had to re-evaluate and modify our expectations.

My God, they've given us a mammoth task! Dad told the Fathers the other day that he wanted to shut the shop down for a few weeks while things are being reorganized, but they didn't agree. Dad's reply was terse and to the point, "Well, we'll do our best," he said, "but let me tell you, it's like trying to change a flat tire while the vehicle is still running down the road."

Even though we've had four months of intense study, our knowledge of the language, culture and ways of these people is slim indeed. We'd be having an even a tougher time if it weren't for the intelligence of Fr. Vincenzo, the new parish priest. (He's the one that we'd met in Rome when he was there for advanced theological studies.) Father knew we'd need an English-speaking administrator to keep us out of trouble, so he hired Laurenti Ntiruhungwa, a former Tanzanian tax department employee, to fill that role. Not only is he competent, he also has a bubbly sense of humour. Every morning when we go to the workshop office, he greets us with a bright smile that lights up his round, shining, ebony face. Laurenti is just the antidote we need to counteract the stresses of this job.

There had been no qualified foreman in the mechanics shop, so when Edward Kimome came to the bunker to apply for the job Dad was quick to put him on the payroll. Kimome was trained by the British, so is a pretty good fit. Three years ago, when he reached 55, he was forced to retire from his job with the Department of Public Works but he's not yet received one shilling of his retirement pension. Kimome is married to a much younger lady and there are five small children to support. Until he came to work for the mission, his family was living on what little they could grow in their small *shamba*, the sale of eggs from their few hens, and revenue from the *mandazi* (doughnuts) his wife has been making and selling at the market. Dad promised to take him to Singida to consult with the government authorities to try and get some action on his pension.

Girish is back in town, so we're once again enjoying evenings with him in his tiny rooms beside the Sisters' laundry, gossiping and drinking hot sweet cardamom-flavoured Indian tea. Yesterday Girish had other guests: Alex Isinika, retired Tanzanian police superintendent, and his diminutive Indian wife, Darcy. As a boy, Alex attended Lutheran missionary school, where the principal recognized his potential and mentored him through his studies, up to and including post-graduate work in Scotland. Even though he's well into his 70's and his crinkly crop of hair is turning grey, Alex carries his tall languid frame with the authority of a police officer. He has a wonderfully respectful way of speaking when he's with us. If he uses a Swahili expression he thinks we'd be unfamiliar with, he does an "on the spot" translation. It's good to be meeting so many local people we can communicate with in English.

The long rains have begun to taper off but we're still visited by an occasional spectacular storm. Early one evening, before the sun had completely set, low black clouds descended and shaped the sky into an ominous vault that hovered above us. The swallows that nest in the eaves of our dwelling stopped their rustling, and as we walked from there to the main mission, we felt a tension in the atmosphere, still and eerie, yet crackling with expectation. We had just reached the shelter of the porch when I felt a charge of electricity that caused my hair to stand on end. Bolts of fork lightning and ringing claps of thunder ripped open the sky and turned the evening bright as noon. Then the clouds burst open and spilled rain in such a fury that, within seconds, the area was turned it into rivers of mud.

Standing there on the porch looking out at the storm, we saw something we've never seen before. Blue flashes of light were skipping up and down the metal power pole that stands just outside the mission. It had become alive with lethal high-voltage electrical current. It was 'electrifying' to watch. (And I mean that in every sense of the word). Assisted by the saturated ground, the electrical current surged from 220 volts to a level so high the lights in the mission house brightened to such an intensity we felt they would surely blow. Then flames appeared through the little window of the cubbyhole where batteries were being charged. Dad opened the door and saw that the battery charger was on fire. He immediately threw the main switch. The flames died down, but the charger was "toast".

When the rains subsided and things settled down and we finally sat down to dinner, Fr. Vincenzo was in a state. "We need someone to study and rework this whole electrical system before we're all fried in our beds!" he fumed. When we told him that our friend George Moore, a qualified electrician, and his wife Muriel were planning a visit, he asked us to call them and ask if George would be interested in having a look it. Well, we made contact with the Moores who thought it over and agreed to stay with us long enough for George to do the study and make recommendations, even though he's not interested in doing the work. But, it will be several months before they can come. Until our house is ready there is no place for them to stay. In the meantime, we're giving that power pole a wide berth, especially during a thunderstorm.

Bro often says that God has created so many insects in Africa that even He has yet to catalogue them all. Indeed, there are many, and each sort, except for the cockroaches that never seem to rest, has its season in the sun. Insects that have lain dormant under the earth during the dry months suddenly spring to life during the rainy season. One Sunday afternoon, while resting on our lumpy cots, I noticed a number of black antlike insects about three quarters of an inch long, crawling up the outside of the window screen. I got up and stepped out the door to take a closer look. They were emerging from a two-inch hole not far from the doorstep. "I'll stop this," I said to myself. I went back in, grabbed the insecticide liquid and poured some down the hole. That's what triggered the real invasion! Within seconds, a black mass of insects erupted from the hole and kept coming by the hundreds, falling over each other in their haste to escape the insecticide. Many came toward the step where I stood, so I sloshed more liquid onto the ground in an arc around my feet to create a barrier between them and me. Still they kept coming! I moved back inside and watched through the window as they proceeded over the step, up the wall and onto the window screens, where, for a moment, they hung so thickly, they partially obliterated the light. Then, as the poison penetrated their bodies, they began to fall. I was overcome with nausea and needed to get away from the repellent scene that I'd created. I said to Dad, "Let's get out of here." As we walked out the door, it was impossible to avoid stepping on the mat of dead black things that crunched under our feet.

Later the same day when we returned to the bunker after supper, we saw that our bookshelves were teeming with other smaller, more benign ants. They were crawling along the book spines and were lodged within the pages of every book. We had to take each book from the shelves and shake the invaders out.

And, that's not the end of the insect assaults. Six-inch snaky things have been coming up through the shower drain. They love the insecticide. In fact, they enjoy swimming in it. Dad had to kill the last lot with a mallet from his toolbox. He brought his arm down with a heavy swing and when he looked around to clean up the squished bodies, there was no trace that the snaky things had ever been there. (We wonder if they had been dissolved by the liquid.)

One day we tried to get away from our stressful existence by making a run to Dodoma, but it was hopeless. A swampy section of the road was blocked by a long line of container trucks that were stranded, one behind the other, mired in the mud. There was no way for them to turn around. One had tried to pass, but he too got stuck in the gumbo. To top it off, he'd also lost his steel container when it slipped off the trailer and now lay bent and broken in the ditch. The drivers and their *tunboys* (helpers) had set up camp beside their vehicles and turned what could have been an upsetting situation into a carefree time as they shared food, smokes and boisterous conversation. Some had fired up small kerosene burners and were cooking rice and *ugali* (cornmeal porridge). Children from the nearby village of Kintinku walked along the muddy verges selling hard boiled eggs, fruit and vegetables. A few truckers had the foresight to bring along live chickens to supplement their diet during the long wait for the road to dry up. They carried these in baskets on the roofs of the vehicles.

We didn't stay long to chat with the truckers. Black clouds were boiling up on the horizon, so we turned around and headed back to Manyoni before another deluge descended and did further damage to the road.

Well, dear ones, that about wraps up this episode. Keep sending photos, especially of the kids. We don't want to entirely miss their growing-up years.

Love,

Mom and Dad

****

To our friends:
Manyoni, Tanzania
June 18, 1989

Dear Loverna and Bob,

Loverna, we didn't realize how much our recent letters conveyed our level of depression until we received your most uplifting Bible verse. It is typical of you, dear friend, to think of others even at a time when you yourselves are going through great losses. You must surely be mourning the recent death of that special lady, Auntie Gertrude, and missing your daughter Jen and family, who've chosen to move away from the Yukon.

Because I know you'll pass this letter on to all the family and friends, I've chosen to write the reading out in full.

Isaiah 58:10

And if you spend yourselves on behalf of the hungry and satisfy the needs of the oppressed, then your light will rise in the darkness and your night will become like the noonday. The Lord will guide you always. He will satisfy your needs in a sun scorched land and will strengthen your frame. You will be like a well watered garden; like a spring where waters never fail. Your people will rebuild the ancient ruins and will raise up the age old foundations. You will be called "Repairer of Broken Walls"; "Restorer of Streets with Dwellings."

What a message! As we go about our daily lives here in the mission, we'll try to keep focused on the promise of that verse. Thank you again for your thoughtfulness.

Since our last letter things have begun to look up in the workshop. We have acquired two new Tanzanians staff members, an administrator and mechanics foreman, to lighten our load, plus the Fathers have approved many physical improvements to the shop. Thus, the construction of two new offices and a secure parts room is almost completed, the centre courtyard has been paved, and loads of junk have been carted away.

The students are now stripping down a wrecked Toyota pickup, Cyril's first training aid for the teaching of mechanics. They're happily polishing, painting and labelling every part and laying each one out on a table. They'll assemble and disassemble them until they understand how every part of a vehicle works. Dad has appointed one of the more competent young men as the new mechanics instructor. For the first time in, who knows how long, the students are having organized instruction. Fr. John is still pressing ahead with the construction of our new trade school. It will be wonderful!

Things have always been better in the carpentry section than in the mechanical because Mzee Peter is in charge. He has things well under control, so, apart from seeing that there is enough timber and supplies and the saw blades are sharpened, we pretty much leave him to it. We do have new procedures for taking furniture orders, though, which Laurenti, our new administrator, sees to.

The morning routine at the workshop begins at 7:30 with a general cleanup of the area. Our office is swept and tidied by Joshua, a man who's been handicapped by polio. He gets around by crawling on his hands and knees, but does a very efficient job by wielding a short-handled broom. (Cleanup is not done at closing time because all the workers leave promptly at 4:00 to spend the last few precious hours of daylight in their fields.)

The rainy season is finally over and the roads are passable again. The dry season has begun and the grasses and trees are shrivelling up. The wind is downright chilly and, at times, whines around the bunker. The sky has become a monstrous grey dome that creates a feeling of hopelessness, making our dwelling more bleak than usual.

Because of this, we leapt at Girish's invitation to go with him to his hometown of Singida for a weekend break. "I want to introduce you to my family," he said. "And, there's an American lady I want you to meet." We were so eager to leave, it took us only a few minutes to throw a few duds together and hop into the vehicle for our getaway. In his hurry, Cyril backed into a low-hanging limb of a tree and bashed in the back of our Isuzu Trooper. (He'd forgotten that the spare tire mounted on the back extends the length of the vehicle by a full two feet, just enough to misjudge the backing distance.) That gives you an indication of the stress we've been under! Apart from the fact that the door doesn't fit as snugly as it once did, no serious damage was done.

The roads were still deeply rutted from the truck traffic that had passed during the rainy season. Weeds have taken root on the piles of dirt and gravel dumped on the roadside for repairs, which never seem to get done. (We've been here over a year and have yet to see a grader working on any of the roads.) Our progress was slow, but we were thrilled to have a chance to go somewhere at last.

Girish's mom and two of his brothers live in a series of concrete-block rooms that range round a central courtyard. Mama Vishani, though Tanzanian-born, still wears the Indian sari. She's the tiniest lady, but a real powerhouse when it comes to putting vegetarian Indian food on the table. When we arrived, she was perched on a low stool hovering over a charcoal brazier preparing a meal. Tantalizing aromas of cardamom, coriander and cumin floated up from the cooking pots that sat on the floor beside her. (The boys, in an effort to make things more comfortable for their mom, first bought her a gas stove. When she refused to use that, they bought her an electric stove. Now the two stoves stand idle, side by side against the kitchen wall, while she persists in doing things the traditional way.)

At dinner time we, along with the boys, sat down at the floral oilcloth-covered table that was groaning with the many plates of poori, rice, dal and vegetable curries. We waited for a signal from Girish to begin. "It is not necessary to say a blessing," he said, "Mama has already blessed the food while putting together the ingredients."

In keeping with the custom Mrs. Vishani did not join us at the table. "Mama, she will eat after we have finished," Girish explained.

Girish, of course, stayed at the family home with his mom and brothers, while we were quartered at a nearby guest house run by Tanzanian nuns. It's very simple, yet clean and safe behind the locked gates. Being close to the mosque is its only drawback. Several different Muslim sects are represented in Singida, and every morning each sect had its turn to call the faithful to prayer. The first wailing call beginning with "*Alluha Akbar*" (God is Great) came from the minaret at 4:30 a.m. Then a half hour later another chant from a differing sect cascaded over the town. These incantations continued every half hour until each faction had been heard. It was almost daybreak before silence was allowed to descend. (We would have been impressed by such devotion had the faithful muezzins actually climbed the tower at that time of morning, but, alas, it was all done by pre-programmed tapes.)

However, at 6:30 a.m. the cathedral bells began to chime, shattering even those few moments of blessed quiet. It was time to get up for Sunday Mass. Bishop Mabula himself presided over the three-hour service in the beautifully designed and decorated cathedral. The elegant marble altar in the shape of two adjoining African drums was imported from Italy but most of the art work, hanging batiks and carvings, was produced locally. In spite of the narrow seats and upright backs of the uncomfortable pews, we took pleasure in the surroundings and the sound of the African voices in choir.

After breakfast it was time to visit Lois Swanson, the American lady Girish had spoken about. Lois is amazing! She is a person so totally imbued in her Christian faith that every fibre of her being radiates love. Originally from Michigan, she came to Tanzania as a young missionary at the age of 18 and has lived here for 35 years, serving as secretary to the Lutheran Bishop. During all that time she's never once had a bout of malaria. Her North American–style home sits on a large grassy plot of land under a huge flamboyance tree. It was so relaxing. Lois has an old piano, so, after supper, we persuaded her play. Her chubby fingers were amazingly dexterous. After playing a few piano pieces, she brought out a vocal score from *The Sound of Music* and accompanied me while I sang, "The Hills are Alive with the Sound of Music". I had not realized until then how much I missed singing. It was the first time since arriving in Africa that I had sung, and it felt glorious.

Later, Girish drove us to a residential area in a leafy subdivision where we met his friend, Dr. Ulome. The doctor had taken his medical/surgical training in Cuba, with whom Tanzania has a close relationship. It's not uncommon to meet professional people who've trained in Russia or Cuba because of Tanzania's ties to these communist countries. Dr. Ulome has the reputation of being one of the finest surgeons in Tanzania, but the operating room at the local hospital is so poorly equipped, he seldom gets to practice his surgical skills. What a pity!

As we took our leave from Singida next morning, Girish promised us that, the next time we come to visit, he'll take us on safari to the Canadian Wheat Project farms that lie an easy drive to the north. Last year, at the Canada Day Celebrations in Dar, we had met several of the Canadians who are stationed there and it will be great to see them again.

When we arrived back in Manyoni we found that our furniture had been delivered. It's being stored in one of the containers behind the mission until it can be moved into our new house. Work on it is moving ahead quite quickly now. The carpenters have hung the doors and put in the wooden window frames, and all the walls have been plastered. Every day after work we walk over to the site to see what progress has been made. It's the highlight of our day!

We're excited that two new Canadians have come to join our mission: Dr. Lillian Lome, a retired doctor in her late 60's, and Maureen, a 20-something university graduate. They'll be stationed at the maternity clinic in Chibumagwa with Ana. The clinic is now up and running at full tilt. Ana and her Tanzanian nurses tend to maternity patients who come from all the neighbouring villages for prenatal care and deliveries. Ana feeds the moms once they are admitted, but many come to the clinic far before their due dates and camp out under the acacia trees, hoping to be pampered. What do they think this is? Club Med? Some have come as early as seven months' gestation, so Ana has to ask them to go home and return closer to their due dates. Because of the great need, the clinic's focus has grown to include all manner of nursing and doctoring, which should keep both Ana and Dr. Lillian busy.

Maureen has chosen to involve herself in education at the Chibumagwa village primary school. She's made it her mission to try to make it into one of the finest primary schools in the valley. Good luck with that!

We had a chance to attend the grand opening of our mission hospital at Itigi. It's named St. Gaspar's Hospital, for the founder of the Missionaries of the Precious Blood. The 375 bed facility will serve 17 villages in the Rift Valley. The President of Tanzania, Ali Hassan Mwinyi was on hand to "cut the ribbon" and we were close enough to the action to snap a few close-ups of him and his wife. Later in the week he was in Manyoni to open the new mosque. Several children, too short to see the President from the ground, climbed into a scruffy tree that overhangs the mosque and got a "bird's eye" view of the ceremony. (It reminded me of the story of Zachias in the bible, the very small man who climbed into a sycamore tree to get a better look at Jesus.)

Every day is like a roller-coaster ride. We never know what highs and lows we're going to experience. (Sometimes, in retrospect, we feel that because we have "wheels," we're fair game for manipulation.) For example, a week after we'd been in Singida, Girish breezed into our office with a long list of items needed to finish our house. "Why didn't you tell us you needed these things when we were in Singida?" I asked sharply. He stalled, giving innumerable excuses, all of them lame, and in the end claimed we'd get better quality and prices if we were to go to Dodoma.

"Right," I exclaimed, getting up from behind the desk and walking over to where Cyril was leaning over the hood of a vehicle. "Wrap things up here and get packed. We have to go to Dodoma," I said.

"What? Now? " Cyril asked incredulously.

"Yes, now," I replied, "I'm fed up to the teeth with these endless delays." So that was that! In moments, instructions were given to the staff, cases were packed and we were off.

En route we detoured down the escarpment to Chib for a brief visit with Ana, Dr. Lillian and Maureen. It was good to see them again, but we lingered only long enough for a quick chat over coffee while Girish borrowed the vehicle and drove into the village to pick up a bag of locally grown rice to take to his brother Bippin who works in Dodoma. (We do so enjoy experiencing Tanzania with Girish, and if he wants to use shopping for us as an excuse to make deliveries to his family, well, we're OK with that.)

The trip was going as well as it normally does over the rocky, rutted road until we came over the crest of a hill. Looking down, we saw that a horrific accident had taken place. A bus had missed the bridge approach and plunged into a deep ravine. Only the rear wheels were left clinging precariously to the road. I whipped out my small camera and took a couple of quick shots. But my actions were not quick enough to go unnoticed by the two white-clad policemen who, looking to us like tiny black dots from where we stopped, were taking measurements at the scene some 300 yards beyond. As we walked down the hill toward them, the larger of the two strode to meet us, and separating me from Cyril and Girish, bellowed, "Lady, you have just committed a crime! Don't you know it's an offence to take photographs of policemen in uniform on duty? Do you want to go to jail?"

"Well, no, actually, no, I don't want to go to jail!" I stammered. "I had no idea it was a crime to photograph policemen." A verbal tug-of-war ensued, with threats coming from the policemen and apologies coming from me. They wanted my camera; I offered to destroy the film.

Then Girish stepped into the breach and came to my rescue. "Right," he said to the policemen, "get into the car. Let's go to police headquarters and see what Chief Superintendent Mgambo makes of this harassment of a missionary lady who's come to help our people!"

"You know Superintendent Mgambo?" they asked, somewhat cowed.

"Know him?" said Girish, "He's my best friend!" Then he took them around the back of the vehicle and showed them the 100-pound bag of rice.

"You see that rice?" asked Girish. They nodded. "Well, it's a gift for Superintendent Mgambo. We're on our way to see him now."

Miraculously, the confrontation ended then and there, with the policemen offering apologies. One of them even scribbled his address on a scrap of paper and asked me to send him copies of the photos if they turned out. (Yes, they did turn out, but no, I did not send him copies. Had I done so, I would have provided him with proof of my own culpability.)

Saved by a bluff and a bag of rice! Bravo, Girish!

"Hotelling it" in rural Tanzania can be a bit problematic. Ever since that punishing night at the Dodoma Railway Hotel where we endured disco music until 3:00 a.m., we were not keen to check in there again, so Girish's brother recommended the Jamboree, a new hotel that had just opened up. It's pleasantly located in a large garden with a sweeping drive, has a nice restaurant and seemed a step up from the other one. But our first impressions were dead wrong. It was horrible! All night long there was noisy conversation in the halls. Doors banged and furniture was dragged scraping across the bare concrete floors. But most irritating of all was the clack, clack, clack of the high-heeled shoes of the "midnight angels" as they paraded, giggling, clients in tow, hour after hour along the uncarpeted corridor. Believe me, this is one Jamboree you don't want your Boy Scout troop involved in!

On the positive side, our shopping went well. I think we checked out every hardware shop in the town, purchasing our bits and pieces. We found locks at one *duka*, hasps at another, bathroom taps at yet another, and so on, until we'd collected every item on the list. Then we went to a large government-owned warehouse to buy steel posts and chain-link fencing. It took three hours to get that done (no kidding!) as paper was passed from desk to desk, accumulating a rubber-stamped image at every stage. (Indeed, nothing is approved in Tanzania without the official ubiquitous rubber stamp.)

We were spared another aggravating night at the Jamboree when Sandy Notley, a new friend (widow of the late Grant Notley, former leader of the NDP in Alberta), took pity on us and invited us to stay at her home. She and Eleri, a lady from Wales, work for the Anglican Church and share a nice quiet place on the outskirts of Dodoma.

Interestingly, Sandy has become a very close friend of Alan Kreutzer, one of our missionaries who's teaching at the seminary nearby. They're meeting every morning for tea; we sense a budding romance.

Well, dear friends, it's time for me to get to work taking inventory.

'Til next time,

Love,

Leona and Cyril

****

To our daughter Kim, son-in-law Blair and family:
Manyoni, Tanzania
August 1, 1989

Dear Kim, Blair and kids,

It's almost six weeks since we wrote home, but that doesn't mean we've forgotten you. On the contrary! The arrival of all your letters and photos keeps our spirits up. With our days full of new, exciting and exhausting adventures, there's often no energy left at the end of the day to put pen to paper. It's great to be able to write just one letter and know that everyone in the loop eventually will get it.

We remember that Robert is one year old today. We're visualizing him sitting in his high chair in your Calgary home eating birthday cake and gleefully ripping the wrappings off his gifts. How sweet it would be if we could be there at our grandson's first birthday party: to be in a place where we belong, where we know what's going on. We often feel out of control here, thrust on a confusing trajectory to we know not where! We're frustrated by how much we don't know and by our inability to interject some order into our lives. Ana says there is no word for "frustration" in Swahili which indicates the depth of the variance in our two cultures. But, we're slowly learning to "go with the flow" and deal with matters as they come up as the Africans do.

For instance, when Sister Carmen sent word from her mission at Mitundu that there was a problem with a "galloping cement mixer" and asked Dad to come round to look at it, we dropped our plans for the day and off we went on the four-hour drive, taking Temaeli Kingu, our Italian-trained electrician, along. The problem was solved when, after much head-scratching, it was discovered that someone had simply put on a wrong-size pulley that caused the mixer to rotate too quickly and dance across the floor. Although the work we'd come to do was accomplished in a matter of minutes, we had to stay overnight because of the length of the journey. Sister put us up in their lovely chalet-style guest house overlooking rolling golden acacia-dotted hills. What a welcome contrast to the bunker back in Manyoni!

Sister had taken a seminar on snakes, and over breakfast next morning taught us how to identify a poisonous bite by examining the position of the teeth marks on the victim. That is information I hope we never need to use!

Snakes are an ever-present danger in Africa. In fact, a few weeks ago, Fr. John had a close call with a deadly green mamba. We, along with Fr. Vincenzo and Fr. John, were seated at lunch around the large square table in the mission house when Juliana, the cook, rushed in from the garden shrieking, "*Nyoka nyoka!*" (Snake! snake!) We rose as one and moved quickly outside to where a group of native farm workers stood poised for action, rocks in hand, and knees slightly bent. All eyes were on the tin roof of the carport where a mamba had wriggled to the edge and was winding itself like a green ribbon down the frontal post. Reaching the ground, it crawled under Fr. John's Landrover and disappeared. One of the workers squatted down and peered up into the undercarriage. Pointing toward the front axle, he said, "*Yuko chini* " (He's under there). Fr. Vincenzo, schooled in African skills, picked up a rock and stood with the others, rigid and ready, waiting for the snake to reappear. When it didn't dislodge itself, Dad suggested that someone drive the vehicle out to see if the snake would drop out into the open. That's when Fr. John, looking as cool as ever in his smart slacks, Safari sunglasses and Gucci shoes, stepped forward and climbed into his vehicle. He remained calm even though it took him a moment to activate the glow plugs and start the engine. Still unruffled, he backed out into the yard and when the snake still failed to appear, began to drive forward along the tree-lined garden path. Then, all hell broke loose! The vehicle slammed to a stop, the driver's door flew open and Fr. John leapt out shouting, "*Nyoka ndani!*" (Snake inside!) The mamba shot out behind him, dropped to the ground and wriggled up into a young banana tree. I couldn't see the snake once it was camouflaged by the greenery of the palms, but the sharp educated eyes of Fr. Vincenzo and the Tanzanian crew could still pick it out. With unerring aim and deadly purpose, they loosed a barrage of stones toward it, turning the tree into a shredded mass of vegetation. Then, one of the men lifted the dead mamba from the torn foliage with a long stick and dropped it into a pit. Fr. John was visibly shaken. He told us that, as he was driving forward, the mamba's diamond-shaped head poked through a gap in the shoddily-screened air vent in the dash of the vehicle and probed the air with its forked tongue.

When we went back in to finish our lunch, Fr. John had difficulty swallowing. Fr. Vincenzo disappeared into the cellar, brought back a bottle of wine and poured it into four tumblers and as we drank it, we talked about the awful possibilities, "What if no one had seen the snake crawl up into the undercarriage?" we wondered. "What if no one had seen it climb through the vent and into the car?" "What if Fr. John, unaware of the danger, had gone out later to start his car?" The consequences were just too terrible to contemplate.

Don't worry about us. That sort of thing could not happen in our vehicle. Ours is well constructed: not shoddy like Fr. John's Landrover that has so many faults Dad's words for it are unprintable!

We were in Dar es Salaam a few weeks ago when Bro arrived on his semi-annual visit, bringing with him a troop of young Canadians. For several years, back in Toronto, groups of high school and university-aged kids have been raising funds for the mission, packing containers and so on, and every year some are chosen to come to Tanzania to see for themselves the work that's being done. (Ted and Ana were two recruits from among the earliest groups.) It was great fun to see the young folks fired up with excitement on their first trip to Africa.

Fr. Domenic said a special Mass to welcome the kids and afterward Dad felt drawn to introduce himself to an English fellow who, along with his statuesque African wife, were mingling in the crowd. Dad and Jim Lamb hit it off immediately. The two bantered back and forth exchanging witticisms and in a matter of minutes a wonderful bond was forged.

Jim is blonde and chunky with a jowly "Churchillian" face. He's originally from Yorkshire, but has lived in various exotic parts of the world working as an engineer with the World Bank. After meeting and marrying the gorgeous Anna Nguma, a lawyer by profession, he settled here in Tanzania. They have two little girls, Linda, nine, and Beverly, five, who have those stunning good looks often seen by the blending of African and European races.

When the Lambs learned we were about to celebrate our 35th anniversary in a few days, they invited us to their place for a barbeque and anniversary cake. To get to the Lambs' house, which isn't very far from the mission guest house, we went off the main road and followed a winding trail through cassava and vegetable plots until we came to a high fence of tightly-woven grasses and palm fronds. At the gate of the same construction, we honked the horn and a guard came out to open up. Behind the fence, we found their cozy concrete-block and stone house that is surrounded by a garden of fan palms, bougainvillea, gladioli and jasmine. The flowers are Anna's pride and joy. Anna does not practice law anymore. She's chosen to stay home to raise the girls and fashion floral arrangements which she sells to embassies and high commissions.

Jim's hobby is flying model aircraft, perhaps because of his experiences in the Royal Air Force — another connection with Dad, who also served in the RAF. Jim proudly showed us his collection of remote-controlled airplanes that he'd built in his workshop.

Dad and I have been invited to stay with the Lambs whenever we come to Dar, which is a wonderful option.

We did a lot of shopping for our new house in Dar and timed our visit to the Nyumba ya Sanaa (House of Art) to coincide with our lunch break. (We've taken a real liking to their chicken escalope and chips.)

We looked up some of the folks we'd been to Swahili School with. It was great to see Geoff Hayes again who's working as an administrator with the Anglican Diocese. (He's the fellow who drove with us from Dar to Musoma across the Serengeti when we had our near miss with the lone buffalo.) Then, we had tea with an American Mennonite couple that we'd met at language school. Kent is an accountant and was expecting to teach in a college, but the local group he's with thought he'd come to run a chicken farm. What a screw-up! (At least our assignment bears some resemblance to our skills. We don't think we'd stick around long if they asked us to run a chicken farm.)

Back in Manyoni the Canadian kids have been put to work digging the foundations for our new trade school so that Fr. John's crew can get on with laying the concrete bricks they've made. It was amusing to see the white kids toiling away in the hot sun while strong African men sat watching from under the shade of a mango tree.

Ana invited us and the young Canadians down to Chibumagwa for lunch of *wali na kuku* (rice and chicken). She was called away from her meal to treat a small village boy who'd been brought to the clinic. The lad had been beaten and his legs had been burned during an initiation rite. He'd been made to dance around an open fire, but when he couldn't move quickly enough to suit the older boys they prodded him on the legs with a burning stick. Ana was furious! As she bound up his sores, she lit into the old man who'd brought the boy in. The man kept saying, "It's the custom," to which Ana replied, "It may be the custom, but it's evil!"

A few nights ago, just after we'd fallen asleep in the bunker, we were jarred awake by the rat-a-tat-tat of a semi-automatic weapon being discharged back of the farmyard. We hunkered down in our beds and waited for the sequel that we felt would surely come. In moments, pandemonium reigned! The mission dogs began to bark, shouts erupted and footsteps pounded past our door, so close we could hear the heavy panting of the runners as they fled. Then all was quiet until we heard a soft tapping at our window. It was Bro coming to tell us the event was over. Thieves, attempting to rob the paint container, had been interrupted by local security officers who've taken them to jail.

Well, there you have it! Life for you folks back in Canada must be very dull indeed compared to the excitement here, eh?

Don't forget to include those birthday party pictures in your next letter. We really need those connections with home.

Love,

Mom and Dad

****

To our sons, Kurt, Dave and Chris:
Manyoni, Tanzania
September 1, 1989

Dear Dave, Kurt and Chris,

Ted has just survived another flying adventure that further boosted his reputation for "daring-do". Everyone, especially you three pilots in the family, will find it fascinating.

We simply have to write this saga separately from other news.

On July 17, Ted was expected to fly the mission plane, *Queen of Heaven,* back to Manyoni from Dar where it had been taken for servicing. When he didn't appear that evening, the mission-to-mission radio connections from Dar to Manyoni crackled alive with anxious inquiries. At length, the story came through that shortly after passing over Morogoro his engine seized and he was forced to make a crash landing. It is such a harrowing tale that we asked Ted to tell the story himself. It's so much more meaningful than anything I could possibly relay. This is what he wrote:

Dear Leona and Cyril,

It all began with a very tiny oil leak. During my pre-flight checks, I found there was always a smear of oil on the outside of the aircraft engine. At first, the loss was negligible and it caused me no concern. But as the flying time increased, the volume of oil I had to replace in the engine block steadily grew. When it was to the point of causing me concern, I booked the *Queen of Heaven* in for a service with the firm at the Dar International Airport. Upon inspection, the head mechanic assured me that it was a minor issue: just a gasket replacement. I waited the suggested number of days and then returned to collect the aircraft. I found they did not have the proper gasket and had ordered one brought in. You know how this story goes…and of course it will arrive, "*sasa hivi tu*!" (right away).

A few days later, I returned to the airport without a doubt in my mind that all would be in order. But true to Tanzania (and probably all of Africa), the wrong gasket had been sent. According to the mechanic, if I was a little more patient, all would be in place by the next morning. Something did not compute about this statement. I couldn't see how the *Queen of Heaven* would be ready the next morning if he didn't have the proper gasket yet. But I put it out of my mind and just wrote off my confusion as the result of my mechanical ignorance.

True to his word, the *Queen of Heaven* was ready the following morning. I was so happy to be under way again, back to Manyoni, out of the thick humidity and chaos of Dar with its distinct permanent odour of decaying compost. I collected Fr. Sebastian and we were on our way. Everything checked normal during the pre-flight routine, the taxi to the runway and takeoff. About 15 minutes into the flight (I'm guessing at the time span), the gauges on the aircraft's control panel were showing signs that something was amiss. The oil gauge was beginning to show that I was losing oil pressure, but the engine temperature showed normal. A loss in oil should cause the engine to start heating up. I radioed ahead to the Missionary Aviation Fellowship (MAF) in Dodoma and spoke with their head mechanic about my observations. He suggested that I monitor the gauges very carefully and set the plane down as soon as I could. At this point in time, I was over some very dense brush; not a chance to put down here. Up ahead a ridge of mountains lay directly in my flight path. I assumed that once over the mountains, I would put the *Queen of Heaven* down and take a good look at the problem.

I never got the chance. No sooner had I completed that thought, when there was a mini-explosion that jolted the aircraft. Just as rapidly, my windshield was covered in oil. The aircraft started to vibrate violently. It shook so badly, I thought it would disintegrate. The engine could not hold RPMs, and I was losing altitude rapidly. Realizing that the engine turned on was not assisting me in staying aloft, I cut it so we would not be shaken to pieces. I immediately trimmed the aircraft for "glide attitude" to minimize altitude loss without "stalling," and started to search frantically for a place to put down. Having flown this flight path many times before, I knew that somewhere up ahead was an abandoned dirt runway that used to service a hospital before major roads linked the rural hospital to civilization. At the same moment that all this was happening, I put in a mayday call to MAF, as I was still on their radio frequency. They quickly responded to the call. I explained to them briefly what was happening and conveyed my intentions. They realized the immense pressure that I was under at this very moment and that I needed every ounce of concentration. They advised me to concentrate on landing the plane safely without any worry about communicating anything further until safely on the ground.

One of the many blessings I encountered that day was the fact that I was flying at over 11,000 feet to give me plenty of altitude to clear the mountains. As a result, I had some extra precious moments to search for a clearing. The lack of visibility through the windshield made it almost impossible to look ahead. I shouted at Fr. Sebastian to snap him out of his panicky stream of questions, and told him to search out of his side window for the airstrip while I did the same on my side.

When I finally spotted the narrow dirt opening surrounded by mature sugar cane fields, I was almost directly over top of it. I realized that I was too high and would overshoot the runway, but I did not have enough altitude to go around and try a second approach. I had only one shot to make the landing. I slapped the control down, giving me full flaps that almost stopped the plane dead in the air. I tromped on the left rudder pedal and put the *Queen of Heaven* into a "side slip". Pointing the nose directly down so as not to stall in mid-air and drop like a rock, the *Queen of Heaven*'s starboard wing was pointed for the apron of the runway.

The sideslip manoeuvre turns the plane sideways while moving forward and down. This allows one to stay on course and lose altitude rapidly at a controlled speed. This technique put the starboard wing of the aircraft pointing to the runway, as well as the nose and landing gear, perpendicular to the airfield. To make a safe landing, the pilot must abort the sideslip when the desired altitude has been reached before touchdown so that the nose and wheels of the aircraft are pointed in the right direction (in the same direction as the runway).

Because of the necessity to lose so much altitude, I was forced to maintain a sideslip attitude until the aircraft was literally ready to touch ground. There was only a fraction of a second to abort the sideslip and straighten out the *Queen of Heaven* for touchdown. God was with us! The landing was perfect! We touched down at the very start of the runway, which allowed for an easy roll, until the *Queen of Heaven* lost all momentum and stood still.

I slumped in my seat and let out a huge sigh of relief. I reached for the radio mike and informed MAF that we were safely on the ground. I could hear the cheering in the background as MAF dispatch offered congratulations. Speaking with MAF later on, they told me that their whole ground crew, mechanics and office personnel, were all gathered around the radio after our mayday call, waiting for the radio to crackle to life with good news.

Shaken by the ordeal, we opened the doors and stepped down from the aircraft. My legs were shaking uncontrollably. It amazed me that I had seen no houses before landing, but people started to stream out from the sugar cane fields onto the runway. I approached an elderly man near to me. He had the traditional kanga wrapped around him, very dirty and worn with age. He walked with a tree branch worn smooth by many years of use as a cane. His wrinkled face confirmed that he had experienced many years of hard life. I looked at him with his earlobes stretched to the point of touching his shoulders and expressed how grateful I was that he had come to see that we were OK.

He almost looked disappointed. He told me that they heard the aircraft engine quit and saw the plane go down. Thinking that we had crashed and died, they came to see what was left and to take home what they could!

No sooner had this elderly man awakened me to the cruel reality of survival in this land, than a beat-up Landrover tore on to the airfield, kicking up a trail of dust as it headed straight for us. A heavy-set man, his stomach protruding from his military uniform, (telling me that he obviously had a much better life than the skinny souls walking barefoot out of the fields) marched right up to my face and asked to see my permission forms for landing on the airfield in his jurisdiction. I explained to him our predicament which almost cost us our lives, and of how fortunate we were to have this airfield on our flight path in order to make an emergency landing. The sergeant continued to insist that if we did not produce the proper papers, he would be forced to imprison us. The universal law of permitting emergency landings had no effect on him. Familiar with the Tanzanian economic situation, I knew that the sergeant's girth was not a result of his military wages. I offered him financial compensation. I agreed to the payment of a "fine" for landing in his jurisdiction without permission. This immediately ended the conflict and the sergeant once again sped off in his Landrover after an amount of shillings was handed over.

Fr. Sebastian and I slept overnight in the *Queen of Heaven*, as there were not enough daylight hours for MAF to send a plane for us. The next morning we were picked up by MAF in a Cessna similar to the *Queen of Heaven*. In Dodoma, we made arrangements to have our aircraft repaired and flown out.

When the repairs were complete, the MAF mechanics showed me where my oil problems came from. They produced the gasket that had been installed in Dar es Salaam. On it was clearly stencilled, "If you can read this notice, this gasket must be turned around." In Dar es Salaam, the gasket was put in the wrong way and the mechanic there just used a pencil to punch holes in the gasket to line it up with the engine configuration. They forgot or missed punching two holes, so there was an improper flow of oil through the engine.

Cheers,

Ted

We hope the story won't end there. Someone must be held responsible for the damages. We sense a legal battle shaping up! We'll write more personal news next time.

God bless and love to all,

Mom and Dad

****

To our son Chris:
Manyoni, Tanzania
September 15, 1989

Dear Chris,

So, you're going to marry that lovely Irish girl! Roshean and her daughter Kaitlin will be splendid additions to our family. How we'd love to be home for your wedding next month, but we just can't ask Bro for more time off, considering we've been on the job for such a short time. When we told Bro you were getting married, he encouraged us to pressure you to get married here, but we know that's not possible. There'll be lots of time for you to come later, however, before our term is up. How about a second honeymoon here in Africa in one of the game parks? Wouldn't that be romantic?

Maybe there'll even be some improvements in the horrible road conditions by the time you come. The President's announcement that he plans to inspect the roads in our area has spurred the local authorities to send out the highway crews who've begun to fill some of the deeper potholes. It's the first time in two years we've seen any road work done!

George and Muriel Moore are coming to visit next month so all "stops are out" for the completion of our house. They arrive on October 29 and will stay until after Christmas. That'll give George time to do the survey of the mission's electrical system and still allow lots of time for visiting and holidaying in the game parks. We're so excited! It will be grand to share our new life with them.

Hardly a day goes by without us being touched by some drama. It's as though we've been cast as characters in a soap opera that never seems to end. We're not the only ones to feel this way. Ted and Ana have the same thoughts, and, because we're all, in one way or another, connected to Bro's windmill project, we relate our encounters as episodes of "As the Windmill Turns".

Our latest chapter concerns an incident in the carpentry shop when our youngest carpenter was rushed into our office by the foreman. "There's been an accident with the power planer," he said, propping up Robert who was holding his left arm tightly against his chest. Robert's ashen face and dilated pupils told me that he was in shock. When he opened his fist I saw that the tip of his index finger had been severed. I grabbed the first aid kit, bandaged up his hand and fashioned a sling. Dad brought the car around and we hurried to the local hospital. It was my first visit to this institution, at least while being fully conscious. (Dad had brought me here last year when I'd fallen in the shower, and now, seeing it with total awareness, I'm so grateful that he refused to let them stitch the gash over my eye, and took me instead to the Sisters' clinic.) There was no one about when we arrived at the crumbling concrete building so, supporting Robert between us on the dusty pathway leading to the wards, we called out, "*Hodi, Hodi*," over and over trying to rouse some medical help. Finally, a young nurse shuffled toward us and listened to our story. Then, without saying a word, she turned her back on us and shambled off. We waited a full ten minutes but she did not reappear. We were incredulous! No one, it seemed, was coming to treat our patient. We helped him back into the car and left for the 45-minute drive to the mission hospital in Kilimatindi where he was taken care of.

That seemed enough turmoil for one day, but not so. Later, Laurenti came into the office to tell us that Yonna, our new gate guard, had been arrested. According to the police, he had committed the so-called "grave offence" of neglecting to salute the police officer at the workshop gate. Even though there was no legal basis for his detention, the police held Yonna for a number of hours. Laurenti himself had tried to free him, but it was only after Mzee Peter, our carpentry foreman, a highly respected elder, spoke on his behalf that he was released. Ye gods, what a tempest in a teapot!

Everyone involved with the mission in Manyoni came together last night to have supper with Bishop Mabula who was passing through. Like many Africans, Bishop is a natural born raconteur and kept us captivated long into the evening by his stories of the suffering and deprivation of the local people. After the dishes were cleared away, he leaned back into his chair, folded his arms across his large belly, and in his slow deliberate voice, reeled off one sad story after another.

During the period of the last rains, he told us, the bus he was travelling on was stranded for four days when it got mired in the mud. Many of the travellers had no food or water and there was no way to communicate their dilemma to the authorities. On the second day, while waiting for help to come along, one of the passengers died. Two African nuns, who happened to be on the same bus, removed their veils and wrapped them around the body in preparation for burial under a tree in the wilderness. The Bishop himself administered the last rites.

Another of his stories involved a group of travellers who lost their lives in the Serengeti one rainy season trying to cross the raging Mara River at a spot where the bridge has no side rails. The water had risen so rapidly and so high it completely covered the deck. The driver thought he knew where the bridge was, but misjudged and drove directly into the river, drowning all the occupants.

Then he lightened the mood by telling us about a conversation he'd had with farmers in his area who refused to use oxen for ploughing their fields. "It's cruel to the oxen," they said. Bishop replied that it was odd they had no qualms about sending their wives to do the job they wouldn't expect of the oxen!

It was very late when Bishop wrapped up his stories and we could politely take our leave. As we stepped out into the yard, a shadowy figure fell in beside us. It was one of our more trusted employees. "*Samahani mzee*" "(Excuse me, Sir)", he said. Then switching to English, he continued, "Bad things happen at workshop. Much stealing!" Theft is rampant in Tanzania, even among our workers. They're so inventive, that it's impossible to plug all the holes in our security system. We've made it clear that anyone caught stealing would be dismissed, but the temptation is apparently too great for some. Our more honest workers keep their eyes and ears open and often report to us if there has been a major theft, or if there is one in the planning. Our informer told Dad that one of the mechanics had been issued two new U-joints from the parts room, but had installed only one on a mission vehicle; the other, he had secreted into his toolbox to take away and sell. Dad, armed with the knowledge of the theft, determined to unmask the culprit by test driving the vehicle himself. Every eye was on Dad as he put the vehicle through its paces, driving it around and around the yard. Then, in an exaggerated show of concern, he leaned out the window. Cocking his ear toward the right front wheel, he caught the grinding sound of the bad cross joint. Grim-faced, he drove the vehicle over the grease pit, curtly ordered the mechanics to remove both U-joints and the scam was revealed. (An aura of apprehension had settled on the scene. Others surely knew about the scam, and some had, no doubt, even been accomplices.) It was very sad to see that the thief was no other than an employee we'd chosen to send for further training. To make matters worse, he was a close relative of a high government official. In Tanzania such relationships carry with them a sense of immunity, a culture of entitlement. But Dad, risking political repercussions, fired him on the spot, making clear that he was a man of his word, without exception. (Unfortunately, we had elevated the fellow to chief mechanical instructor, so we were left scrambling to train the next in rank to take his place.)

Our other disappointment was the betrayal of trust by our neighbour, a young man who'd gained the confidence of one of the Fathers and had been given accommodation in the other half of the bunker. We'd observed that this fellow (let's call him Mustafa), a student in the mechanics' class, was receiving a rather large number of calls on the workshop phone. It was annoying to have him called out of class so often, and I resolved to speak to him about it, but before I had the chance, matters were taken out of my hands.

To make a long story short, the chap had been taking orders for spare parts and materials on the workshop phone, and when opportunity arose, used his trusted position with the mission, which gave him access to the mission stores, to steal parts and materials. These, he stashed away at his former girlfriend's mother's house. But "love hath no fury", so when he later spurned the girl, her mother called the police and reported the thefts. "Mustafa" was in the middle of a soccer game when word reached him that the police were on their way. In a panic, he fled the field and took off across the African plain, still wearing his soccer uniform and boots. The police later arrested him in Singida, and when they searched his quarters next door to us, found that he'd set up the place as a "show room" where he had displayed samples of various things available from the mission stores, such as nuts, bolts, hasps, door handles, etc. What a con artist! Must admit though, he really has a western entrepreneurial spirit.

We never cease to wonder at what a small world it is. What are the chances of meeting someone from your home town 10,000 miles away? That's exactly what happened recently when we were finishing lunch at the Nyumba ya Sanaa in Dar es Salaam. A familiar-looking couple walked in to the dining room where we were seated. Dad gaped at the fellow and whispered, "Isn't that Dr. Steele?" There directly in front of our table stood a forlorn-looking Dr. Peter Steele and his wife, Sarah! Dad asked tentatively, "Dr. Steele?" Peter wheeled around and almost embraced us in his excitement. Words tumbled from his mouth as he unburdened himself, telling of their unhappy experiences since arriving in Tanzania just the day before.

Even though both Peter and Sarah are world travellers, Tanzania proved to be a daunting experience for them. Within minutes of arriving, they found themselves caught up in money-changing scams and shakedowns by unscrupulous police officers who, using threats, conned them into surrendering a portable radio, camera and $1,000 US in traveller's cheques. The Steeles were so upset they abandoned a trip to Zanzibar and planned to take the next plane out to Zimbabwe. We couldn't spend as much time with them as we'd liked, because we'd been invited to dinner at the Lamb's place and didn't feel we knew Jim and Anna well enough to bring extra guests. But we did take them for a long drive along the beach and back to their hotel before saying goodbye.

From time to time, we're still invited to experience new and interesting cultural events. The latest unexpected pleasure was dinner with Girish at the Hindu temple in Dodoma. Before entering this place of worship, as is the custom, we removed our shoes at the door. At one end of the temple a glitzy altar draped with tinsel held brilliantly-coloured images of Hindu gods and goddesses. Girish took us for a walk alongside the altar and introduced us to some of the deities. Brahma, the creator, sits at the apex of the hierarchy of gods, and on either side of him are positioned, Shiva, the destroyer, and Vishnu, the preserver. These three are believed to be physical manifestations of a Supreme Universal Soul. Images of lesser gods such as Hanuman, the monkey god, and Ganesh, the god with an elephant's head, as well as myriad others, were also present. (Hindu scriptures boast a pantheon of 330 million gods, but in fact, many are reincarnations.)

Women wearing bright flowing saris and Punjabi suits moved gracefully around the temple, putting out platters of pungent vegetable curries and cardamom-flavoured rice. When time came for dinner, we were each given a large tin plate and invited to serve ourselves. Although it's the custom to eat with the fingers while squatting on the floor, Girish, being respectful of our age and culture, brought us chairs and spoons. When everyone was settled, the sound system was turned on and gentle sitar music filled the room. The total experience was an exotic feast for eyes, ears and palates.

This has to be a very short letter, Chris, because we're spending every available hour to finish up at the house in preparation for George and Muriel's coming next month.

We'll be thinking especially of you and Roshean on October 7, your wedding day.

Love you all,

Mom and Dad

****

***To our friends*:**
Manyoni, Tanzania
November 3, 1989

Dear Bob and Loverna,

Finally, two years after the initial promise, we were able to say, "Bye -bye bunker." We've moved into our new home and our lives have been transformed! Here, no creepy crawlies come up from the drains, no squawking swallows nest under the eaves and there are no battling bats above the doorway. No longer do we have to move ourselves toward the pale 40-watt bulb and squint to find a little light; at last we can read comfortably in the beautiful natural light that comes in through the wide windows. How lovely it is to rest in this peaceful location away from the hubbub and traffic at the mission gate. The only sounds we hear are the creaking of the nearby windmill, the whoop of an occasional far-off hyena and the singing of the Barabaig warriors as they reel past after a night of drinking *pombe* (homebrew) in the town.

It's great to live our lives as a family again, to be free to plan our own meals and to invite friends to share them.

Settling into the house before George and Muriel arrived was no "mean feat". We found that, three weeks before they were due to arrive, Girish, our contractor, had fled. Half the floor tiles were left unlaid, so we had to abandon the workshop and devote every minute of our time to finishing the job. (Girish later resurfaced, full of apologies for leaving us. He'd been called home to Singida to attend to a family emergency.)

The glossy Ikea-like furniture from Italy was delivered to the house in bits and pieces. Everything was jumbled together with no assembly instructions. It was a nightmare until Ted and his brother John, who'd come from Canada for a visit, came to our rescue and helped us in the Herculean task of assembling the kitchen cabinets, beds, tables, etc. Now that it's all done, I'm glorying in the bright, sunny house I'd visualized two years ago.

What an amazing six weeks have passed since our last letter home. Life here in Africa is like being in a Technicolor movie, compared to the black-and-white existence of North America. There've been so many events; I hardly know where to start.

We'd promised ourselves a getaway to celebrate Chris and Roshean's wedding on October 7 and were happy when our friends Bibi Lois Swanson and Girish agreed to guide us north to the Canadian Wheat Farms. From Singida, we headed northeast toward Basuto along the rough roadway which winds past huge *kopjes* (jumbles of rocky outcroppings). Once we'd cleared the rocky area, the vast savannah opened up, and we could see, in the distance, tribesmen of this area herding their humpbacked cattle: the tall, lanky Barabaig wearing simple brown cloaks and the shorter, more colourful Iraqw in red-chequered wraps. An occasional lone acacia tree popped up here and there, providing a little shade from the brutal sun.

Lois directed us toward the wheat farms that lay under the shadow of Mount Hanang where the Canadian advisors live. Even though they didn't know we were coming, all the Canadians gathered for a meal at Joe and Norma Campbell's cozy prefab bungalow.

The Wheat Project comprises a series of seven 10,000-acre farms. It's the brainchild of Canadian Prime Minister Trudeau and Tanzanian Past President Julius Nyerere. Conceived in 1970 to ease food shortages, it's become the focus of much controversy because the farms have displaced the Barabaig tribe from their homelands. The plains where they once roamed freely have been converted into a sea of waving wheat. Farming is done using high-tech methods, creating little work for local people. In the fullness of time, history will judge whether or not the project has been a success.

After our holiday at the farms, we returned to Manyoni and made final preparations for George and Muriel's arrival before driving to Dar es Salaam to pick them up. Their KLM flight came in early, but we were already at the airport, fairly jumping up and down with excitement. It was wonderful to see them! Muriel emerged fresh and radiant in a flaming red dress; but George looked tired. We checked them into the unit next to ours at the mission guest house and then took them for a drive along the sea front. When we returned to our rooms we pored over pictures of Chris and Roshean's wedding which the Moores had brought. (Thanks, Bob and Loverna, for standing in for us as Chris's surrogate Mom and Dad.)

There were quite a few folks for dinner at the guest house in Dar es Salaam that night, including Dr. Lillian Lome, the Canadian doctor working with Ana at the maternity clinic and Fr. Domenic, the local parish priest. But there was concern because Ted, who'd brought the well-drilling rig to Dar a few days earlier, was missing from the supper table. No one had seen him for two days, but since he's a very independent sort of guy, we shrugged off our fears.

But our optimism was misplaced. In the middle of the night, Fr. Domenic called through the opened louvers of our window, "Cyril, get up. There's been a terrible accident. Ted has been hurt and is in hospital. We have to go now. Dr. Lome is coming too." We jumped into our clothes and reported the news to the Moores telling them that we were on our way to the hospital. With Cyril at the wheel and Fr. Domenic up front, we drove apprehensively through the darkened roadways into Dar es Salaam. We found Ted in intensive care at Muhimbili Hospital, a large dreary sprawl of cement buildings. He lay on grey grungy sheets, his hands and feet restrained by strips of cloth tied to the chipped enamelled bed frame. In his agitation he had worked his body down the length of the sagging mattress until his feet extended through the bars at the end of the bed. His head was bandaged and his handsome face, now purpled with bruises, had begun to swell. A breathing tube in his mouth kept his airway open. It was shocking to see this vigorous young man in such a state. One of the nurses, attired in protective red rubber boots, moved toward us and ordered us to remove our shoes. We did so, but trod carefully in our stocking feet to avoid stepping on bits of stained dressings and a rusty blood-encrusted razor blade that lay on the floor. Fr. Domenic and Lillian immediately took on their professional personae. Fr. Domenic launched into a barrage of questions in rapid Swahili, "What happened to Ted? Who brought him in? What treatment is he being given? Who is his doctor?" The nurses all stared mutely at him.

Lillian, the doctor, immediately had a sense of Ted's injuries. "This young man has been beaten," she said. Then turning to the nurses, she berated them for leaving Ted in a state of obvious discomfort. "Help me move him up to the head of the bed. Don't you see how uncomfortable he is? He'd be better off lying on the floor than this way." The nurses still looked at her blankly and refused to move until Fr. Domenic said sharply, "*Yeye ni daktari*" (She is a doctor.)

Eventually, a senior nurse appeared and we learned the name of the attending physician. With an orderly as guide, Father and Cyril drove off into the night to find him at his home. Lillian and I stood, one on each side of the bed, talking softly to Ted while stroking his hands and the tops of his feet until his agitation ceased and he rested more calmly. It seemed forever before Cyril and Father returned. They had found the doctor, but were told nothing more except that everyone involved in Ted's case would be conferring next day at 9:30 a.m. We were told to return then.

Fr. Domenic recognized one of the junior nurses as being an acquaintance from Manyoni. He smiled at her, and taking her aside, explained who Ted was and what was expected of her and the other nurses. Then, turning out his pockets, he withdrew several wads of cash and handed a bundle of shillings to each of them saying, "Take good care of him."

We left the hospital then and slogged our way through muddy rutted tracks to find the local police station. While Lillian and I waited in the vehicle, Cyril and Fr. Domenic went inside the "hole-in-the-wall" station. The police, they said, were sullen and reluctant to give out any information, but a felon, face bloodied, popped his head up from behind the police counter and related his version of events.

This was his story: A Tanzanian soldier was killed when the vehicle Ted was riding in crashed into a group of soldiers outside the military base. The impact tossed the soldier's body up onto the hood and through the windshield directly at Ted. The vehicle then rolled, over and over. The driver and other occupants fled, but Ted, being injured and vulnerable, was beaten into a coma by the other soldiers and left for dead.

We had no idea how the felon knew this. Nor did we know who had taken Ted to hospital, nor the chain of events leading to the Canadian High Commission being informed. (The High Commission had called Bro in Toronto when they were unable to get the news through to Manyoni.)

We left off trying to get any more information and made our way back to Fr. Domenic's place where we each had a shot from his stock of Beirut scotch. (Ghastly stuff, but it helped relax us.)

Next morning the Moores came with us to Muhimbili hospital where they got their first glimpse into the inner workings of a Third World hospital.

Plans were being worked out to "Medivac" Ted by Swiss Air Ambulance to Rome. Later we went to the Canadian High Commission Office, where we met with the First Secretary. The staff was excellent and everything possible was being done to help Ted. Even High Commissioner Rose popped his head into the room to say, "*Pole!*" (Sorry — pronounced "poley").

The First Secretary asked Cyril to sign for the few remaining possessions found on Ted's person when he was admitted to hospital: a comb, a silver chain and a few shillings. And it was she who told us that the driver and the others who were in the car with Ted were employees of a British construction firm. (We learned later that the company had spirited them quietly out of the country rather than face the wrath of Tanzanian justice.)

Before we left Dar es Salaam, Ted was much improved. He was taking sips of water and beginning to talk.

George and Muriel are standing up very well in spite of having been swept so swiftly into the African cultural milieu. Between hospital visits, we tried to be good hosts and took them to eat at our favourite cafés, for drives along the Indian Ocean and walks through the exotic streets of Dar es Salaam.

Returning up-country, we were forced to stay overnight once again at the infamous Jamboree hotel in Dodoma, where George and Muriel experienced another cultural zinger. They'd been booked into a room right beside ours, but when the key broke off in their lock, the manager relocated them to a rather unsavoury section of the hotel. There, the "night angels" and their clients haunted the hallway right outside the Moores' room. I don't think our friends got much sleep, what with all the giggling and clacking of spike heels on bare concrete. Ah well, such is life in the "big city" of Dodoma!

Next day, we continued on our way to Manyoni. Baobab trees were in flower along the route, their white bell-shaped blossoms dripping with yellow-tipped stamens. The blooms were so large they fit neatly into the palm of the hand. I picked one, but it wilted and turned brown within minutes of being separated from its stalk. Like many other floral species, baobabs bloom near the end of the dry season - they seem to sense the impending rains.

Back in Manyoni, after we'd eaten dinner with the Fathers, it seemed rather inappropriate for Fr. Vincenzo to ask George and Muriel if they wanted to see the black mamba that had just been killed in the mission yard, but being good sports, they agreed. Father summoned one of the farm workers who brought in the snake's six-foot-long body suspended from a stick.

What an orientation the Moores have had to Africa - their minds must be reeling!

Until next time!

Love to all,

Leona and Cyril

****

To our son Mark and daughter-in-law Christian:
Manyoni, Tanzania
November 18, 1989

Dear Mark and Christian,

Your letter and the package of photos came in the mail today. Thanks so much. Each letter and photo that we receive tugs at us and a twinge of guilt creeps into our hearts. Yet, this is the only way we're able to stay in each other's lives. We are beginning to make a difference here and we hope you can all forgive us for choosing this particular path at this time. We feel that one day we'll all be enriched by our experiences here.

George and Muriel Moore have been with us since late October. Their company has given us strength and relief from the pressures that never seem to go away. While George is studying the mission's electrical system, Muriel is burning up the treadle on the sewing machine. In a matter of days, she has transformed a bolt of red gabardine into sofa cushion covers and has draped the living room windows with classy creations in black and white African print.

We were lucky to find that sewing machine; eight machines had been sent from Italy, but when the container was opened only this one was found. "What happened to the others?" you may ask. Probably stolen by corrupt customs agents or truckers! George spent more than a few anguished hours assembling the thing. Like our furniture, it arrived in bits and pieces scattered about in a shipping crate - without any assembly instructions.

We're delighted to tell you that Ted, who was brutally beaten following a vehicle accident in October, is recovering nicely. He was sent by Swiss Air Ambulance to Rome where he had plastic surgery on his torn ear and cheek and broken hand. He's now home in Canada, close to his family, to complete his treatment.

He and Miriam, his fiancée, are expected to be married in December on schedule and, God willing, they'll return to Tanzania. We miss Ted so much. Without him, Tanzania is a poorer place. In the meantime, another young Canadian, Derrick, is doing his best to hold the water project together.

Before resuming our work after our sojourn in Dar, we took George and Muriel on a magnificent safari. Fall, just before the onset of the rains when the grasses and streams are drying up, is the best time to visit the game parks. This is the season when the animals gather in abundance at the water holes.

For me, planning a trip is almost as much fun as the trip itself. But here in Africa, travel takes on a more critical dimension. We felt responsible for George and Muriel's well-being, so our first concern was to bring enough water and emergency rations. Along with the jugs of water and cases of pop, we packed in some canned tuna, a case of pork and beans and a few cans of Crosse and Blackwell fruit cake that we found in the food storage container. The Sisters contributed a dozen hardboiled eggs and we were given a round of cheese by Fr. Vincenzo from his cheese-making enterprise. Juliana, the mission cook, baked a batch of buns for us and we picked two bunches of bananas and a dozen oranges from the mission garden. (And, because one never knows if fuel will be available along the way, we filled the jerry can with diesel and locked it into place on the rear of our Isuzu Trooper.)

We found accommodation in Singida, our first overnight stop, at the simple but clean guest house run by local African Sisters. The only restaurant in town had run out of food so we spread a towel on the coffee table in the common area, opened our food baskets and laid out our dinner. Who could find fault with bananas, oranges and hard-boiled eggs, protected as they are from contamination by their natural outer coatings?

Next morning we ticked off the villages on our map as we progressed to our next destination, the Canadian/Tanzanian wheat farms. There are no road signs anywhere in this part of the country and one vehicle track looks the same as any other. We'd been this way before with Tanzanian friends who showed us the route, but on this trip without their guidance, we were lost. I believe that we'd still be wandering the African plains were it not for the expert directions that we received from local folks. If we stopped and asked, "*Barabara hi itakwenda wapi?*" ("Where does this road go?") the person would often hop in and escort us to the very spot we wished to go.

The whole crew of Canadians had gathered at the wheat farms, and together we enjoyed a beautiful roast pork dinner prepared by Norma and Joe Campbell. Anyone who has lived outside their native homeland knows the thrill of meeting fellow countrymen and relaxing in a familiar cultural milieu.

Our next stop was Lake Manyara Lodge, which, our map told us, could be reached by driving straight north through the town of Mbulu and beyond until we came to Karatu. From there, a short drive east should bring us to our destination.

We arrived at the lilac jacaranda boulevards of Mbulu easily enough, but then things got tricky. Tracks from Mbulu radiated out spoke-like in all directions. We stopped, surveyed the terrain and chose the one we felt would lead us most directly to the lodge. The route we chose was glorious. It wound, climbing higher and higher until we were riding on the slender ridges of the golden grassy hills that folded one into another. As we progressed, the trail became less defined and the foliage between the tire tracks was so tall it brushed up against the undercarriage of our vehicle. No other vehicle approached us during the two-hour drive and we began to feel apprehensive; there never is much traffic on remote trails, but here we were truly alone.

When we glimpsed the large soda lake on our left, we began to wonder if we'd made a gigantic error. According to the map, the only lake in this area was Lake Manyara and, if we were on the correct path, it should be on our right. At this point we began our descent to the marshy flat lands, heavy with reeds that lay at the bottom of the hills. The road came to an abrupt end at the bank of a wide river that intersected the marsh. But, on the section of map where we believed ourselves to be, there was no river. Where on earth were we?

Tire tracks could be seen entering the water where a vehicle had forded it earlier, and, looking across the river, we could see them coming out the other side. Dad threw the Trooper into four-wheel drive and with trepidation we followed the tracks. The tires slipped and skidded on the rocky riverbed and the water came up level to the bottom of the doors, but we emerged on the other side unscathed.

George was in agony. He'd developed a sore neck and splitting headache and was in desperate need of a place to lie down. I gave him my seat in the front, reasoning that there he would be less jounced about.

It was now nearing sunset, but we pressed on. What else could be done? Finally, we came to the end of our track and stopped at a village that intersected with the main road. This must be Karatu, we thought. If we just take a right here, we'll find the lodge. But just to make sure, we decided to ask a local.

I approached an old man who was pedalling away on his sewing machine in front of his shop. "*Samahani, Mzee*," ("Excuse me, sir.") I said. "Could you tell me how to get to Lake Manyara Lodge?"

Without skipping a beat on his treadle he snorted, "*Manyara mbali; mbali sana.*" ("Manyara is far away, very far.") And I was dismissed. I stalked back to the car and told the others that he'd been no help at all. "Silly old fool! He lives here and doesn't even know the way to Lake Manyara Lodge."

"Well, you'd better ask someone else then," Dad said. He was testy now. "I don't want to spend the night in the car." Now we were both on edge. I looked around and spotted a police station. In a gesture of support, Muriel hopped out and we went in together. Spreading our map on the counter, I again asked the route to the lodge. The policeman roared with laughter. Pointing to the map, he showed us that we were 90-degrees off course in choosing the track we did. We were now at the village of Magugu.

There were still many more kilometers to go before we could recover from our mistake, but eventually we did arrive at the lodge, albeit in the dark, some two hours later.

Our food stock was in need of replenishing, so Muriel and I thought that if each of us were to order two boiled eggs for breakfast we could eat one and save the other for lunch. Three of us did this, but George had had enough of hard-boiled eggs and, rebelling, ordered his eggs scrambled. Guess who had to settle for beans at lunchtime?

The road through the Serengeti was appalling. The grey washboard clearly had not seen a grader blade in many years. Dust filtered in through the crack in the ill-fitting back door of our vehicle and, as the day wore on, the air became uncomfortably warm.

The sun was at its most intense by mid-day. Heat rose from the earth and quivered in layers above the African Plains. Blown by the hot dry winds, the long tawny grasses lifted and fell like a sea of rippling wheat. Heat waves shimmered on the road ahead creating mirages of shining waters. The wheels of approaching safari vehicles split the heat waves, pushing them aside as though splashing through puddles.

By a river crossing, a group of giraffes marked with bright jagged spots moved languidly among a stand of acacia trees. Stretching their long necks, they nibbled on the high thorny branches. We could clearly see the deep limpid eyes and the tufts on the stubby horns of the two males who crossed necks and began a mock battle.

Further along, we stopped near a baboon family sitting at the side of the road. The female had eyes only for the baby that she cradled against her breast. She looked down on it as fondly as any human mother would. The male, who was chewing on a twig, got up and moved closer to his mate's side. From his place as protector, he scrutinized us with penetrating eyes. Dad and George went “ape” with their cameras. (No pun intended.)

And so it unfolded. Mile after mile of incredible sightings of animals in their natural habitat!

Muriel was enchanted by the animals and endowed them with human characteristics. This seemed especially true of the Thomson’s gazelles to whom she waved as we passed.

It’s common to see single ostriches striding across the plain, but rarely does one see, as we did, a group of twelve females moving together. Muriel and I imagined that they, although voiceless, were communicating with each other through the to and fro movements of their long necks.

We spent our next night close to the Kenyan border at Lobo Lodge. Carved into the side of a huge *kopje*, it overlooks the vast expanse of the Serengeti. We four were the only guests in the dining room, which meant that each of us had two impeccably dressed waiters at our beck and call. (We ordered the topi stew, which was superb.)

Retracing our steps, we added a stop at the Ngorongoro Crater. It’s cool on the crater rim, being heavily forested and at an altitude of 7,000 feet. We checked out two elegant tourist lodges, but found they were priced beyond our budget. In lieu of that, we followed a weather-beaten sign leading us through the mists and deep into the forest to the Rhino Lodge which is operated by the Tanzanian Wildlife Fund. What luck, I thought, here we can stay two nights for the price of one. (I never could resist a bargain.) It looked fine from the reception area, so we registered for two nights without asking to see the rooms. What a ghastly mistake! The stench of mildew permeated the rooms, and the ceilings, stained with jagged yellow water marks, sagged from years of neglect in the moist jungle. Black, short stubby hairs clung to the sides of the chipped enamel communal bathtub forming a grotty ring of filth. (It was as if some one had shaved in it while sitting and soaking off the Serengeti silt.) The mattresses were lumpy and damp; so damp, in fact, that George slept in his raincoat. I had come down with early signs of malaria and started my chloroquine regimen. (One does not wait for a diagnosis of malaria. When the first symptoms appear, one immediately begins treatment.) It was a rough night for me as I lay, alternately shivering and sweating, on the soggy bed.

But things looked brighter in the morning. The mists were clearing and the chill of the night had dissipated. My malaria symptoms had eased; the chloroquine tablets were beginning to take effect. We had survived the rigours of our first night at Rhino Lodge.

After a surprisingly good breakfast in the lodge dining room, we picked up our packed lunches at the reception desk and returned to the crater. We were allowed to take our own vehicle down into the basin but were required to hire a guide from the Ngorongoro Conservation Authority. For the "princely" sum of 100 shillings (equivalent to 50 cents), we engaged Julius. Unfortunately for us, he badly needed a shower, so we travelled with the windows open and the fan at full blast to freshen the air.

On the winding, rocky descent to the bottom of the basin we passed several spear-carrying Masaai warriors herding their humpbacked cattle. Their red togas and ochred hair created an impressive sight against the grey rocky banks. (Only the Masaai have permission to take their cattle into the crater which is part of their traditional homelands.)

Many types of African creatures live in that unique bowl. Flamingos, crested cranes, buzzards and secretary birds were all there as well as elephants, rhinos, hippos, lions, hyenas, wildebeest, wild dogs and gazelles of all types, and Julius knew exactly where to find them.

We stopped to eat our packed lunch at the Hippo Pool where hippos bobbed, submerging and surfacing, like gigantic grey boulders. After we'd eaten, Julius pointed to an area behind some bushes and announced, "It would be safe to 'reduce' ourselves over there." (Would that "reducing" ourselves weight-wise were so simple.)

A group of German tourists, also having lunch at the Hippo Pool, excitedly told us that the Berlin Wall had come down. What a momentous occasion! We'll always remember exactly where we were when that infamous wall came down.

At the end of the day we returned to Rhino Lodge. (Hey, it was all we could afford and, anyway, we'd already paid up.) After supper we spent as long as possible drinking Safari beer in front of the feeble fire in the bar before settling down in our dank quarters. (I don't know about the others but I slept in the grungy cotton clothing I'd been wearing for the last two days.)

We left the area next day and stopped at the touristy village of Karatu so that George could do some shopping. The market there is notorious for its sullen hawkers who prey on gullible tourists by mixing over-priced fake trinkets with authentic Masaai crafts. But George was "on to them"; sorting through the junk, he came away with two 'honest-to-goodness' Masaai spears and a short blunt club called a knobcarrie.

At the end of the day we arrived at Tarangire, a matchless pearl in the string of Tanzania's parks. We had saved the best for the last. Just inside the boundary of the unfenced park a beautiful waterbuck stood, half hidden by a thorn thicket. Elegant horns swept back from his head giving grace to his bearing. A ring of white surrounded his black muzzle and another ring lay like a necklace on his chest. I felt like wrapping my arms around his neck to feel his soft thick pliant grey coat. His perfection took my breath away. Dad shut the engine down and we sat in stillness. The waterbuck and I looked long and hard into each other's eyes until, breaking the spell of our connection, he bent his head and began to graze on the stubby grass.

We spent three wonderful days at the Tarangire Safari Lodge. From the patios of our green canvas tents that sat on the escarpment above the curving and gently flowing Tarangire River, we could watch the animals coming to drink, each group in its turn. They approached from as far away as the eye could see. Moving steadily over the sunburnt grasses, they passed through the patches of light and shade around the acacia and baobab trees and converged on a bend in the river where the bank had been displaced by a wide expanse of firm river sand. There, they had only to stand, lower their heads and drink. Zebras, barking with a distinctive "Yip, yip, yip", were the first to claim the water. Close on their heels came their snorting, grunting companions, the wildebeests. The gazelles, mincing their way along like society ladies in slender pumps arrived next, leaving the majestic elephants to bring up the rear. Each drank their fill then moved off. We marvelled at the order and discipline of this daily procession to the river. Who other than a Superior Intelligence could possibly be responsible for such beauty and timelessness?

Each of the tents at Tarangire sits on a concrete pad with adjoining walled and covered toilets and showers. At 10:00 p.m. everyone was ordered into their tents with strict orders not to go out until morning. The power plant was shut down and guards armed with spears began their patrol. We crawled into our cots and listened to the sounds of the African night. Zebras moved among the tents during the wee hours, munching grass like small striped horses, and in the morning, we found heaps of steaming elephant dung on the walking path to the dining room.

All too soon our safari was over. Duty dragged us from this foretaste of paradise and, like unwilling children, we faced the reality of our work-a-day lives in Tanzania. Reluctantly, we returned to Singida where we had business to attend to with the Immigration Department.

Our friend Girish who usually helps us with such things was away, so in his place his brother Menoj accompanied us to the office. Here, we jumped through bureaucratic hoops in the hope of unravelling government-imposed red tape. Shameless immigration officers at the Dar es Salaam airport had been up to their old tricks again. As they had once done on my passport, they'd stamped Muriel's passport with an exit date earlier than her return ticket shows. (If one is not careful in checking these dates, the officials can make life very difficult. They have been known to intimidate hapless visitors by accusing them of breaking Tanzanian law. Then, they might try to extort a bit of foreign currency in exchange for allowing the person through to board his plane.)

But, even after the government official corrected the exit date on Muriel's passport, we were not yet finished with the Immigration Department. Because Dad and I plan to go to Kenya with George and Muriel at the end of their stay, we needed tax clearance certificates. Even though our residency permits specifically prohibit us from earning any money while in Tanzania, we still have to affirm that we're not skipping the country owing taxes. Then, permits to re-enter Tanzania were required. What a rigmarole we went through! This bureaucracy took the better part of three hours, but Menoj was unflappable. Working smoothly and efficiently with the regional officer, he did not rest until all our papers were in order. Thank goodness for Tanzanian friends!

While we sat on our straight-backed chairs in the bare concrete office waiting for the wheels of Tanzanian government to turn, we were kept entertained by the antics of a huge rat that was on the windowsill. He sat preening his whiskers and attending to his long, bare tail. Silhouetted against the thin curtain, he seemed twice his actual size. Muriel leaned over to me and asked if he was inside or outside and I couldn't truthfully say.

Well, my dears, that wraps up the saga of our safari and leads us back to work in Manyoni. Must run! So much to do!

Cuddles for Baby Stephen.

Love,

Mom and Dad

****

To our daughter Kim, son-in-law Blair and boys:
Manyoni, Tanzania
December 10, 1989

Dear Kim, Blair, David and Robert,

Our grand safari into the Serengeti with George and Muriel Moore is over, but it doesn't mean that our adventures together are at an end. Far from it - even in this small African town of Manyoni, we can still share aspects of our new life with them. We wish you folks could experience similar events in person, but, because that's not likely to happen, you'll just have to live them by proxy through these letters.

When we arrived back to Manyoni three weeks ago, we found that Fr. Vincenzo had hired household help for us. We never thought we'd be in a position to have a cook, house girl and gardener. In fact, we felt rather guilty about it. In some ways it seems absurd, but on the other hand, it provides employment for three more people and frees me to help Dad reorganize the workshops and training centre.

Our cook, Gemma, was the first to report for work. She's not at all like Aunt Jemima! On the contrary, she's young, slender and has the classic beauty of a model: fine features, high cheek bones, perfect teeth and deep dark eyes. And there's a dependable quality about her. This lady will have no difficulty in managing the household!

There's an oval brand on the forehead of her copper-toned face that marks her as an Mgogo - a person of the Gogo tribe - and we recognized her as the bride whose wedding we had attended in Chibumagwa months earlier. Gemma has been living up to her name and proven she's every inch a real gem.

She often brings the youngest of her three children, chubby round-eyed Patrick, to work with her. He's so cute and so good. We've yet to hear him cry! Dad can't resist rubbing his hands over his little "steel wool" cap of hair.

Then there was Valeriana, who was our house girl for a mere two weeks. Gemma must have had reason to suspect Valeriana's honesty because she began counting the flatware at the end of each day. When, one day, two place settings were missing, Gemma confronted the shamefaced girl who brought back the "loot". Shortly after that Valeriana was replaced by Gracie, who now does the sweeping, dusting, mending and laundry.

We had brought a vacuum cleaner from Italy and it was great fun to watch the looks of astonishment on Gemma and Gracie's faces when Muriel fired it up and demonstrated its use. At first the ladies seemed fearful and were reluctant to take the hose into their own hands as though it were some nefarious tool. But, ever since Muriel showed them the physics of it, they're happily availing themselves of its labour-saving aspects.

Fr. Vincenzo also hired an *mlinzi* (guard) for us. We don't know where he found this fellow, but he's most peculiar. He's more frightened of the sounds of the African night than we are, and has taken to hiding in the 45-gallon steel drum that Girish's crew had left on the porch. He cries piteously, "Mama, mama!" and begs to be let into the house. When a small snake slithered across the driveway, rather than protecting us by killing it, he ran shrieking toward Dad and begged *him* to kill it. Now he's taken to bedding down in the drum and is sleeping long before we are; the sounds of his snores amplified by his metal cocoon. Some watchman!

One day, just as we were sitting down to dinner with George and Muriel and our Tanzanian friend Baldwin, the first rain of the season arrived releasing billions of tiny flying ants from the ground. They swarmed like a flurry of snowflakes through the window screens and swirled around the hanging lamp above the table. Then, dropping their transparent wings, they fell onto the table and into our dinner plates. I jumped up and grabbed the vacuum cleaner and tried to suck up as many as I could while Dad, George and Muriel rushed around flinging tea towels over the remains of our food. Only Baldwin sat calmly finishing his dinner, now spiced with the salty flavour of flying ants.

"Relax," he said, with a slow smile, "it's only a disturbance."

We tried to continue with our meal but it was impossible. A powerful wind came up and, blowing horizontally, pushed the rain through the window screens creating a mighty spray that spewed into the dining room. Water poured down through the clerestory windows that stretch all along the centre of the house where the two roof levels meet. We were being flooded! In minutes we were wading up to our ankles in water. We opened the doors at the back of the house and using every available mop and broom, swept the water out, down the steps and into the yard. (Girish, the building contractor, will have some explaining to do.)

Each day as the rains continue, something new crawls out of the ground. Once, after a spectacular downpour, we saw children scurrying about gathering something from the ground. They were chatting and called out to each other whenever a fresh patch of goodies was found. When I went outside to see what all the excitement was about, they proudly showed me what they'd collected. Their chipped basins were full of large brown caterpillar-like winged insects. Some of the wings had fallen off and were stuck to the sides of the containers. The children called them *kumbikumbi*. Gemma told us that they're very rich in fat and protein, and when fried up with peanuts make a delicious snack. Maybe we'll be brave enough to try them sometime.

Girish is back in Manyoni doing some work for the mission. We enjoy having him around. One day he dropped in and insisted on cooking an authentic Indian meal for us. He'd brought with him all the ingredients, including a scrawny plucked chicken. Muriel looked at it with scepticism as Girish asked, "Do you think you can help me tenderize this thing?" I'd brought my pressure cooker from home and now was the time to show how efficient it could be. I pulled it out from the back of the cupboard where Gemma had exiled it. (I'd tried to demonstrate its use to her once, but she was terrified of the hissing and flatly refused to have anything to do with it.) "Here you are," I said to Girish, "This will tenderize your chicken." He was game to try it, but just as the pressure was building up, he became nervous. Standing back from the stove he said, "Stop it now Mama, stop it, that's enough!" So, against my better judgment, I lowered the heat and the cooking stopped. Later, as we chomped away on what your Dad referred to as "Olympic chicken" (all sinew, no meat), Girish was convinced it was the pressure cooker that made it so tough. Sometimes you just can't win!

Girish tells us he's on the hunt for a "trailer". (That's what he's calling a prospective wife.) In Hindu tradition, the names of eligible men and women are posted in the temples around the country. The parents are then involved in screening likely candidates for a match for their son or daughter. Girish and his mom have just returned from Mombassa, where they met an eligible girl. (We learned later that this was the so-called "family emergency" that took Girish away from work on our house, leaving us with a half-tiled floor.) The young people do have a say in the choice, and in this case, Girish flatly turned the young lady down. He didn't say why, exactly, other than that she was very large. Earlier they'd gone to Mbeya in the south in their search for a bride. In this case, the girl had gone out to the bar with friends and refused to come home until Girish and his mom had left. He's not having much success in the romance department! Dad told Girish to hurry up and make a choice so we could go to a Hindu wedding while we're still here in Tanzania.

Last week Ana sent word that there was mischief afoot down in the Rift Valley: the water supply for her maternity clinic and dispensary had mysteriously dried up. So off we went with some of our crew and discovered that opportunistic villagers had tapped into the line and were diverting the water to their cows. (We DO understand that cows are very important in the life of the Gogo people but we felt putting cows before sick people was going too far.) The folks at the government water department agreed with us and gave us the go-ahead to do whatever was necessary, so we plugged off the line to the cows and redirected the water back to the clinic. The culprits, we heard later, were not only stealing the water, but had been selling it to others along the line.

We felt we'd earned a respite from the hurly-burly of life in Manyoni, so one day we took the Moores to the village of Heka to meet Father Crema, the legendary author and lecturer on tribal customs. He's the only white person within miles, and we sensed that he, like us, is often lonely. Father loves company and welcomed us by pouring out five glasses of sparkling burgundy, the finest of his homemade vintage.

"This is my presidential wine," he said. "I serve this only to my friends. I have other inferior, more potent stock that I reserve for loosening the tongues of visiting government types. I call that one politician's wine; '*In vino veritas* - in wine, the truth', as the ancients Romans used to say."

A grizzled old man wrapped in a brown canvas sarong was sitting just outside Father's house massaging his left leg which was wrapped in soiled brown bandages. A twisted walking stick lay beside him. Assuming we were part of the Sisters' medical outreach program come to treat him, he feigned an exaggerated wince.

Through Father's interpretation we conversed with him. He was curious to know how we'd arrived in his country. When we told him we'd come by *ndege* (airplane), he sniffed and told us he had no need of airplanes because he had the power to transport himself on the back of a hyena. Indeed, he claimed to have done so many times.

Superstitions run deeply here. Some would go further than merely believing that riding on the back of a hyena is possible;

they cling to the notion that some people possess magical powers that enable them to turn themselves into hyenas, lions or leopards who roam around terrorizing their enemies.

At one point, the old man asked Fr. Crema for help in finding a fourth wife. But when Father mentioned a comely young woman in the village, the old fellow nixed that idea, saying, "*Hapana! Angependa kucheza kwenye ngozi ya ngombe, lakini, mimi siwezi, nimezeeka sana..*" (No! She'd want to play on the hide of a cow, but I can't. I'm too old!) He wants a cook, perhaps?

A very sad event occurred a few days ago. One of our workers, Joshua, who'd been handicapped by polio, was suddenly taken ill. His family loaded him into a wheelbarrow and pushed him off to the local hospital, where he was given some medicine and sent home. Later, he quietly passed away in his hut. No autopsy was performed, so the true nature of his illness remains unknown. Indeed, no facilities exist for performing post mortems here in this part of the country. Early next morning, before daybreak, Mzee Peter, our carpentry foreman, visited the hut and measured up the body. Coming back to the carpentry shop he laid out the dimensions and built a coffin to accommodate Joshua's body. Mourners assembled that very afternoon outside Joshua's mud-and-stick dwelling where his body lay. They sat or stood quietly under the mango trees, murmuring softly. An air of calm acceptance had settled on the scene. There was no wailing or anguished sounds of mourning, only a soft keening could be heard from the women inside the hut. Life had been particularly hard for Joshua; yet in accepting the limitations placed on him by his handicap, he epitomized the African mentality that is at peace with destiny. Father Vincenzo arrived and entered the hut where he put on his white vestments and began to perform the rite of Christian burial. The coffin was brought out and passed hand to hand along the line of men who stood from the door of the hut to the waiting Toyota pickup. While passing the coffin, each of the men raised a knee on which the coffin rested briefly as it was moved along the line. When it reached the vehicle, it was slid into the pickup box and driven to the burial site. Father led the group in prayer and sprinkled holy water on the coffin; then it was lowered by ropes into the grave. Everyone walked quietly past and taking a handful of earth tossed it down onto the coffin lid to symbolize Joshua's connection with the earth. The young men of the village, who by custom must open and close the graves, began immediately to shovel the earth in. People quietly moved away from the gravesite and gathered under a copse of trees to take a bit of *ugali* (porridge) or other refreshment. We offered our condolences to Joshua's widow in the customary way by saying, "*Pole*," and made our way back to the mission.

When we drove into the yard we saw that mission truck was backed up to one of the containers and boxes were being off-loaded. The quality work clothes that Bro had promised had arrived. Boxes upon boxes of mechanic's and carpenter's coveralls, pants and denim jackets were there and we, along with George and Muriel, had great fun "shopping" in the container to find just the right colour and size for each of the students and workers. George picked out a flaming orange pair for our electrician, Temaeli. It seemed an appropriate colour for someone in that occupation.

There were some amazing discoveries in the boxes. Some items of clothing were huge. Would you believe pants up to a humungous size 56-inch waist? One afternoon before Christmas, we called everyone together and Dad played Santa Claus, giving each of the men a pair of coveralls and each of the women a denim jacket. Georgie, one of our mechanics, is a very tiny man with perhaps a 26-inch waist. We couldn't find a pair of mechanic's coveralls small enough for him, so we gave him a pair of carpenter's overalls that fit and threw into the bargain one of the large pairs of pants. Two Georgies could have fit into them. Everyone laughed at the absurdity of the size of the pants, no doubt visualizing Georgie in them, but it was Georgie who had the last laugh. He took them to the local tailor and had a suit made out of them.

The next event was the graduation ceremony for the students who'd successfully completed their studies. All the mission personnel joined the grads and their parents in celebrating at a *tafriga* (graduation party) in their honour. The large outdoor carpentry area was swept clean and transformed into a convocation hall. We followed the form of graduation ceremonies used everywhere. There were speeches and toasts and even a valedictorian address by one of our top students before Dad presented the certificates. Following this, the womenfolk served dinner from the huge kettles of *pilau*, a rice, meat and potato-based stew that had been simmering for hours over an open fire in the workshop yard. To complement the food, Father Vincenzo brought in enough soda pop for everyone and placed a few bottles of Dodoma Red, a local wine, at the head table.

After the meal, the chairs were cleared away and the dancing began. Soon the floor was crowded with dancers moving to the heavy rhythms emanating from a boom box. Muriel astonished the African assemblage by joining them. They'd never before seen a white woman dancing. (The Italian Sisters are the only other white women here and they certainly had never been up on the dance floor!)

I was thinking that maybe your Dad had had too many glasses of wine when he also stepped onto the dance floor and started to perform his version of a "chicken dance". I wondered if this was appropriate for a person of his position, but the Africans, drawn to him by his buoyant nature, loved it. (Dad continues to deny that he'd had too much wine and refuses to admit he performed anything resembling a "chicken dance".)

As the evening wore on and the African beat became more and more intoxicating, the dancing of the young men, gyrating and sweating, took on a decidedly sensuous tone. Primal instincts, it seemed, were being given free rein! It was time for the elders to wrap the whole thing up!

But before they could call an end to the festivities, black clouds rolled in and a violent thunderstorm struck. The power cut, the music came to a halt mid-beat and we were left standing on the dance floor in total darkness. Nothing could be heard above the deafening drum beat of the rain on the corrugated iron roof. The party was over!

Concern went up immediately for the welfare of two of our *fundis* (workers), who'd earlier gone down to Chibumagwa to repair the clinic generator and hadn't yet returned. Dad, being a good boss, commandeered another *fundi,* and throwing our Isuzu Trooper into four-wheel drive, went ploughing through the mud and muck down the escarpment. They needn't have worried. The two missing men were found tucked snugly into bed in the hut of a friend. In the morning, after the storm had passed, we found that robbers, taking advantage of the darkness and confusion, had broken into the parts room and stolen two very expensive Toyota leaf springs. But, in spite of these troubles, we felt that, all in all, the evening had been a resounding success.

We couldn't let George and Muriel go home without visiting the *mnada* (the local market) that's held every Saturday morning, so, on their last weekend in Manyoni, with Baldwin directing us, we took them to the market grounds on the outskirts of town. The wares were incredible. Row after row of colourful *kangas* lay on the grass beside a collection of hand-fashioned cooking pots. A cattle auction was in progress and a large barbeque made from a half steel drum was glowing with hot charcoal. On the grill, every part, and we mean EVERY part of goats and cattle, including eyeballs, penises and testicles, was being roasted. George, feeling slightly queasy, snapped a quick photo before averting his eyes. But, the most intriguing of all the items for sale were the sandals fashioned from cast-off tires. Being the only Europeans at the market, we'd already drawn considerable attention, but when George flopped down on the grass and took off his shoes and socks to try on a pair of steel-belted radials, a large crowd gathered around to gape at his very white feet. One small boy pulled at the hem of his mother's kanga and blurted out in Swahili, "Mama, Mama! *Angalia, miguu myupe ya yule mwanume*!" (Mama, Mama! Look at that man's white feet.)

At a section of the market, euphemistically called the "bar", Baldwin agreed to humour us by daring to drink a one litre plastic mug of *pombe* - homemade beer from a barrel of frothing brew. Baldwin gamely finished his drink in "one go" and handed the mug back to the attendant who swished it around in a *debe* of cold water. Then, dipping it back down through the yellow-grey foam, he refilled it with *pombe*, and passed it on to his next customer, an elderly Barabaig warrior.

Pombe can be ready for market in only six to seven days. Maize chaff, called *pumba*, is mixed with water in old petrol barrels and left to ferment in the sun for four or five days. Then the whole mess is boiled for about ten hours until it looks like stiff porridge. The next day, more boiling water is added along with ground sprouted maize and left for another 18 hours. It's filtered then and sugar or honey is added. When it's deemed ready for consumption, the brewer must drink a little of it first to prove that it's not poisoned.

Several calves and goats were tethered nearby to be slaughtered as needs arose. We wanted some meat for Sunday's dinner so I chose a plump goat and asked the butcher to reserve a hind leg for me. We left then, not wanting to be present for the slaughter, and returned later to pick up my purchase.

As we left the market, goat leg in hand, we were followed by a vendor intent on showing us what he had in his large round covered basket. I tried to ignore him, but Dad was curious. "Come on," he said to me. "Be a sport. Let the man show you his merchandise." So, to get the fellow off our backs, I agreed and allowed him to get close. With a grin, he lifted the cover and exposed a mass of writhing cobras. Muriel and I screeched, and although the men tried to be macho they, too, beat a hasty retreat.

Rereading this, I can hardly believe that all that took place in such a short time. Imagine, all those adventures crammed in between an unbelievably full work load within the space of a few weeks. Exciting, yes, but sometimes we yearn for the safe predictable life that we had in Canada.

Soon it will be Christmas. It'll be the first ever that we, as a married couple, will spend away from home and we're beginning to miss the warmth of family. If we hadn't looked at the calendar we'd have had no indication that Christmas was fast approaching. In Canada there will be signs of the holiday everywhere: the round of concerts, the shopping, the lights, but here in Manyoni there is none of that.

We're going to spend Christmas in Dar es Salaam with our friends Jim and Anna Lamb so it's sure to be special. After that, we're going to take George and Muriel to Zanzibar before they leave the country. They'll be going back to Canada from Kenya, so, in order to see them off, we're joining them on a MAF (Mission Aviation Fellowship) flight that will take us from Dodoma to Nairobi.

Please remember us as you celebrate Christmas. Do take lots of pictures of the little ones opening their gifts.

Love,

Mom and Dad

****

To our daughter Laura:
Manyoni Tanzania
January 15, 1990

Dear Laura,

It was grand having George and Muriel with us long enough to experience much of our life here in Tanzania. They helped us in so many ways. We spent Christmas week with them in Dar es Salaam where, apart from the climate, there was little difference in the celebrations. Christmas carols drifted out onto the streets through loud speakers from the small *dukas* (Asian shops) and parts of the city were decked out in traditional twinkling lights, albeit, not on pine trees but on palms. On Christmas day, we went to Mass with our friends Jim and Anna Lamb and their girls, Linda and Beverly and then enjoyed a traditional Yorkshire dinner that Jim had prepared: roast pork, gravy, vegetables and Yorkshire pudding. It was wonderful.

Jim and Anna didn't have room to accommodate all four of us, so we and the Moores took rooms at the New Africa Hotel in downtown Dar. The rooms were fine, but our sleep was disturbed, night after night, by the African beat of a raucous disco coming from the floor above. The music began its throbbing at 10:00 p.m. and carried on until the wee hours. But that wasn't the end of it! The revelry was then replaced by rowdiness and fighting as patrons reeled out into the streets below. It was "*deja vu*" from our night at the Dodoma Railway Hotel. (In retrospect, we should have thrown on our clothes and gone up to join the party, which, by the way, is what we did on New Year's Eve - but I'm getting ahead of my story.)

After our final night's stay at the New Africa, we found that our turn signals and parking light assemblies had been "ripped off", literally as well as figuratively. Shreds of wiring were the only things left in the cavities where the lights had once been. Rings of thieves had been busy. Having previously patrolled the areas where cars were left unattended, they had taken inventory, matched it with requisitions from "customers" and returned in the cover of night to fill their orders.

On New Year's Eve we drove out to Mikumi Wildlife Lodge to spend the night. You may think that "wildlife" would refer only to the wild animals in the park, but on this special night the term belonged to man and beast alike. The partying was spectacular! But this time we were a little smarter and instead of holing up in our rooms, fuming about the noise from the disco, we put on our "glad rags" and boogied with the best of them.

We had one more treat in store for George and Muriel before they left Tanzania, and that was a trip to Zanzibar, the spice island. Our Air Tanzania flight from Dar es Salaam was overbooked, but even so, everyone was given a boarding pass. It was a free-for-all. Passengers tried to bulldoze their way ahead of us, but we were undaunted. Dad made himself as broad as possible by extending out his elbows, while Muriel and I, like chicks trying to get under the protection of the mother hen, fell in beside him and walked stolidly up the airplane steps. Once on the plane, we grabbed whatever seats were available. But George, who had politely stood aside to let others pass, was left wandering up and down the aisle with no place to sit until the stewardess took him by the elbow and led him directly into the cockpit. Courtesy does have its rewards! Not only did he have the benefit of a chat with the pilots, but also a superb view of the dazzling island jewel as we skimmed over the tops of coconut palms on our descent to the wide runway that parallels the ocean.

A row of antiquated taxis stood at the curb at the exit from the terminal building. Each one seemed as rickety and beat-up as any other, so we chose one whose driver waved a sign boasting, "Taxi No. 1". He tossed our luggage into the trunk, closed the lid as far as it would go and, after tying it down with a piece of twisted twine, drove us to our hotel in the middle of a coconut grove.

The Bwawani Hotel was, in an earlier time, a great beauty. Graceful Swahili arches form the basis for the hotel's structure like the fine bones of an elegant woman's face. But, the lady had aged. The white adobe surface that was once her alabaster skin had lost its loveliness. Burnt by the sun and ravaged by the salt air, it had darkened and begun to peel.

The lovely dining room showed that parts of the "old girl" had been given a facelift and the rooms were spotless. (Our only complaint was the steady dripping from the overhead water pipes in the exposed bathroom ceiling which created puddles in front of the toilet.)

We took a tour of this intriguing island and as we were driven through Zanzibar town and into the countryside, our guide enlightened us about its fascinating history. For over 2000 years traders have been coming to Zanzibar from India, Persia and Arabia. Aided by the trade winds, they sailed back and forth in dhows, traditional Arab ships propelled by lanteen sails. Most traded in spices and ivory, cloth and gold while others were involved in the slave trade. As we walked through the streets and into the spice groves, the heady scent of cloves, cardamom, nutmeg and cinnamon hung in the air and I fancied that we were being accompanied by the exotic strains of Rimsky-Korsakov's Scheherazade.

Zanzibar is 97% Muslim, having been settled by Omani Arabs and Shirazi Persians (Iranians). In the labyrinth of narrow alleys of Stone Town ancient palaces with brass studded doors and carved geometric designs told of a time when Sultans lived extravagant lives. Sultan Barghash was the most ostentatious. He maintained a harem of 100 concubines and their attendant eunuchs. (This, in addition to the four wives that Islam allows.) The Shirazi Persians intermarried with the local Africans, and, from these unions, a new bloodline, the Swahili people, developed. These people were content to tend to farming and fishing and left the lucrative trades in slaves, spices and ivory to the Omani Arabs.

European explorers including Burton, Speke and David Livingstone all began their expeditions into the East African interior from Zanzibar. In fact, the house from where Dr.

Livingstone planned and outfitted his medical missionary expedition is still standing.

Stanley also left from Zanzibar in his search for Dr. Livingstone. (Their legendary meeting, where Stanley is said to have asked, "Dr. Livingstone, I presume?" is believed to have taken place in Ujiji near Lake Tanganyika.)

A Canadian couple working in Zanzibar on a Canadian University Services Organization (CUSO) project joined us for dinner at the hotel. Myron is teaching computer skills in the town, while Jenny's work with the Department of Women's Affairs takes her to some exotic places. We were riveted by her story of a recent face to face encounter with the "Cult of the *Shetani*", a cult of evil spirits.

Jenny told us that on an outing with Zanzibari co-workers to the tiny island of Tumbatu, a sophisticated gentleman in their group picked a certain beautiful white blossom and presented it to her. A few of the others backed away, overcome with fear. They believed the tree to be guarded by the "*Shetani*" and that the blossom must not be picked on any day except a Friday. To show contempt for this taboo is to invite possession by the devil in the form of paralysis. (It must be a terrifying thing to hold to a proscription so strongly that going against it could result in paralysis, yet that is the belief.)

Jenny tried to reassure everyone that such a belief is mere superstition, but a few days later she received a message saying that a relative of the fellow who'd picked the flower had taken to her bed in a paralytic state, unable to move her legs. Jenny returned to the island and tried to convince the lady that what was happening to her was psychological and that no "*Shetani*" had placed a curse on anyone. Under Jenny's coaching, the lady was convinced to take a few steps. It took the better part of the day before she could walk again and the curse of the "*Shetani*" was deemed obliterated.

We had read that the islands of Zanzibar have long been centres for witchcraft; an undercurrent of black magic, seldom witnessed by foreigners, courses through main stream Zanzibari cultural belief. Belief in the "*Shetani*", we have heard, is so prevalent that many homes and businesses hang scraps of paper inscribed with Arabic verses from the ceiling beams to protect themselves from its horrors.

Well, the lady from Tumbatu's recovery may not have been miraculous, but catching our flight out of Zanzibar came close. Although we went to the airport well ahead of time, we found the area crowded. A throng of Muslim women in traditional long black body coverings called *buibui* milled around outside the terminal building hovering over huge wicker baskets overflowing with fresh mangoes, papayas and breadfruit. They were waiting for their flight to Oman that was due to depart the same time as ours. There was chaos at the check-in. People shoved and pushed along the width of the counter rather than forming a single line. Dad, George and Muriel waited outside while I stood my ground. I leaned over the counter and stood flapping our four tickets and passports at the frenzied agents, hoping someone would attend to me. A Norwegian fellow beside me stuck a $20 bill into his ticket. In moments he was taken care of. Seeing my dilemma, he said quietly to the agent, "Take this lady's tickets too, please," and I was included in the manoeuvre. I called the others and we went through together and boarded our flight, but not a minute too soon.

Jim picked us up at the airport in Dar and after a night at the Bahari Beach Hotel we motored back to Dodoma to catch our flight to Nairobi, the Moore's departure point for Canada. After another noisy night at the Jamboree Hotel in Dodoma, Brother Alan drove us to the tiny airport. Before boarding the small aircraft operated by MAF (Mission Aviation Fellowship), George almost got us into trouble with the law when he was seen trying to photograph the plane that had just landed. Luckily, Girish's brother, who works for MAF, moved in and warned George against clicking the shutter. George didn't know that it was "verboten" to take pictures of government establishments. Thank God for our Tanzanian friends who keep us out of trouble - maybe even out of jail!

The MAF flight was great. Everything was orderly and everyone had an assigned seat. Before taking off, the Norwegian pilot offered a prayer for a safe flight and for hassle free movement through Kenyan Immigration on arrival.

In Nairobi we booked in to the immaculately kept Flora Hostel operated by Italian Consolata Sisters; it's an affordable option to the pricey hotels that cater to the safari crowd. Volunteers from all over East Africa were staying there. It was a great opportunity to swap stories and empathize with each other. That's when we found out that we're not the only ones having difficulty dealing with cultural diversities!

In Nairobi we browsed in the classy shops in the arcade of the Hilton, took a tour of Karen Blixen's estate and visited the Melville Giraffe Centre where Rothschild giraffes are being raised. (The keepers had named the tallest giraffe John Paul, in honour of Pope John Paul II who'd made a recent visit to East Africa.)

On the final night we dined at the upscale Tamarind restaurant where, I must admit, the tensions we'd been under were loosed by the fair amount of wine we consumed. I guess we were laughing rather riotously, because we drew the attention of an American family of four who were seated nearby. One of them came over and said to us, "You folks seem to be having such a good time. Do you mind letting us in on the fun?" We said we'd be happy to include them in our conversation. They ordered another bottle of wine and pulled their chairs over to our table where we sat long into the evening exchanging stories of our experiences on this continent. They'd just come back from an opulent Five Star safari and were full of the wonder of it, but, they told us, the colourful anecdotes of our life in small town Africa were much more exhilarating.

But, now our holidays are over. We've said goodbye to our Canadian friends and we're back to the isolation of Manyoni.

We sure miss you guys!

Please everyone, send your Christmas photos.

Love,

Mom and Dad

****

To our friends:
Manyoni Tanzania
February 10, 1990

Dear George and Muriel,

It was sad saying good-by to you in Nairobi and we carried that feeling of loss throughout our flight back to Dodoma. As the plane swooped down for our landing, we could see the clouds of dust being kicked up by vehicles on the lonely track below us. Knowing that was the route that would take us back to Manyoni made us feel even more forlorn.

Brother Alan was at the airport with our car and after we dropped him off at the seminary, we cheered ourselves up by going to the tree nursery and buying as many saplings and flowering shrubs as could fit into the vehicle. Julius, our gardener, has planted them all and they are thriving beautifully. Every time we go out to the garden to see the strawberries ripening, we think of you folks arriving back in Whitehorse at -24 degrees Celsius.

We're back on the job facing the same daunting tasks as before: trying to combine the operation of the training centre while looking after the mission's technical needs and running a commercial enterprise. Our resources are stretched. There is simply too much work and too little time. A new school term will be starting soon, so we have the extra duty of selecting the first year students. With our head teacher, we've been sifting through over 100 applications for the ten spaces that have opened up in the mechanics' course alone. How can we ever choose? They all seem so deserving.

As maddening as our problems are, they're small compared to those faced by a live-in parent run trade school in the nearby village of Mkwezi. It was heart-breaking to see the pitiful conditions there. The training areas were housed in rough dilapidated structures; the worst being the plumbing shop where bits and pieces of pipe and plumbing accessories had been dumped into one corner. The floor and desks were littered with stinking bat droppings, the bats themselves curled up asleep hanging from the rafters. The school has no tools nor text books nor any other type of teaching aid. Outside, in the *jiko* (kitchen), at an open fire pit covered by a battered tin roof, an old lady was preparing the students' lunch. She stood, stooped over a heavily smoking fire, stirring a huge vat of *ugali* (corn meal mush) with a long flat wooden paddle. From time to time she would step back and wipe her smarting eyes with the hem of her *kanga*. But each time she was forced to move back in to give the pot another stir.

We visited briefly with the principal in his office, a cramped musty room. Yellowed files and papers lay on the hand hewn-desk and bulged from the battered metal filing cabinet. The only decoration was a tattered, fly-specked map of Communist North Korea pinned on the wall behind the desk. We felt moved by how hard these people are trying to give their young people an education against incredible odds.

When we came home from our trip to Mkwesi, we found Maureen sitting dejectedly on our new red couch. "Maureen," I said, "whatever has happened?"

"I've been fired," she replied sulkily, her large blue eyes welling with tears.

"You've been fired from teaching at the village school in Chibumagwa?" I asked incredulously. This is very funny when you remember that Maureen, who has a Master's Degree, was fired by the head teacher, a male who has the equivalent of grade seven. The whole thing has to be understood in the African cultural setting. Maureen, a young single woman, who carries no status in this society, had caused the male teacher to lose face.

When Maureen first arrived at the school, she found that the lessons were haphazard and attendance was spotty. In fact, pupils were often called out of class by the head teacher and ordered to work in his *shamba* (field). Not one of the kids from that village had ever progressed beyond the primary level, so, Maureen, determined to change that, took over their advancement as her personal goal. Without consulting the head teacher, she scheduled extra classes after school and on Saturdays, pouring every ounce of her energy into upgrading the young folks. But, in over-reaching her authority she angered the village teacher who told her to 'hit the road'.

(Also, incidentally, by insisting that the pupils be in class rather than hoeing in his *shamba*, she'd deprived him of all that free labour.)

Little dramas like that continue to unfold on an almost daily basis. For example, this morning a clapped-out Landrover screeched to a stop outside our kitchen door and before the plume of dust had settled, out stepped the local police chief and his driver. The chief, swagger stick tucked under his arm, pulled himself up to his full 5' 7" height and strode up the walk. His driver, a tall languid fellow, fell in beside him. Cyril, still munching on a piece of toast, opened the door and faced the policeman who bellowed, "Your foreman, Kimome, has been disrespectful to me!"

We left our breakfast, and, with the policeman's Landrover following, drove directly to the workshop where we called our foreman into the office. Kimome was clearly nervous as he told his side of the story. According to him, the police chief had demanded that an administrative rule we had set in place be bypassed and that he be served immediately.

It was that rule that had created the impasse between the two. We'd been having a lot of difficulty collecting for work done on government vehicles, and it had come to our attention that questionable private deals were being hatched between some of our workers and outsiders. So, to put a stop to these shady dealings we'd instituted an LPO (Local Purchase Order) which had to be signed by the chief administration officer of the organization who was sending the vehicle for repair. The policeman, evidently thinking himself to be above the rules and regulations, had come without this official document, while Kimome was insisting that he, along with everybody else, must present a validly signed document.

After getting our foreman's account of the events, we invited the policeman to join us. His driver, beret slanted at an angle, muscled his way into the office as well and leaned insolently against the door jam. We offered the pugnacious policeman a chance to sit while Kimome, knowing he'd have our support, stood confidently beside the desk holding an LPO in his right hand. Kimome's authority was being challenged and the workers who milled around outside the open office door knew this.

When the policeman launched into his tirade again, alleging refusal of service, Kimome was undaunted. "No Sir! I did not refuse to serve you!" he replied, slapping the copy of the required form into the open palm of his left hand with each syllable. "What I requested was that you present a validly signed "L", (slap!) "P", (slap!) "O", (slap!)."

The tension was palpable. Challenging a policeman in Tanzania is unheard of. As the verbal exchanges went on, Kimome's stature rose more than a few notches in the minds of the workers who hovered around listening outside the open door. At length we managed to assuage the policeman's irritation by patiently explaining the reasons for the rule and firmly reiterated that Kimome was simply acting on our instructions. It was important for our workers to realize that we would stand behind them, providing they did their jobs to the best of their abilities, and we were gratified to see that our foreman held such loyalty to us, even in the face of possible arrest.

Back on the domestic front, Gemma continues to "do us proud" with her delicious and well-balanced meals. One day, after we'd eaten one more of her pasta suppers I asked her in Swahili why she had never cooked *ugali* for us.

She gave a little chuckle and with eyes wide with scepticism asked, "*Unapenda ugali*?" (You like *ugali*?)

"Well, I'm not sure," I said, "But we'd like to try it." Then I turned to Cyril and asked, "Wouldn't we?"

He nodded but I knew he wasn't entirely convinced. Anyway, Gemma took us at our word and next day there was *ugali* sitting on our plates like small mountains of stiff white porridge surrounded by a slurry of boiled greens that Gemma called *mchicha*.

"How do we eat this stuff?" Cyril asked Baldwin who'd dropped in and, naturally, stayed for supper. Baldwin broke off a lump and rolled it into a ball. Then, making an impression in it with his thumb he dipped it into the *mchicha* and efficiently scooped it up and popped the lot into his mouth.

"Mmm," he said, "*Nzuri!*" (Good!)

It was Cyril's turn to try. He followed Baldwin's example. Then, pulling a face, he cast a wary eye to see that Gemma was out of earshot before blurting out, "Yuck. It tastes like wall-paper paste!" and pushed his plate toward Baldwin who gleefully accepted the extra portion.

After Gemma left for the day, I excused myself and went into the kitchen and prepared scrambled eggs for Cyril.

We sure miss you folks. Thank you again for visiting us and helping out so much. Temaeli, our electrician, wants to be remembered to you. He sends his thanks for everything you taught him when he worked alongside you studying the mission's electrical system. Gemma often asks about you too. As a matter of fact, she just popped her head around the corner and asked if I was writing to you. When I replied, "Yes," she said, "*Sema habari, Mzee na Mama Moore.*" (Say hello to Mr. and Mrs. Moore.)

Cyril has just poured out two shots of single malt scotch from the bottle that you brought from the Duty Free. It's "sun-downer" time. Time to enjoy that civilized British Colonial tradition of relaxing with a cool drink at the end of the work day. And, boy, do we need it!

Love,

Leona and Cyril

****

To our son Kurt, daughter-in-law Carole and kids:
Manyoni, Tanzania
April 15, 1990

Dear Kurt and Carole,

It was a shock getting your letter telling us about Laura's poor health. She writes regularly, but never said a word about her problems. Thank you for looking out for her. Of course we'll come home! We'll be arriving in Victoria on May 12 and have an open return ticket so can stay as long as we're needed. Bro has been very supportive about us coming home under the circumstances and we've been moving along quickly to get all the bits and pieces together for our trip.

Bro has arranged our flights through a special deal with Air Zambia. (We call his deals, and there are many, "Bro's Specials".) They're really, really cheap but there's always a trade off in convoluted itineraries.

Our routing on this one will take us from Dar es Salaam through Nairobi, Lusaka, Monrovia, New York (JFK), New York (La Guardia) , Toronto, Vancouver, Victoria. It'll be 36 hours from the time we leave Dar until we arrive in Toronto. Then we have our connections through to Victoria. And, the return flight will be even more gruelling. Aarg, our aching backs!

As soon as we received your letter asking us to come home, we checked the validity of our documents. (All our papers must be in order, if we intend to travel internationally.) Since then, we've had no end of trouble. It started when we found that our passports were due to expire shortly, so a few weeks ago we drove to Dar es Salaam where we persuaded an extremely disagreeable woman at the Canadian High Commission to attend to our needs. We went straight to the offices on Samora Avenue as soon as we arrived and filled out our passport application forms. Then, after having our photos taken at the little "hole-in-the-wall" photo shop on Biashara Street, we returned to the High Commission where we were introduced to the "immigration officer from hell"!

This aggressive official, whose apparent unpleasant duty it was to serve us, ushered us into her office, and in a heavily-accented Quebecois accent announced, "The person who usually attends to these matters is away leaving me to deal with it. And let me tell you, I'm not terribly happy about it!"

Shocked by this rudeness, I felt my back stiffen. I matched her belligerent tone, "Well, we're not terribly happy about it either!" At this point Dad nudged his foot against my ankle, and, in a sidelong glance indicated that I should "cool it". We did, after all, need those passports.

I knew that my eyes had taken on a steely glint as I handed over the completed forms. She took them, then leaned forward and snapped her plump fingers in my face demanding, "Your passports! Give me your current passports!"

I produced them, and, still stunned, waited for the next imperious demand. The photos came under scrutiny next, and, although we'd just come from the photographer and were wearing the same clothes and hair styles and were sitting directly in front of her, the officer told us we'd need a guarantor. We explained we didn't know anyone in Tanzania on the approved list of guarantors because, for this country, the category of "Clergy" had been removed. So, even the Bishop in whose diocese we serve would be ineligible.

"But," I suggested, waggishly, "we do know the Cardinal. Is the category of "Cardinal" on the approved list?" (I'm not above dropping names when it suits my purpose.) Her look told me she was not amused by my attempt at sarcasm. (I suspect she knew that we knew full well that "Cardinal" would fall under "Clergy".)

Then, in a show of exasperation, she pulled some forms from her desk, and, hefting herself out of her chair, ushered us back to the waiting room with the command, "Fill these out! They'll do in lieu of a guarantor. And, there's a fee for this. We do this to teach people a lesson."

I was, at this point, seething, but made no response. Dad also remained outwardly cool. We did as we were told.

But we weren't finished yet. The next hurdle was "proof of citizenship". Perhaps it was naive of us to assume that our passports, on which we've travelled worldwide as proof of Canadian citizenship, would be accepted at our own High Commission, but, this was not the case. When our officer asked us to produce birth certificates or citizenship papers, we explained that these precious documents were secured at home in Whitehorse, and that, obviously, they'd been produced in the first place to get the passports.

Logic was lost on our civil servant whose only retort was to read aloud the regulations on the back of the application forms and insist on the documents being produced. Finally, at our suggestion, she agreed to telex the Passport Office in Hull, Quebec, where our original passports had been issued, but not before saying, "Lucky for you we have telex connections to Hull."

We left then, somewhat bemused. Returning two days later, we found that she had indeed contacted Hull who had verified our story. But, still being obtuse, she'd issued only interim passports for six months. (Still teaching us "lessons", I suppose!)

We'll get home OK on them, but when we get there we'll have to sort things out to get full term ones.

Dad and I have told our story of "bureaucracy gone berserk" to our British and American friends. Everyone was dumbfounded by it and none had ever had a similar experience.

I felt compelled to write a letter to Minister of External Affairs Joe Clark telling him of the appalling treatment we received. It'll be interesting to see what response we get from his office.

As if the problems at our own High Commission were not bad enough, we still had Tanzanian governmental bureaucratic hurdles to overcome. Shortly after getting back to Manyoni, we braved the awful roadway to Singida to get tax clearances and re-entry permits from the regional government office where we were subjected to another attempt at intimidation.

Dr. Lillian is leaving next month so we took along her passport to get the tax clearance stamp she needs to leave the country. We ourselves needed two stamps: tax clearances and re-entry permits.

We'd heard that if ever we were in a tight spot with immigration authorities to call Bishop Mabula who brooks no nonsense from anyone. So, in a pre-emptive move, we paid him a courtesy call as soon as we arrived in Singida. After tea and an exchange of pleasantries, he obliged us with a written endorsement on a government form affirming that we were who we said we were, and were doing what we said we were doing.

Then, armed with the Bishop's affirmation, we felt ready to tackle the business of bureaucratic rubber stamping.

The Tanzanian official was no less officious than the one in our own High Commission and things proceeded much as we expected. This officer, a skinny sour-faced man, welcomed us at the door of his bare cubicle by hooking the leg of a chair with his foot, and dragging it across the bare cement floor. Then he nodded at Dad to sit down. (I believe he thought that I, being a mere woman, should remain standing.) Dad pulled up another chair for me and handed over the paperwork we'd prepared. We waited while he perused our documentation. As if on cue, he shook his head and spoke his first words, "This is not the proper form!" Then whipping out a long green sheet of paper he continued, "This is the form you need." Dad asked where we could get the green form and he replied, "You'll have to go to our offices in Dar es Salaam for it."

This was altogether too much. Go back to Dar es Salaam? Go back and return here under these road conditions? Undertake another four days drive? No way, I thought. The man must be joking!

I dug in. "No," I said. "Bishop Mabula has assured us that we have the correct papers. We have just come from his office; why don't we call him now?" And, that was the end of it. Spreading the passports on his cluttered desk, he grabbed two rubber stamps and began vigorously stamping until all was accomplished. Then, without a word, he jerked his head toward the door indicating he was finished with us.

But that doesn't quite end the story. When we got back to Manyoni we discovered a problem with the stamp on Lillian's passport. Reading the fine print, we found that tax clearances can be issued no earlier than 30 days ahead of the time of leaving the country. Lillian was due to leave in 35 days so the stamp would already have expired when she arrived at the airport. What to do? No way were we going back there! So, finding a black pen, Derrick, our partner in crime, simply added two loops to the number 13 and turned it into an 18. Nobody has said a word to Lillian and no one but us is any the wiser.

We're not sure who has the most officious immigration agents, Tanzania or Canada. You be the judge!

It will be good to see you all again in just four weeks. God willing, Laura will be well again soon.

Hugs for Brittany, Ben and Patrick!

Love,

Mom and Dad

****

To our sons Chris and Greg and their families:
Manyoni, Tanzania
July 5, 1990

Dear Chris and Roshean and Greg and Carolyn,

Although we enjoyed seeing everyone again, our visit home was bittersweet. The burden of Laura's illness hung heavily over us. We felt we wanted to bundle her up and bring her back to Africa with us. God willing, she'll continue to improve. We know that everyone will be watching out for her. Do call if you need us to come home again and we'll be there in a flash.

We've just received your telephone calls telling us the wonderful news that two new grandchildren have arrived. And within three days of each other! How fantastic is that? Congratulations, Chris and Roshean on the birth of Christopher Jr., and Greg and Carolyn on the birth of Jocelyn.

When Roshean's call came in we were at the workshop which is about one eight of a mile from the telephone. Then, later in the day, when Carolyn called, we were at our house, which is about the same distance away. Each time, the mission cook, who'd taken the calls, had to walk over to where we were. By the time we were able to get to the telephone, fifteen minutes must have passed. Thank you both for keeping the lines open for so long. Those calls must have cost each of you a small fortune, but it was worth every penny for us to hear the news from the Moms themselves.

We look forward to getting lots of photos of the new babes. We don't want to miss too much of their first weeks and months!

Our trip back to Tanzania was gruelling but uneventful, except for the mysterious loss of a hundred dollar bill from Dad's wallet. One minute it was there, and the next, it was gone! Ah, the mysteries of Africa! Was it witchcraft or just plain old clumsiness? My guess is that it was stuck to the wad of bills he'd pulled out to pay for our night's lodging in Lusaka and the cashier, finding it and delighting in his windfall, simply pocketed it.

Now that we're back, we seem to be visited by one trauma after another. Indeed, a week doesn't go by without unexpected twists and turns. The first shock we received was when we arrived in Manyoni and found that our house had been burglarized. Our *mlinzi* (guard) had been captured and his hands tied behind his back. The thieves were unable to smash their way past the iron window bars, so, instead, they beat a hole through the door with a huge rock. They'd ransacked our cupboards, and although Fr. Vincenzo had cleared up much of the mess, we felt violated at seeing our personal items scattered about. But, we enjoyed a sense of triumph! The stupid robbers missed taking the most valuable things in the house. Dad's red metal tool box containing $500 worth of tools still sat at the door, the vacuum cleaner and my electronic piano were in their regular spots and the $700 worth of Tanzanian shillings that I'd stuffed into a brown paper bag before tossing it to the back of the cupboard was still there. The bandits managed to get away with a pair of red-handled Italian-made pliers, binoculars, wall clock, steam iron, a large supply of antibiotics and anti-malarial tablets, two single bed foam mattresses and covers, an old battered suitcase and, the greatest loss of all, our radio/tape deck. However will we manage without that devise that provided us with our only contact with the outside world and the ability to listen to our beloved Schubert tapes?

The police have already arrested four men from Singida and are holding our guard for questioning. (The guard is said to be "helping the police with their investigation" which is a euphemism for, "We're holding him until he can clear himself of complicity in the affair"- a common practice.)

Some of our belongings have been recovered, but we can't get them back until after the trial. In the meantime, they're locked up at the mission for safekeeping because there's no secure storage area at the jail. The preliminary hearing is to take place shortly. Fr. Vincenzo, as head of the mission, will be acting on our behalf. We're going to attend to see how the wheels of Tanzanian justice grind.

We were beginning to recover from the shock of the break-in when one of our workers, who'd been handicapped by polio, was hit by a truck while riding his hand-propelled tricycle in town. Jonas was admitted to the local hospital where we found him lying in a huge ward on a chipped enamel cot covered with a tattle-tale grey sheet. What a dismal institution that is! Cobwebs were hanging from the roof rafters, bits of blood-stained gauze lay on the dusty cement floor and the rank odour of urine and feces intermingled with and overpowered the strong antiseptic smell of Dettol. Most astonishing of all, we saw that the attending doctor was drunk. Reeling toward us, he reeked of booze and was so incoherent he couldn't answer our questions. One of the nurses stepped in and took us aside. She suggested that we get the patient out of there and to the mission hospital in Itigi, but when we called them to send the ambulance they said it couldn't be started. They'd let the battery go flat! In the end Fr. Dino loaded Jonas into his Toyota and delivered him to Itigi himself.

And so we move through our days bemused by one unexpected incident after another. Our naivety seems to be part of our problem. Indeed, more than once, we've allowed ourselves to be taken advantage of. Recently we became dupes in a "con game" that two of our workers had cooked up. One of them came to us with tears in his eyes, (Africans are wonderful actors!) telling us that the wife of a co-worker had passed away in Itigi hospital. Dad, without even being asked, told them to take the shop pick-up and go to Itigi to get her body. So, off the two of them went. But, when they didn't return after three days, we became suspicious and made enquiries. Girish told us that he'd seen the two driving around Singida in our pick-up, doing God knows what. There had been no deceased wife's body to pick up in Itigi. She had, in fact, passed away several years ago!

But, our naivety notwithstanding, we feel we've begun to break through the barriers that divide our culture from that of our African staff. Our working relationship is improving. We were impressed with the way Laurenti and Kimome had looked after affairs at the workshop in our absence. The most impressive thing they did was recover a starter motor and alternator (two very expensive items), which had disappeared from the stores. They handled the situation beautifully. Calling all the students and workers together they announced that, unless the items were returned in three days, all pay would be stopped and all classes cancelled. The threats worked. On the morning of the second day, Fr. Vincenzo found the items lying just inside the mission gate.

We've introduced you to Temaeli and Elly, two of our other trustworthy workers, in earlier letters, but now we'd like to flesh out their "cameos" so that you can appreciate them as much as we do.

Temaeli is the mission's electrician who does a creditable job untangling crossed wires and restoring electricity whenever there's a malfunction. His competence was recognized early by Fr. Dino who sent him to Italy for training. Being viewed as a favoured one, Temaeli stands solemnly apart from the others. In addition, he belongs to a very strict evangelical religious group that brooks no thievery or deceit. He's fluent in his tribal language as well as Swahili, Italian and English. George was impressed with his intelligence and integrity and was happy to have him alongside while he studied and wrote the recommendations for the mission's electrical system.

Copper-coloured Elly, our genteel stores-man, is scrupulously honest and is a fantastic organizer. His record keeping is impeccable; we call him "Mr. Neat Nut", although not to his face. When Dad went into the stores and took out a light bulb without going through Elly's ironclad security system, Elly rushed out after him waving a requisition form and politely but firmly insisted Dad must sign just like everybody else.

It's very chilly here at night but the temperature soars during midday and the hot dry winds are beginning to scorch the land. Already, we yearn for a rain shower but there will be none until mid-November. The weather has become quite depressing, but, on the positive side, our house is beginning to look more like a home. We just took a stroll in the garden and saw that the hibiscus, frangipani and bougainvillea bushes we planted in February are thriving under the care of Julius, our gardener. He's also covered the strawberry plants with the cloth mesh we brought back from Canada. (The birds will not get this year's crop.) And, we've beautified the front yard. There's a type of short ground cover that grows wild in the ditches, and we hired some of our students to dig some up and transplant it in front of our house where it has spread to form a soft green lawn that never needs cutting or fertilizing. Then, we had our carpenters build red shutters and install them beside every window. With the material left over, they constructed a tiny red picket fence, about one foot high, to encircle the lovely frangipani that grows in the centre of the turn-around at the end of the driveway.

A lot of work has been done on the mission's new trade school and we hope to have the grand opening soon. In the meantime, Dad and I are working on a timetable to schedule classes for the entire day, not just for one hour in the morning before the generator starts up. That will be wonderful!

Must go! So much to do!

Hugs for Jocelyn and Christopher Jr.!

By the way, did you hear that the Armstrongs are coming for a visit?

Pray for us!

Love,

Mom and Dad

****

To our friends Bob and Loverna:
Manyoni, Tanzania
August 20, 1990

Dear Bob and Loverna;

We're so excited! In exactly two months you'll be arriving. We've already booked accommodations for your safari and promise you an unforgettable experience.

Make sure your inoculations are up to date and remember to bring all your medications. Your doctor will prescribe anti-malarial tablets. We take proguanil (Paludrin) once a day and chloroquine once weekly. Even with this regimen it's possible to have "break through" malaria, but don't worry; the mission clinics can administer treatment should this happen. There is a new drug called mefloquine (Lariam) that's being touted as being wonderfully effective against malaria, but it can cause serious side effects in some people. In fact, some embassies have asked doctors in their countries not to prescribe this drug because so many travellers have been experiencing vivid dreams and depression, and a few have even become psychotic. In my mind, it can be a very dangerous drug. Anyway, your doctor should help you sort all that out.

You'll also want to bring broad-brimmed sun hats, tanning lotion and DEET. Print film may be available for your camera here, but we wouldn't vouch for the freshness of it, so you'd better bring a big supply. (Slide film is not available at all.)

When you come into the country, as well as showing your passport, you'll have to present your International Certificate of Vaccination that Public Health will give you following your immunizations. And, you'll have to fill out a Currency Declaration Form declaring all the foreign currency that you're bringing into Tanzania. Every time you exchange dollars for Tanzanian shillings, the money exchanger will record the transaction on the back of the form. Keep that form! When you leave the country, a tally may be done to prove that all your transactions were valid and not done on the black market. Oh, and it doesn't end there! Before you leave the airport, you'll have to exchange $50 US. That should tide you over until we can get to a bank.

There are a few things we'd like you to tuck into your bags for us: a large supply of Trac 2 razor blades, AA, C and D batteries and some Ziploc food storage plastic bags. Do you remember the old sticky flypaper coils that our parents used to hang from the ceiling? Don't know if they still make them, but if you find some, bring them along too. (Flies are a real nuisance here.) Also, bring black garbage bags large enough to stuff your suitcases into. You'll need them to keep the dust out of your belongings when we're driving on the dirt roads. Be sure to pack your binoculars. You don't want to miss out on that game viewing!

We expect to be at the airport in Dar to meet you, but if something unexpected should happen and we don't show up, take a taxi to the Embassy Hotel and wait for us there. If we still don't show up, go to the Canadian High Commission offices to track us down.

While you two are caught up in the whirl of activity getting ready for your trip, our lives continue in unique African fashion. Yesterday we went to the preliminary hearing on the court case dealing with the break-in at our house. Four suspects have been charged with the robbery. The proceedings were held in the town courthouse, a semi-open area built of cement breeze blocks and covered by corrugated iron roofing. While waiting for court to convene we sat in the last row of backless benches beside two of the armed guards who were a little "slap-dash" in their decorum. At one point, one of the guards lost control of his bayoneted rifle when the string that had replaced the leather sling gave way. As the rifle fell clattering to the cement floor the bayonet grazed the back of the woman sitting in front of him. Had the safety latch not held, the weapon could have accidentally gone off and wiped out half of the people in the court!

As in the British court system, the judge entered through a door behind the bench to cries of, "Oyez, oyez, all rise!" He was not robed, but like the crown prosecutor and clerk of the court, was neatly dressed in suit and tie. Fr. Vincenzo, representing the mission, appeared as the victim in this case and was cross-examined by the suspects, who, of financial necessity, conducted their own defence. The questions posed by the four suspects tried to cast doubt on the mission's ownership of the items. During the questioning, the clerk methodically reached under the table and brought out some of our belongings retrieved by the police: our soft-sided suitcase, two cloth mattress covers, our binoculars and a pair of Italian red-handled pliers that belonged to the mission. Fr. Vincenzo may not have recognized our belongings but he did recognize the pliers, so, when the thieves said they'd bought the items in town, Father replied, "Well, if you bought those pliers, then someone else stole them ahead of you."

After a short recess, court resumed. In that brief time, the inventive thieves had changed their minds about where they'd acquired the items, and produced a receipt from a mysterious merchant in Singida. The judge, not all that gullible, has ordered the merchant to appear at the next court date. The saga continues!

By the way, Bob, we saw a big Rotary wheel downtown advertising that an International Rotary convention will be held in

Dar during your time here. It would be fun if you could attend a session. Maybe you'd even be able to meet President Mwinyi, who is himself a Rotarian. Wouldn't that be a "hoot"?

We're so looking forward to your visit. See you soon.

Love,

Leona and Cyril

****

To our son Kurt, daughter-in-law Carole and family:
Manyoni, Tanzania
Nov. 1, 1990

Dear Kurt, Carole and kids,

Loverna and Bob are with us, and after recovering from their rather traumatic entry into the country, are having a great time!

On the very first hour of their arrival at the airport in Dar es Salaam they ran into difficulty with the authorities. (But then, who doesn't?) It wasn't much fun for them when the incident happened, but it's rather funny now. Dad and I had been up on the observation deck and saw them disembark from their British Airways flight and walk across the tarmac into the airport. We went down to the arrivals gate and waited for them to appear. We waited such a long time that we were getting antsy. Every other passenger, it seemed, had claimed his luggage and had passed through the gate in front of us. Through the glass doors we could see that the arrivals lounge was deserted; yet the luggage carousel continued to turn, taking the last three bags round and round. Still Loverna and Bob did not surface. Had we had not seen them get off the plane; we'd have thought they'd missed their flight. We were beginning to be concerned when finally they appeared. Loverna was ashen-faced and shaken, but Bob had a smug look of triumph on his face.

"What took you so long?" we asked. "We were getting worried."

Loverna's voice was trembling as she replied, "We were almost refused entry into the country."

As we bumped along, dodging the bathtub-sized craters on the horrible roadway to the Lamb's place, they told us their story:

(By way of background, for those of you who aren't aware of it, every person entering Tanzania must carry an international vaccination certificate issued by the public health department in their home country proving they've been vaccinated against yellow fever. There is small print on the back of it that says, "The validity of this certificate shall extend for a period of ten years beginning TEN days after the date of vaccination". It was this part of the document that got the Armstrongs into trouble.)

Yellow fever vaccine is not available in Whitehorse, but this was not a problem for them. They were travelling through Vancouver so arranged to have it done there. Then, after a few days in London, they blithely carried on to Tanzania.

When Bob and Loverna handed over their documents to the immigration official they saw him open their immunization cards and begin counting back to the date of the vaccination. Here was a master looking for a loophole to extract a bit of "*chai*" (a bribe). Lo and behold, he found his opportunity and shrieked, "Are you trying to break the laws of our country?"

"Of course not," Bob said. He was confused but tried to remain calm.

"Then why did you not get this vaccination in time to enter our country?"

"I don't understand," Bob replied.

The official didn't reply, but moved out from behind the counter. Taking Loverna by the arm, he led her into a small cubicle. Then he took Bob into another place and began grilling him. Loverna was very frightened. She was now apart from her husband yet within earshot of the exchange of words between the official and Bob that went something like this:

"Why are you trying to break the laws of our country?"

"I am not trying to break the laws of your country. I don't know what you're talking about."

"Why are you lying?"

"Sir, I am not lying. I truly do not know what you are talking about."

"If you are not trying to break the laws of our country and are not lying, why did you not get this yellow fever vaccination ten days before you tried to sneak in here?"

"We're not trying to sneak into the country. We did not mean to do something illegal. The nurse did not tell us about this rule. It is not our fault." Then Bob pulled out his trump card, "Furthermore," he said, pointing to his Rotary lapel pin, "I am a Rotarian and Rotarians don't tell lies." (Wisely, Bob remembered that we had told him about the Rotary convention that was on in Dar es Salaam that very week, and that the President of the country, Ali Hassan Mwinyi, was himself a Rotarian.)

That did the trick. Maybe the official thought that Bob was a "mighty potentate" in Rotary. At any rate his tune changed and, after wishing Bob and Loverna a pleasant stay, let them go.

Dad whooped with laughter at Bob's use of his lodge connection to get out of a tight spot; especially the bit about Rotarians never ever lying. (He thinks that bit is a whopper in itself.)

It was like a marvellous Christmas celebration when we arrived at the Lamb's house and Bob and Loverna brought out gifts for everyone. We took a photo of Jim grinning openly and toasting us with the first glass of scotch from the bottle of Glenfiddich that George had sent for him.

There is such welcoming warmth in the Lamb's home. I truly don't know how we would survive without their hospitality. Even though their house is tiny, we didn't have to stay in a hotel. They found room for all of us. Bob and Loverna were content to sleep in Jim's workshop which he'd converted into a spare room complete with air-conditioner just for their visit. (Loverna, with her dry sense of humour commented, "That's the first time I've been lulled to sleep by the movement of model airplanes circling around and around in their orbits while breathing in the faint smell of model glue!")

As we settled for bed, Jim reminded us not to step outside for any reason during the night. Demon, his dog, was out of his run and beginning his nightly patrol. Demon will vigorously protect his family from any being who might venture into the yard without Jim's presence. The dog has even done battle with a hyena. At the sugar estate where Jim once worked, a hyena - and you know that they are "meaner than sin" - had bitten through the wire mesh fence and challenged Demon. The dog grabbed the hyena by the snout and, clamping down on its bone-crunching jaws, held it there until Jim arrived with his rifle and put it out of its misery. That story is mighty believable when you see Demon's big black figure moving about in the shadows like a reincarnation of the Hound of the Baskervilles!

But, let me get back to the wonderful experiences we shared with our Bob and Loverna.

Just as we did when George and Muriel were with us, we drove along the sparkling Indian Ocean, sat under the grass cupolas at Kunduchi beach and watched the dhows dip and swerve among the breakers while drinking safari beer and eating *karanga* (roasted peanuts). We enjoyed spicy samosas at the Kili rooftop restaurant, and later, at the Nyumba ya Sanaa, tucked into the house specialty, tender chicken escalope and chips.

We walked down the same dusty streets of Dar es Salaam, passing the old leper who still sits at the corner of Cathedral Square. His eyes are now partially covered by a whitish film that has increased his blindness, and his left leg has been amputated above the knee. In response to the chink of coins that Bob tossed into the tobacco tin by his side, he turned toward us. Then, with intense concentration, he tried, unsuccessfully, to scoop out the coins with his deformed fingers. We can't help but wonder how he gets to his spot on the pavement every day. Even with the help of his gnarled stick, he surely cannot walk far on his one swollen and bandaged foot.

We stopped in at the Canadian High Commission offices to let Bob and Loverna "sign in" and to get out of the tropical heat for a while. Bob is not handling the heat at all well. Sweat was running down and dripping off the tip of his nose as we stood in the air-conditioned office.

We didn't go directly back to Manyoni as Fr. Francis and Brother Allan invited us to stay overnight in Dodoma. Now that they can accommodate guests at the new seminary, we don't have to stay at the seedy Jamboree Hotel with its parade of giggling "night angels" to shock and/or amuse our guests. (Actually we think Bob was a little disappointed to miss the show, given that George had told him all about it!) Instead, it was the seminarians who were amused by Bob and Loverna who whipped out large rubber elephant noses from their bags and stuck them on their faces. Those two are such fun!

Each of the bedrooms at the seminary has its own toilet and shower. We think they need to lower the water pressure on the toilets, though, because every time we flushed the water rushed up in a grand swirl and splashed over the edge of the bowl and into our shoes. (We all got caught on that little idiosyncrasy more than once.)

To save time and eliminate backtracking, we decided to take the Armstrongs on their safari to Tarangire National Park directly from Dodoma. So, next morning, just as the pale yellow sun was breaking across the horizon, we headed out. Even at this early hour, the villagers were already on the move. Small boys in tattered brown shorts wielding herding sticks were ushering cattle and goats out from the thorn bush *bomas* (corrals) and into the fields to graze on the dry scrubby terrain, while women walking single file with vessels balanced on their heads made their way to the water holes.

The road was atrocious. Huge boulders and giant potholes so badly impeded our progress we were forced to creep along. Dust filtered in through the crack in the bent back door of the Trooper and settled into the creases of our faces. It was a long and tedious day, but when we finally arrived at our own personal paradise of Tarangire, we all agreed it was worth the drive. (We didn't get lost on the infamous road from Mbulu to Magugu, so George and Muriel can safely say they're probably two of the few Canadians to have had that adventure!)

We stayed in the same tented camp as we did when the Moores were with us. The first thing we did was to dash into the little covered areas back of our tents and shower away the dust. It was a new experience for Bob and Loverna to stand under the thin spray and see rivulets of red mud trickling down their bodies and swirling down the drain.

On both nights we were haunted by lions that moved among our tents, their bodies occasionally brushing against the guy ropes. From time to time, their bone-chilling throaty roars reverberated back and forth across the river valley. I wanted to roll up the window flap on our tent and look out at them, but did not, knowing that to make eye contact with a cat is to invite a challenge. (And, hey, there was only a feeble piece of canvas between us and them!)

The lions terrified Loverna. She had, she told us, lain for two sleepless nights in a cold sweat of fear, actually feeling the hairs on her arms standing on end. Bob gave her no comfort at all; ignoring her frantic whispers, he snored blissfully through the whole exotic performance.

Each morning, down in the river valley, a pride of lions lay sunning themselves on the eastern sand bank across from where the other animals come to drink. They still came, each group in their turn, but with an acute awareness of the lions on the other side of the river. The zebras and wildebeests, skittish with anxiety, barked and snorted in voices that seemed higher than usual. Some stopped and rolled back and forth in the dust before their final approach to the river. Perhaps their instincts told them this would help obliterate their scent.

The elephants, undeterred by the presence of the lions, maintained a more dignified attitude. Taking their time in approaching the river, they stopped to wallow in the muddy pools that lay some yards from the river bank. Worming their trunks deeply into the water holes, they drew up the murky water; then, withdrawing their trunks, they swung them up and over their backs and spewed out the cooling slurry.

As always, we were reluctant to leave Tarangire. Delaying our departure, we took one last walk along the gravel path in front of the tents and looked down the embankment to see the beginning of the animals' daily parade to the river. Then, it was time to move on.

Rain had come in the night and settled the dust, making it easier to look back onto Lake Manyara as we climbed out of the

Rift Valley. The baboon colony was still there at the side of the road. They seemed prepared to climb all over our vehicle if we were to stop for a long backward glance, so we moved along higher up on the escarpment edge and looked down on the white ringed lake, so large as to seem an inland sea. The flamingos were there in their thousands. Wading through the shallow water on slender legs, they dipped their long necks into the brine to locate and eat the shrimp that would eventually turn their whole bodies pink.

Gibbs Farm was as lovely as I remembered it from our first visit two years ago. The lilac jacarandas lining the path between the coffee plants hung heavy with flowers, and the ornamental pond was alive with darting gold fish. The hibiscus blooms are enormous this year, and, on several of them, tiny shimmering black birds probed their long curved beaks deep into the blossom centres.

We stayed overnight in two of the stone and thatched cottages that are just as charming inside as out. The lions' roars of the previous night were displaced by a chorus of crickets and bull frogs that chirped and croaked unceasingly until the first glimmer of dawn. Then, as though responding to a conductor's baton, they suddenly stopped, and our world was enveloped by an eerie silence. After a few moments, the doves and finches awoke and filled the void with a million songs.

We went down into the Ngorongoro Crater again. It was, as always, a special joy. Loverna was rendered almost breathless by the beauty of the animals, especially the crested cranes and flamingos in flight.

The four-wheel drive system on our vehicle "packed it in" while we were down on the crater floor, and Dad had to drive it up the steep escarpment in low gear, high range. He knew the only way he could get us out of there was to keep the engine revs high. So, he pressed down on the pedal and up we flew, bending and swerving around the tight narrow turns. Had the revs dropped and the engine powered out, we'd have been stuck there until a park ranger could come to rescue us.

Elephants are often seen moving freely in and out of the shrubbery along the escarpment, and we prayed that none would be on the road as we sped upwards. Damien, our guide, well aware of the danger, kept shouting, "Slow down, slow down, *Mzee*!" and Dad, gripping the wheel ever so tightly shouted back, "I can't slow down! I have to keep the revs up!" Loverna and I kept up our prayers and Bob just held on.

When we made it safely to the top of the crater rim, Dad pulled off the road, shut down the engine and, heaving a sigh of relief, bent down and touched his forehead to the steering wheel. Damien was the first to break the silence with a heartfelt Swahili prayer, "*Kumshukuru Mungu*" (Thanks be to God) and we all burst into applause for Dad in appreciation for a difficult drive well done.

Well dear ones, I see that I've reached the last bit of space on this, the last of our airmail letters, so I have to wrap this up. I'll continue writing the "Adventures of the Armstrongs" another day.

Love to all and God Bless,

Mom and Dad

****

To our friends George and Muriel:
Manyoni, Tanzania
Nov. 21, 1990

Dear George and Muriel,

We promised you folks a sequel to our "Adventures with the Armstrongs", so here's Part Two.

There was too little time to take the Armstrongs into the Serengeti. We were concerned about the length of time we'd be away from our post, considering that we'd have to drive them back to Dar for their flight home.

So, from Ngorongoro, we drove directly to Arusha where we stayed overnight. We had no problem replenishing our food baskets from the produce of the lush plantations and vegetable gardens situated under the cooling shadow of Mt. Meru. But, finding bread was a little more difficult. The clerk at our hotel told us to go to the movie theatre. "There'll be bread for sale there," she said. It seemed a funny place to buy bread, but we did as we were told. Sure enough, within minutes of us arriving at the theatre, a battered van rolled up, and the driver hopped out to off load several boxes of freshly baked whole grain loaves into the lobby of the theatre where we made our purchase.

From our hotel, we could see Mt. Kilimanjaro rising in the northeast. It's often shrouded in mist, but, on the morning before we left Arusha, the mantel of cloud had lifted and we were afforded a perfect view of her snowy head.

With work in mind, we headed straight back toward the mission. Still, even taking the most direct route, it took us three days to get back to our post.

On our first day homeward, we passed through the town of Babati that had, seven months earlier, been ripped in two by flash floods. The spring rains had fallen with such ferocity that, within hours, adjacent Lake Babati was flooded. The connecting river, unable to carry away the wall of water, burst its banks and, opening a new outlet, tore through the centre of town. Surging along the main street, it wiped out the mud brick buildings that lay in its path and etched a ditch so wide and so deep that the roadway was narrowed to a thin strip barely wide enough to let a vehicle pass. Rubble and bits of twisted rusty roofing still lay in the gulch where it had fallen. Temporary walkways, in the form of boards, had been laid across sections of the gully where pedestrians precariously made their way across. It has been over half a year since the flooding, yet no appreciable repair to the town has been done.

We stayed overnight with the folks at the Wheat Farms who were as warm and hospitable as always. On this visit, Charlie Wheat, the Mechanical Advisor, and his wife Carolyn hosted us. Again, the whole crew gathered for a party in the evening and it was fantastic.

On our drive to Singida next day, we stopped under a copse of trees to have our lunch. In moments, hordes of children, like ants coming uninvited to a picnic, emerged from the nearby huts and surrounded our vehicle. They stood there peering at us until, feeling uncomfortable by their stares we were forced to move along.

In Singida, we stayed in the very same rooms at the African Sisters' guest house as when we were together, but didn't have to break into our emergency food baskets because we were invited to Girish's Mom's place for an authentic Indian meal of *poori* (deep fried puffy bread) and curried vegetables followed by mouth freshening "bitings" of fennel seed and raw sugar crystals. After dinner, Girish insisted that we join him in watching a four-hour Indian movie on his VCR. We had long finished the "bitings" and were half asleep before the movie drew to a stupefying close. Indian movies are not known for their dynamic story lines. Rather, the producers try to make up for shallow plots by filming endless scenes of chunkily built heroes cavorting across the screen in pursuit of vapid heroines in swirling saris. (Cyril says that watching one of these movies is equivalent to one year's penance in expiation for his sins.)

It was Halloween next day and Bibi Lois Swanson had us over to her home for a traditional American supper. The dining room was decorated with black and orange streamers and a serviette with a Halloween motif lay on each plate. Jack-o-lanterns, fashioned from African gourds, stood on the window sills, their candles flickering out into the African night. For the most primitive of people who might happen to pass by Lois's house, it could be a very scary thing to see these grinning apparitions. But Lois has taken care throughout the 38 years she's been in Africa to try to demystify this rather silly North American custom.

In the after-glow of supper, surrounded by dear friends, we were filled with such a sense of belonging and privilege that we coaxed Loverna to Lois's old piano and asked her to play her favourite thanksgiving hymn: "Take Thou my Hand, O Father." (Even Bob singing along in his off-key baritone didn't bother us one bit.)

But, no day is perfect, and this was true on this particular day. When we arrived back at the Sisters' guest house, the old guard was ranting and drunk. He refused to open the gate and let us access our rooms. After a few minutes of his obstinacy, I got sharp with him and reamed him out in Swahili. This verbal "dressing down" eventually penetrated his befuddled brain and he shut up and opened the gate. (I didn't know my vocabulary was so good.)

Ted and Miriam have come back to Tanzania. The whole town is beside themselves with happiness! Ted is looking quite well. Apart from some scarring above his eye, there's hardly any indication of the trauma he suffered after the car accident and the beating he received last year. The water project crew, delighted to have Ted, their intrepid blonde hero and his bride back, hosted a welcoming celebration at the parish centre. We were invited to join Ted and Miriam and Fr. Dino at the head table under a canopy of red bougainvillea blooms that had grown up between the rafters of the corrugated iron roof. There, we enjoyed the usual festive meal of *pilau* (a stew of rice, potatoes and meat) and tomato and onion salad.

It was natural that music and dancing should follow the meal. But, we were somewhat bemused when Loverna, our refined and genteel friend, schooled in the finest of western culture, was carried away by the moment and walked out onto the dance floor with Mr. Kimome and led the assemblage in a lively loose-limbed jive. Soon, everyone, including Bob with his "two left feet," was up and gyrating in a most uninhibited fashion.

But, a cloud was cast over the gathering when, at the close of the evening, Ted broke the news that he and Miriam will not be staying in Manyoni. They'll be moving to Dodoma, where the water project is being relocated. We're disappointed they won't be our neighbours, but I'm sure we'll see a lot of each other. It was touching to see the guests, with heavy hearts, get up and come forward one by one to shake hands with the guests of honour as they made their way out of the venue.

During the last week of the Armstrong's stay in Manyoni, we took them to visit two Tanzanian families so they could see for themselves the humble way of life in rural Tanzania. First we took them to visit Alex and Darcy at their farm where we shared a delicious pot of tea flavoured with lemon grass. These folks are suffering unusual economic hardship. Blight has affected their cashew trees reducing their crop from two tons to zero, honey badgers have cleaned out all the honey in their honey logs and a number of their chickens have been killed by wild animals. But, like farmers the world over, they maintain a stolid stoicism and look forward to next year for a reversal of fortunes.

Our next visit was to the Kimomes' home where we celebrated the birth of their twin baby daughters. In the tiny front room of the adobe house, a rough hewn table sat unevenly on the cracked cement floor. On it rested a doily-covered tray that held six chilled soft drinks, six glasses and a basket of samosas. No matter how humble the home or how stretched the family's resources, an African is at his most endearing when playing host. Some refreshment will always be found and served from the finest vessel. We four guests managed to squeeze onto the faded floral couch that sat against the wall near the door. Across from us sat the Kimomes, each one holding a sleeping twin. Three older children hovered about solemnly eyeing the bottles that sparkled in a shaft of light coming in through the open door. Garlands of tinsel were draped in loops from the wooden rafters under the flat tin roof and a yellowing outdated calendar hung from a nail high above the one barred window. There was no glass or mosquito screening over the window, just wooden shutters that could be closed from the inside.

Outside, under a tin roof adjacent to the house was the *jiko* (kitchen): three large stones that support the cooking pots.

The family's big red rooster tried repeatedly to come inside the house, but Bob, not realizing that the rooster lived in the house with the family, kept blocking his way by sticking out a foot. Finally the rooster, fed up with being prevented from taking his rightful place in the family home, took wing and, squawking raucously, swept through the air above our heads and landed on the back of the couch.

On the way back to the mission, we encountered a dreadful scene. A young man, his face covered in blood, was being dragged through the main street by two policemen. The young man lunged at our car shouting for Fr. Dino. He grabbed the door handle where Loverna was sitting and was able to partially open it, before Loverna managed to yank it shut and lock it. We did not want to be involved with a police incident! We mentioned it to Fr. Dino next day, but he had no idea who the young man might have been or why he was calling for him.

On the morning that we left Manyoni to take the Armstrongs back to the coast for their trip home, Loverna asked Cyril to stop for a final farewell. She turned in her seat and took one last look at the cross on Manyoni Mountain. Then, before we descended into the Rift Valley, she asked him to stop at the edge of the escarpment. There, we paused for a moment and gazed out over the flat wide expanse that follows the curvature of the earth.

En route, we stayed overnight at the seminary in Dodoma and enjoyed a rich evening of celebration. It was Brother Alan's birthday and the cooks had put on a spectacular feast.

At dawn we were awakened by the rich resonant tones of African voices coming from the chapel. The seminarians had gathered to sing Matins, their morning prayers. The sound was uniquely African, yet as compelling as the chant of medieval monks.

But the Armstrongs' adventures were not yet complete. From Dar es Salaam, we took them to Zanzibar. By chartering a neat little Piper Seneca six-seater that zipped us in and out of Zanzibar during off-hours, we avoided the conflict and confusion we'd endured when we flew with the national airline.

Still, there were hassles. The regulations in passing from one part of Tanzania (the mainland) to the other part of Tanzania (the island of Zanzibar) are still in place. I don't understand the relationship between the two, but one has to have passports stamped, currency declarations balanced and departure fees paid on leaving one part of Tanzania and entering the other. (I wonder if we, in the rest of Canada, might one day have such a strange relationship with Quebec.)

The taxi that picked us up at the Zanzibar airport had even more character than even the one we shared with you! This one was a small French car of questionable vintage. It seemed to be falling apart, both inside and out. The trunk had long since lost its clasp and one of the back doors had to be opened by someone rolling down the window from the inside, clasping the glass and the door handle and pulling inward to release the lock. The steering column swayed from side to side and the driver had to turn the wheel half a revolution before the car would respond to direction. To get moving, we required a "pushie" from bystanders. Then, off we went, bucking and heaving, until we were stopped by a policeman for inspection. (He was checking to see that our driver had not violated the "Four Passengers Only" rule.) Because we'd stopped rolling, the engine stalled and we needed an additional "pushie". After progressing a few yards, our vehicle ground to a halt once again and the driver, a wiry wizened Muslim in a *kofia*, leaped out with a wrench and tightened the only remaining two studs of a possible six on the right front wheel. The sound of the engine defied description! Loverna put it this way, "Heavy metal moving along in overdrive while suffering from a combination of malaria and yellow fever!"

When we arrived at our hotel, we were astonished that the driver, with all sincerity, offered to take us on an island tour. It was quite touching in a way; the dear man really had no idea that his services were under par!

We were given the same room at the Bwawani Hotel as before. The air conditioner still wasn't working, and the water pipes in the ceiling still dripped rusty water down onto the very same spot in front of the toilet. Just think of it, almost a year ago since we were last here and still no repairs have been done.

We did go on a spice tour, but, needless to say, NOT with our former cabbie. We walked through the spice fields sampling the exotic fruits and sniffing at bits of cinnamon bark that our guide peeled from the tree. The clusters of cloves, black pepper corns and cardamom pods were not yet ready for picking so we satisfied ourselves by taking photos.

We again visited the Kidichi Persian baths with the attendant row of toilet holes. (Judging from the lack of privacy provided for users of these facilities, it seemed that the Persians were indeed an uninhibited lot.) It's not a very attractive spot. Black mould has grown up onto the decorated stucco walls, and the stench of urine and feces from the resident colony of bats was so overpowering, that we didn't linger long.

Further along on our tour, we stopped near Mangapwani village, where we descended into a natural coral cavern. At the bottom, carved into the side of it, is a man-made cell where, long after the slave trade had been abolished, traders continued to hide slaves.

Back in Stone Town, we wandered through the tight alleyways so Bob and Loverna could see the beautiful brass-studded doors of the Swahili architecture and admire the impressive balconies of the House of Wonders and the massive carved door on the house of the infamous slave trader Tippu Tip.

The old Arab man who'd allowed George to photograph him reading the Koran was still tending his *duka* (although not reading the Koran on that day), and the market was still as it was, and probably has been for many, many years. Hand carts, laden with deep-fried goodies, were still being dragged through the streets by ragged men and boys to their designated selling spots. And, from time to time, through gaps between the crumbling structures, we caught glimpses of the triangular sails of the traditional Arab dhows as they glided gracefully in and out of the harbour.

This time, we visited the Anglican Cathedral that we'd missed on our last trip. Built over the site of the old slave market, it's a monument to the passing of the slave trade in East Africa. The altar has been positioned over the place of the whipping post, and the crucifix that hangs above is said to have been fashioned from a limb of the tree under which Dr. David Livingstone's heart was buried. Other missionaries are remembered in plaques around the nave, but it is Dr. Livingstone that has been given the highest honour. A stained glass window has been dedicated to his memory. While we stood there transfixed in the stillness, a ray of sunshine burst through the window and dappled the crucifix in a prism of light. I imagined Christ on the cross transformed into the figure of a young black man chained to the whipping post and I understood the similarity of the sacrifice and suffering of both.

Nothing is left of the slave market, but it is rumoured that a cellar under nearby St. Monica's guest house was used as a pit to hold the slaves.

There was one thing that Loverna and I wanted to take away from this exotic island more than anything else: a miniature Zanzibar chest. We were so excited when we found the tiny workshop where craftsmen were busy assembling the wooden pieces to make up the finished boxes, carving ornate patterns on them and tacking on the ornamental brass studs. We felt confident we'd be able to make our purchases there and stepped up the two worn stone steps and into the ancient room that smelled of wood shavings and sweat. We looked over the stock of chests and chose two beauties. A surly fellow in an embroidered *kofia* and dirty *kanzu* approached us and we began to negotiate a price. He named a figure for the two boxes in US dollars which was fine with Bob and Loverna. But, when we convinced him that, as Tanzanian residents, Cyril and I had no US dollars and would be paying in Tanzanian shillings, he put caveats on the deal. We had to take both chests and he inflated the price for mine so high that I would be paying much more for it in shillings than the equivalent in US dollars. Well, we really wanted those chests, so we agreed. Bob pulled his money belt from under his shirt, withdrew and signed a traveller's cheque and handed it over to the scruffy man while I peeled off the agreed upon number of shillings. But, once he had his hands on Bob's cheque, the greedy little man changed his mind and wanted even more.

Outside, a thunder storm had erupted and inside tempers were rising. We were now at a state where our shouts were competing with the claps of thunder that crashed around us. Eventually Bob had had enough. He yanked the cheque back from the little man's hand and I stuffed my shillings back into my bag. We stormed out and sloshed through the alley, now ankle deep in water, back to our waiting car.

Loverna was almost in tears over the loss of the chest!

The thunder storm that racked Zanzibar had also swept over Dar es Salaam. When we arrived back on the mainland, we found that trees had been uprooted along the road to Jim and Anna's place and were lying across the path so Cyril was forced to put the Trooper into four-wheel drive to manoeuvre around the obstacles.

Next morning Loverna shared with me her diary entry for that last night. "Three weeks ago," she had written, "I lay in this same bed full of apprehension and excitement for the immediate future. Now, every dream has come true!"

After breakfast we drove the Armstrongs to the airport. The road had become a river and we found ourselves ploughing through walls of water so deep it threatened to enter the vehicle.

We followed a lorry all the way, driving slowly through the wake it had created.

It was sad saying goodbye to Bob and Loverna. We stayed at the airport and watched through the viewing area until we could see them in the departures lounge. They had successfully navigated the pitfalls of customs and immigration and were ready to board their plane. Bob had already bought a bottle of safari beer and lifted it toward us in a final gesture of farewell.

Well dear folks. It's back to work for us. Continue to circulate these letters and remember to keep us in your prayers.

Love,

Leona and Cyril

****

To our friends:
Manyoni, Tanzania
Dec. 31, 1990

Dear Loverna and Bob,

It's New Year's Eve and we're visualizing you folks back from the cross-country ski trails bundled up in sweaters and relaxing by the fireplace sipping hot toddies, while here we sit near the open windows in cool cottons, drinking cold Safari beer.

It was good to know that you arrived home safely. Had we known that your flight was going to be six hours late leaving Dar es Salaam, we'd never have had you up at 5:00 a.m. to drive to the airport through rivers of rain! And what's this we hear about you having to pay *chai* to get out of the country because your passports were not stamped when leaving Zanzibar? That's a new wrinkle in scams. Could your Rotary connections not get you out of that one? It seems the airport authorities were out to get you guys both coming and going!

It's too bad you couldn't have stayed for our graduation ceremonies. It was impressive. One of our grads drew a banner on the blackboard proclaiming graduation day, and I baked a cake for the occasion and decorated it with real flowers from our garden. Using frangipani petals, I spelled out "*Hongera Wanafunzi*" - "Congratulations Students" in the icing. Had you been here we'd have found spots for you two dear friends beside Father Vincenzo at the head table. The students and staff were thrilled with the gifts you left for them. They especially loved the Canada pins and the baseball caps that you had imprinted with "Manyoni Mission Workshop". You should see the pride with which they wear them! We are developing a real "esprit de corps".

We'd invited some Department of Education types from Singida, but they couldn't come because a meningitis outbreak had spread to our area. Five people had died in the Singida region and Manyoni was under quarantine. No passage was allowed either in or out of town for a period of three weeks.

How is it that, when we heard the news that meningitis was moving toward our part of Tanzania, we were home in Canada on leave and were able to get immunized against it? Whether you call it good fortune or Providence, you have to believe that we are two of the luckiest people in East Africa.

The quarantine had been lifted in mid-December, so we could attend the Canadian High Commission's Christmas Party in Dar es Salaam. The gala was held at the residence on the lush lawns that stretch down to the sea. It was a gorgeous night, soft and starry and drenched in the delicate, almost fragile, scent of frangipani. In the sky, the new moon lay like a silver crescent sending glimmers of moon beams that winked off the gentle swells of the Indian Ocean. There was a small piano there and a Sister came forward and began to play. Hands pulled me up and led me to a spot beside her and from there, while looking out to sea, we led the group in singing "It Came upon a Midnight Clear." I was overwhelmed by the privilege and the exquisite beauty of it all.

There was food and drinks and dancing and lots of laughs, a few at my expense; I had the misfortune to lock myself into the washroom of the residence. The High Commissioner himself, always at the service of us Canadians, removed the screen from the bathroom window and handed me a pair of vice grips through the security bars. “Do you know how to use those things?” he asked. I assured him I did and was able to free myself. When I emerged, somewhat embarrassed, a cheering crowd had gathered. This is not the type of attention one wants to attract!

Jim came as our guest, and all the Canadians from our mission attended except for Ted and Miriam. Ted was in the middle of a well drilling project, working to a deadline. He felt he couldn’t take time off, which was a shame. We’d all encouraged him to come. After all, the well would still be there when he got back. God knows these people have survived without us for thousands of years and would do so again if we all pulled out tomorrow. But Ted could not be persuaded. He is nothing if not totally dedicated.

While you two are in the midst of winter woes, our lives continue in unique African fashion. We see many strange events with our own eyes; others, we experience vicariously through the stories of the Fathers and Sisters who regularly visit the outlying villages. Father Vincenzo told us a real humdinger. Most of his encounters in the bush are unremarkable to him because he’s spent so many years in Tanzania, but even he was shaken by this one. As he was delivering his homily in a thatched mud and stick chapel in a remote village, he told us that he’d had a near brush with death. During his homily, he said, he was thrilled to see the congregation sitting wide-eyed and motionless. It seemed that they were listening with rapt attention. Thinking that he must be in fine form, he expanded on his theme. “It’s not every day I have such a receptive audience,” he said to himself. But, after a while, he noticed the worshippers beginning to shift uncomfortably on the narrow pews. Their eyes had moved away from him and were focused on the rough tree branch that served as a roof beam just above the altar. Father, feeling annoyed that he was losing the congregation glanced up to see what was distracting them from his message. There, wrapped around the beam, was a huge cobra, its head hanging down within two feet of Father’s face. He quickly wrapped up his talk, and keeping an eye on the snake, gathered up the Mass vessels, and beat a hasty retreat. “I just got the hell out of there!” he said.

A Canadian nurse friend related a mysterious episode that blended traditional healing and witchcraft. A patient had been brought to her semi-conscious, a victim of snake bite. When he didn't respond to the antivenin injection she'd given him, the family took him away and propped him up against a tree. Then they sent for the witch doctor who formed a ring of stones around the periphery. As the family members crawled into the circle on their knees, the witch doctor performed incantations and poured a herbal concoction down the unconscious man's throat. (A no-no!) The man, without gagging or sputtering, swallowed the medicine. After a moment, he regained consciousness and walked off, seemingly cured.

Scenarios similar to these, like chapters in our own personal soap opera, continue to unfold. Each episode entertains with tales of wonder, intrigue, tragedy or romance.

The latest thing in our "soap" is a romance. Just as we predicted, Alan Kreutzer, one of our missionaries, and Sandy Notley, a missionary with the Anglican Church have announced their engagement. We hosted the engagement party at our house which was attended by all the North Americans in our mission plus Fr. Vincenzo. I prepared a roast pork dinner and baked a cake. Alan and Sandy are going to Canada to be married and won't be returning to Tanzania. We're going to miss them very much.

Well dear friends, tomorrow a new year begins and we wonder what it will bring. I think it's best not to know. As Karen Blixen said in "*Out of Africa*", my favourite movie, "Perhaps God made the world round so we couldn't see too far down the road."

Have a blessed and happy New Year!

Love to all,

Leona and Cyril

****

To our son Mark, daughter-in-law Christian and family:
Manyoni, Tanzania
Jan. 15, 1991

Dear Mark and Christian and little ones,

So we've become grandparents once again! We're so happy that baby Theresa's birth went smoothly. It took almost three weeks for the birth announcement and pictures to reach us, and we were getting concerned. But, now that the wonderful event is over, we can relax. Every time there is a life changing event such as this, we feel torn and wonder if we've made the right choice. On one hand we want to be back in Canada with you, but on the other, we feel we must stay to fulfill our mandate to the mission. Thank you for the family photos that keep us in your lives.

Gemma, our cook, also recently gave birth. Her sister woke us at 3:00 a.m. and asked us to give Gemma a ride to the hospital. We got up and piled into our Isuzu Trooper prepared to drive to her house, but as we turned out of our driveway, her sister pointed to a spot on the side of the road where Gemma was lying. She'd walked as far as she could in hard labour. We loaded her into the car and rushed her off to the hospital where her baby was born 20 minutes later.

African babies are often named after an event associated with the birth, and I secretly hoped she might name the baby after one of us, but no, she called the baby "Romano" after a treasured old uncle. (Ah, well, I guess it's better than being named "Isuzu" after the vehicle he was almost born in!)

Our new school building is finished and we've begun moving in. The rooms are beautifully fresh and airy; natural light reflects off the honey-coloured wooden ceilings and pale green walls. Twelve desks, tossed out of a Toronto school to make way for new ones, have, through Bro's intervention, found their way to us. Our carpentry crew has sanded out the graffiti and applied a fresh coat of varnish making them look good as new. Our crew has moved the training aids (the Toyota chassis and engine components) to the back of one of the classrooms and I've been working with Joseph Sakalani, our head teacher, on drafting the new timetable. We've scheduled periods of English, Kiswahili, trades math, mechanical and carpentry theory, welding and, as Tanzania law demands, weekly periods of *Siasa* (Political Studies). Now that we can teach all day, we're on our way to becoming a real trades college.

Now we have a place for the globe and the books that we'd brought from Canada. Sakalani is beside himself with happiness. As he sits at his desk in the school office preparing his lessons plans, I've often seen him spin the ten-inch globe just for the sheer delight of it.

We try to speak a bit of Swahili each day with varying degrees of success. Dad's efforts caused a few smirks at the shop the other day when he tried to chide Nulla, one of our workers, for his habitual lateness. Nulla speaks no English so Dad was forced to try to communicate in Swahili. He took the bemused Nulla out of earshot and gave him what he told me was a real dressing-down. But, in spite of several lectures, Nulla's lateness continued. Finally one day, when he again wandered into the workshop half an hour late, Dad lost all attempts at diplomacy and blurted out in front of the whole crew, "*Nulla, umelewa! Umelewa tena!*"

Stifled grins broke out on every face. I went up to Dad, tapped him on the arm and asked him quietly, "Why are you telling Nulla that he's drunk?"

Dad said defensively, "I'm not telling him he's drunk. I'm telling him he's late."

"Cyril," I said, trying to be diplomatic, "you've confused the word for 'late' with the word for 'drunk'."

Dad paused for a moment in embarrassment and then asked, "Oh, have I? What should I have said?"

I replied, "You should have said, *Umechelewa*. The word for late is '*chelewa*', the word for drunk is '*elewa*'. It's a simple mistake to make."

I'm not sure who started to laugh first. At any rate once the crew saw that Dad could take a ribbing at his own expense, they all joined in the fun.

Dad's relationship with the staff is solid. He genuinely likes and respects them and they reciprocate with the same affection and high regard. It was a wonderful thing to see them laughing together at the boss's mistake. No one lost face; if anything their relationship has been strengthened. (And by the way, Nulla has not been late again.)

As we mentioned in an earlier letter, the Tanzanian Government has a compulsory retirement policy. Everyone, regardless of position, must retire at 55. Our mechanics foreman Mr. Kimome has been retired from his former job with the Department of Public Works for several years, but in all that time he's not received one shilling of his pension. He's been corresponding with Personnel at the head office in Singida who keep reassuring him that, in the fullness of time, he will get his pension; but, with each communication there was always a request for yet again another piece of validating information. The latest piece of evidence required was too precious to be sent through the mail, so we offered to take Kimome to Singida so he could deliver the document in person. When we arrived, we were invited into the offices where we could speak in support of Kimome directly to the officer in charge. We emphasized his need, stating that, in the interim after his mandatory retirement and before coming to work for the mission, he had had no income at all. The family had subsisted on what little could be gleaned from his small *shamba* and his six hens. Twins were born; an older son and daughter were sent off to secondary school while bills for school fees, uniforms and medical care mounted with little hope they would ever be paid off.

After we had completed our business with Kimome, we dropped him off at the residence of an *ndugu* (friend) and went off to find Girish. Girish had anticipated our arrival and had arranged several outings. First we went to meet his friend, Dr. Ulome, the local surgeon. The doctor had received his medical training in Cuba and was as fine a surgeon as you'd find anywhere. The government hospital where he practiced was short on surgical supplies and medications so there was little opportunity for him to use his skills. Most major surgeries, he told us, were done either at our mission hospital in Itigi or at the Irish Sisters' hospital just north of here at Makiyungu. Since we'd never been there, Girish suggested we take a run out.

The Medical Missionaries of Mary are a delightful group. Predominantly Irish, they radiate Gaelic charm; even those Sisters and lay people who are not Irish are animated by the charisma of that race. The whole medical staff of the well-equipped 160-bed hospital and nursing school is made up of women. Doctors, nurses, lab technicians, x-ray technicians, pharmacists etc. all happen to be women. Not that they have anything against men; it just worked out that way.

That night, back at the guest house in Singida, Dad became violently ill. He woke up with his abdomen painfully distended. Then, vicious cramping started and he was overcome with nausea. I rushed out to find a bucket in the washroom, and he vomited into it over and over again. Kimome was staying in the room next to us and, hearing us, got up to help. I sent him to find Girish who brought Dr. Ulome with him. The doctor examined Dad and took me aside. "I think he may be having an appendicitis attack," he said. "He may need surgery." Oh, my God, I thought and my mind flew in a million directions. Facilities at the local hospital were inadequate; there was no airplane to send Dad to Nairobi, and the road to our hospital in Itigi was so horrible, a sick appendix would surely rupture en route. Then I remembered the Irish Sisters just up the road. "If we can get him to Makiyungu," I asked, "Will you perform the operation?" Dr. Ulome said, "Yes," and went back into the bedroom to prepare his patient.

Something had happened in those few minutes when we were out of the room. When we went back in, we were surprised to see Dad sitting up in bed; the lines of pain were erased from his face, his stomach was no longer distended, the cramping had stopped and the nausea had vanished. The sickness had disappeared as suddenly as it had come. Dr. Ulome had no explanation for it. We thanked God that we were spared the risk of major surgery in a place so remote. Dr. Ulome refused to charge us a fee, saying "What are friends for?" We will find a way to reward him for his kindness.

We returned to Manyoni as soon as Dad was well enough to travel. We were apprehensive about the impending rains that would make our journey difficult. But the rains were long in coming. In fact, they held off for many more days after our return. Indeed, we feared that if they didn't arrive in a timely fashion, the crops might fail. Day after day, with predictable regularity, inky black clouds rolled in with accompanying thunder and lightning that split the sky over and around us in all directions. This powerful light and sound show lasted for weeks before the heavy rains finally broke. But now our yard is awash in rivers of mud and the main road has become impassable. We may be marooned here in Manyoni for months.

The rains have brought out the *wadudu* (insects) again. A scorpion scrabbled out from under Dad's shoe this morning and I scooped up another into the dust pan. When I laid the broom on it, it flung its tail with the stinger over its back and struck at the bristles. Termites are putting up their hills in the middle of the road and the *siafu* (driver ants) are on the march.

In fact, an invasion of these driver ants forced us out of our house last week. We had just snuggled down in bed when we heard a faint plopping sound. Plop. Plop. Plop. It was as though something soft were being dropped. We switched on the light and sat up to see gobs of brown fur moving on the floor, not crawling along, just squirming on the spot.

"What the heck is that?" Dad said.

"I've no idea," I replied. "I've never seen anything like it."

While we were pondering this phenomenon, more gobs fell from the roofing beams and landed on the bed. We could see, from close up, that each gob was an insect, a cockroach or a beetle that had been set upon and was being devoured by masses of tiny ants. Other ants were streaming in through the windows in seething ribbons of activity. They climbed up and down the walls, across the floor and up onto the edge of the bedspread that hung down to the floor.

"*Siafu!*" I screamed. We leapt out of bed, shook the ants out of our clothes, dressed and fled from the bedroom. The whole house was being invaded. *Siafu* by the thousands had entered the house and thousands more were following. They poured in through the screens, under the door, past gaps in the plumbing fixtures and through cracks in the poorly-sealed clerestory windows. The kitchen sink, layered with a thick brown mat of pulsating ants, seemed to have come alive. Grabbing our flashlight and car keys we left the house and drove to the main mission. Fr. Vincenzo had already locked up and gone to bed, but we shone our flashlight at his bedroom window and called his name. He let us in and offered us a spare bedroom.

Next morning, our house was still alive!

"You can deter *siafu* by pouring a line of diesel fuel around the perimeter of the house," Father told us.

But with so many already in the house, what use was there in trying to prevent a few more?

It was two days and two nights before the *siafu* left and we could return to our own home. Like nature's vacuum cleaners, they had destroyed every other insect in their path, leaving only remnants of the hard shells of dead beetles and roaches. When we finished sweeping up and washing the floors with hot soapy water, the house was spotless.

Kimome told us about the loss his neighbour suffered when *siafu* swept through his yard. His prize hen, he said, had just hatched out a brood of dozen chicks. The day after the *siafu* came, the poor hen was seen walking alone around her nest and clucking as though bereft. The farmer, fearing the worst, went to investigate. In the nest he found no living furry yellow balls, only the tiny bleached skeletons of the dead chicks.

No one knows what unseen force drives these ants to form en masse into undulating ribbons of activity intent on destroying every living thing in their path too small or too weak to avoid them.

We hope we haven't scared you too much with these tales of Africa. We can assure you we're in no danger. In the meantime, you have your own challenges with the two little ones to care for. Trust us when we say, "You will survive."

(By the way, our personal pleas on behalf of Kimome seem to have had some influence; he just received his first pension cheque today.)

Love,

Mom and Dad

****

To our daughter Laura:
Manyoni, Tanzania
March 22, 1991

Dear Laura,

Our hearts are much lighter now that we know you've found a job that not only pays the bills, but gives you the opportunity to spread your warm generous spirit to folks handicapped by age or infirmity. But, do be careful. Your illness has been long, and you must save some of that care for yourself.

We've just returned to our work after taking Alan Kreutzer and Sandy Notley to Dar es Salaam to catch their flight to Canada where they'll be married. Their obligations to their missions have been completed, and they won't be coming back.

One by one, our *Wazungu* (non-African) friends are going home. Dr. Lillian left some time ago. Derrick and his wife Liz, who'd been looking after the water project while Ted recovered, were summoned back to Ontario when Derrick's father became ill. And now, Alan and Sandy are gone.

But all is not lost. We find ourselves being drawn closer to our circle of Tanzanian friends: Girish, Baldwin, Bibi Lois Swanson, Jim and Anna Lamb, Alex and Darcy Isinika and their families who continue to offer support and fellowship.

We drive over to visit Alex and Darcy at their cashew farm at least every two weeks. A heavy meshed wire fence hanging with red and white bougainvillea is the only thing separating their simple three-room cement block house from the cattle yard. Black flies flit back and forth from the barn yard to the sitting area and try to settle on the rims of our tea cups. We've learned to follow Darcy's lead by putting our saucers on top of our cups to keep them out between sips.

The road out to their place skirts the cemetery, and when we pass by, I always pray that I'll not fall sick and die while here in Manyoni and have to be buried in that rocky desolate place. Especially so after hearing some of Alex's stories!

Alex has been retired from the Tanzanian police force for some time, and professionalism demands that he speak only in generalities about the cases he was involved in. But, one evening, primed with a liberal draft of scotch from the "mickey" that Dad had brought for him, he agreed to tell us about one high profile case that had reached international interest: the case of the "Lion Men of Singida".

"That was a time of many *shauris* (troubles),"Alex said, taking a sip of scotch from his mug.

In 1946 the British administration in Tanzania (at that time called Tanganyika) called on Alex to investigate instances of people being robbed and murdered by *Wajombo*, creatures who had the ability to morph from humans into lions or hyenas. (This belief, called lycanthropy, is the same branch of witchcraft that led to the myth of the werewolf in medieval European societies.)

The masterminds of the scheme played directly into that superstition. The "lions", Alex told us, were merely humans draped in lions' skins with claws intact. Some accounts have it that the *wajombo* in this case were old women and handicapped boys who'd been captured and drugged, but it seems unlikely that such feeble people could have been induced to terrorize. It was never determined who the main perpetrators were; people were simply too intimidated to testify. In the end, at the trial in 1947, only those convicted of hiring the pretend *wajombo* to do the killing were found guilty and condemned to death.

Belief in witchcraft is still prevalent in certain African societies. Just yesterday, a government sanctioned vigilante group, called the *Sungu-sungu*, was active on the streets of Manyoni dealing with a complaint of witchcraft. I saw them, decked out in their garish feathered headdresses, dragging off a fellow who'd been accused of stalking around huts masquerading as a hyena. But, in the minds of some, such as the old man we met in Heka, this was no masquerade. They actually believed that the detainee had turned himself into a hyena.

The *Sungu-sungu* are a traditional defence group and, as such, have been charged with the job of ensuring that the populace can "sleep peacefully without fear of banditry, cattle rustling and theft" but sometimes they overstep their mandate. Indeed, even folks who have come to help are not immune from their machinations. For example, when Maureen was bringing a patient from Ana's clinic to the hospital in Kilimatinde, she was flagged down by a group of *Sungu-sungu*, ordered out of her vehicle and harassed. When the village elders heard of this, they were furious and took action against the vigilantes, issuing them strict instructions to use common sense when wielding their powers of detention.

Rumours reached us that other *Sungu-sungu* groups to the north have been involved in the killing of old red-eyed women, believing them to be involved with witchcraft. (These poor souls have been cooking over smoky open fires for years, so of course their eyes are red.) The Ministry responsible for the *Sungu-sungu* issued a sharp rebuke saying that such beliefs are misguided. That's easy to say, but much harder to change so primitive a mentality.

A Canadian family has moved into the dusty, dilapidated village of Chikuyu, just a half-hour drive from here. They're living in a cement block house that makes our old "bunker" look like a palace. No glass or screens cover the windows. Sagging, ill-fitting shutters are the only protection from the elements. Mosquitoes and other insects and reptiles can easily come and go. In addition, craters in the floor have opened up where the cement has chipped away, exposing the base of sand and gravel. Laurie has covered the holes with sisal mats so two-year old Amy can toddle around safely. At dusk, when the anopheles (malaria carrying) mosquito is most active, Laurie, Ed, Baby Amy and the two preteen boys, huddle together under a net on the large family bed and read until the light fails.

Ed is digging a cistern and a reservoir to demonstrate to the locals that one doesn't have to be totally dependent on the amount of rainfall. He's showing how water can be safely collected and stored for a time of scarcity. He's also fashioned an outdoor western style chemical toilet and bath house at the back of the house. Laurie told us that one morning after she'd completed her sponge bath and was preparing to leave, she was stopped short by a cobra that had slithered in under the gap in the warped wooden door. It lay coiled between Laurie and the door, blocking her only exit. No one else was at home; there was no one to call to, so she stood stock still, terrified, and began to pray. She's not sure how long she stood praying, but eventually her prayers were answered.

The cobra got tired of lying on the washhouse floor and slipped out the way it had come.

Laurie has taken in an orphaned Barabaig baby, and when we stopped in for a visit, was sitting placidly on a stool simultaneously breast-feeding her pale white-haired daughter Amy, and the tiny jet-black orphaned boy. This family is definitely meant for Africa.

By the way, we have an update to the letter I wrote to Joe Clark, Minister of External Affairs, about the disrespectful treatment Dad and I were given here at the Canadian High Commission Offices when our passports needed to be renewed. It was rather amusing. When we were last in Dar, we stopped in the offices and while standing in the waiting room, a young lady staffer came up to us and asked, "Are you the Lanes?" We weren't sure whether or not we ought to admit to our identities, but when we allowed that, yes, indeed, we were the Lanes, she beamed. "Your letter to Joe Clark was fantastic," she said. "We got a copy of it from Canada and it was handed around the office. You know," she went on, "that woman treated everybody badly but nobody except you two ever called her on her behaviour." "Is she still here?" I wanted to know. "No," the lady replied. "I'm happy to say that, after your complaint, she was posted elsewhere."

In just six more months our contract will come to a close. Already we are feeling conflicted. How ever are we going to settle back into to a North American life of dull predictability?

Well dear daughter, keep well and do preserve your health,

Love you so much,

Mom and Dad

****

***To our daughter Kim*:**
Manyoni, Tanzania
May 27, 1991

Dear Kim,

Even though it happened a month ago, we are just coming to grips with the terrible loss of my dear brother, your Uncle Wilf. It was a great shock to get your call telling us of his death, especially since we'd just received a letter from Aunt Lynn saying how well he was doing. The nurses, she said, already had him up for short walks and he was enjoying solid food. How could this have occurred when the doctors, just weeks earlier, had told her that his brain tumour was benign, and that he'd be well again? This dreadful turn of events has left everyone confused.

Perhaps he was discharged from hospital too soon. Did they not know that he would be going home to the farm where no medical care was available? But, it's pointless to speculate. The only thing we can do now is to support Aunt Lynn and the kids in what ever way we can.

As I think of our childhood growing up in Saskatchewan, I realize that, of all my siblings, he was closest to me. I will miss him very much.

I remember the fun Wilf and I used to have impishly conspiring against my parents when we paired up in a game of whist. If I wanted him to lead with a heart, I might sing a snippet of "Peg o' My Heart" and he'd lead with that suit. Or, he might ask a seemingly innocent question such as, "Dad, who's going to dig the garden this year?" and I'd lay down a spade. We used this ruse time and time again, thinking that they'd never catch on, but they did!

Then there was the time we tied Mom's new copper washtub to the calf's tail and sent the poor creature stampeding off into the pasture in fright, trying to rid itself of the metal object that crashed and clattered behind it. How deliciously naughty it all was! (That latter stunt got us banished to the bedroom where we were ordered to pray the Rosary in reparation for our sins.)

I regret that, in adulthood, our lives had grown apart - what with us living in the Yukon, so far from him and his family in the

Peace River country. There were exchanges of photos and letters, but because travel was expensive and money tight for everyone, we rarely saw each other.

I called Aunt Lynn and caught her at home just as the family was leaving for the funeral. Fr. Vincenzo said a special Mass in remembrance of Wilf in the Sisters' chapel. I wanted to sing for him and tried to do so, but it was not good. The stress of the last days showed in my voice and I was unable to make a clear free sound, but I'm sure he knows that I did my best for him.

Dad and I found some consolation during Easter Week when we attended a marvellous production of the Passion Play. Laurenti Ntiruhungwa, our accountant, had laid aside his ledgers and putting his dramatic talents to work, wrote and directed the play that involved young people from every Christian denomination in Manyoni.

We sat in the open courtyard of the parish centre where a make-shift stage had been set up. The night was warm with only a whisper of a breeze. The cloudless sky formed a black velvet canopy above us, where the stars, uneven in brightness and size, sparkled like raw salt crystals clinging to the inside of an upturned ebony bowl.

I cannot fully describe the authenticity of the costumes that were put together from scraps of faded and grubby homespun fabrics. But, picture the actors in mid-length brown tattered robes, their dark heads swathed in red, yellow and blue striped turbans.

Each scene was simply and beautifully set. Indeed, we felt ourselves seated with the disciples at The Last Supper, agonizing with Christ in the Garden of Gethsemane, present for His trial in Pilate's Palace and helping Him carry His cross to the place of the Crucifixion. There is a natural flare for the dramatic in most Africans and it was a delight to be present for this display of raw talent, where each and every actor remained totally "in character" throughout the production.

(Actually, there was almost too much reality in parts, such as, when the soldiers, costumed in leather, rushed in to arrest Jesus. Charging in with flailing swords, they narrowly missed hitting the actors on stage and very nearly set fire to the flimsy curtains with their flaming torches.)

When the play ended, the audience rose and gave the crew and cast a well-deserved standing ovation. Laurenti was beside himself with delight. I don't think we'll ever forget his face, black and shining like obsidian, grinning from ear to ear.

We wonder why Hollywood almost always gets it wrong when casting the part of Jesus. Trying to bring out His gentleness, they invariably end up depicting Him as effeminate and weak. Laurenti, on the other hand, was able to find, in this small African town, the most incredibly perfect Jesus: masculine and regal, yet gentle.

I wonder what would happen if we were able to wrap this young man in cotton wool and bring him to "so-called" civilization. Would he thrive or would he whither in the artificial light?

In years past, an attitude of intolerance was common among missionary groups: Pentecostals derided the Catholic faith; Catholics refused to cooperate with Methodists, etc. etc. This was a source of scandal for the native population who couldn't understand how these groups could presume to preach the love of God and mankind while denigrating each other. These scandalous frictions were so deep that even now in North America some have a very perverted view of mission work.

Indeed, even when we were last home, folks meeting us on the street would ask the most inane questions! Apologetic, yet feeling they had to bring their lingering doubts out into the open, they asked questions like: "Do you have to be Catholic to go to the mission school or get health care at the mission clinics?" I was absolutely floored. "No, of course not", I would reply, trying to stay calm. "Well, then," they would continue, "I guess all your workers have to be Catholic, right?" And I'd say with a sigh, "No, that's not the way it is."

Thank God, these attitudes have largely gone, at least in our area, and have been replaced by mutual respect - due to the work of creative, committed Christians like Laurenti.

I must close now on that high note. But, my emotions are spent. Notwithstanding the joy we felt in the message of the Passion Play, reliving the tragic circumstances of our mutual loss has taken its toll on me.

I will write again in a few days when I have regained a perspective on life.

Love to all.

Mom and Dad

****

***To our friends*:**
Manyoni, Tanzania
May 1, 1991

Dear Bob and Loverna,

It was great to get your call telling us that Bob's open-heart surgery was successful. You will have had some anxious moments leading up to the diagnosis and through the surgery. It's a good thing none of us knew what was going on inside his chest when you were here in Tanzania. When we think back to his time here, we remember that he was not handling the heat well. Especially in the humid atmosphere of Dar es Salaam, where his shirt was always soaked and sweat poured down his face and dripped off the end his nose. By now he will be home carefully following his doctor's instructions for a complete recovery.

We have passed on the good news to Jim and Anna and all our friends who have been praying for you both as you weather this new storm that has blown into your lives.

A most interesting guest stayed overnight with us last week. There was no one at the mission house to receive him so he came to our place. He was a respectable fellow, well-dressed and carrying a brief case. He announced himself as the chief investigator on the case of Ted's forced landing of the mission plane. He was travelling by train, making the round trip from Dar es Salaam to Bukoba in the north. A family member had died there of AIDS, he told us, and he was going to attend the funeral. The dead woman had been young; her husband had predeceased her and a number of small children were left behind. The rest of the family is now left to comfort the children and find suitable homes for them. He was a very concerned young man and the responsibility rested heavily on him. This was our first encounter with a person who had been personally touched by that disease. He was frank in his discussion about the way AIDS is spread and offered no excuses for his African fellows who behave promiscuously, get infected and bring the disease back to their wives.

We talked about many things during the course of the evening, including the lawsuit pending over the shoddy work that caused the plane's engine to fail. The case should be a simple one. In our opinion, the engine failed due to the incorrect fitting of a gasket. Ted, Bro, and the MAF mechanics had all seen the gasket and had handed it over to the investigating authorities. For some reason, our guest trusted us to see this piece of damning evidence. He was carrying it with him all the way across Tanzania rather than leaving it in his office where he feared it might be stolen. After the dinner dishes were cleared away, he brought out his brief case and withdrew from it the gasket on which was stencilled, "If you can read this notice, this gasket must be turned around."

It was clear that things had happened exactly as Ted had said. The gasket had been put in the wrong way around; the holes did not line up with the configuration on the engine part. The incompetents in Dar es Salaam had punched holes in it to make it fit, but in the process they missed two, and that is what starved the engine of oil.

If you remember Ted's letter that we sent you back in September of 1989, you'll see that this case has been going on for a very long time.

A thunder storm awakened us that night releasing a massive downpour that once again flooded the house. In spite of our efforts to seal them with tar after the last flood, the clerestory windows still leak and there is no hope in trying to prevent the rain from blowing in through the louvered windows that don't close properly. When the rain started to pour in, I tiptoed into the guest room to ensure that the investigator's brief case was not lying on the floor where it could get swamped. Then Cyril and I did as before; we got out all the mops and brooms and waded into the ankle deep water and swept it out through the open kitchen door.

Later in the week, Fr. Vincenzo enlisted our help in organizing a good old-fashioned "garage sale" to raise funds for a children's project. So we rummaged through the shipping container that held the used clothing and tried to sort out the garments into piles of men's, women's and children's. Who could guess that there would be any difficulty in that? Yet, we were astonished by the inappropriateness of items that had been sent from abroad: T- shirts emblazoned with inappropriate or obscene messages, polyester pants for women who do not wear pants and fur-lined boots to a country where the temperature never reaches even close to freezing. What should we do with these things? In the end we discarded the offensive T-shirts. (They can be used as rags in the workshop.) We dumped all the pants in a single pile and the winter boots in with the other footwear and left it to the shoppers to make their own choices.

We backed the truck up to the container door, loaded up the items and took them down to the workshop where we laid out everything before opening the doors for the sale to begin. Like Woolworth's on opening day, folks who had gathered outside rushed in, pushing and shoving. Grabbing items of clothing, they held them up against their bodies to see if they'd fit. It was fun watching the men sorting through the pants pile. One young man picked up a pair of women's pull-on polyester pants in brilliant chartreuse and held them up to his waist. Puzzled, he turned them over back and forth a number of times searching for the fly. Then he consulted with a second young man who'd joined him. He too, looked bewildered and carried out the same close examination of the pants in search of the fly. In the end the pants were rejected in disgust and dumped back onto the pile.

Among the things on the miscellaneous table we had put a lady's Easter bonnet. It was a broad-brimmed straw in canary yellow, bedecked with a multi-coloured floral band that took the fancy of one well-built fellow who bought it on the spot. "How sweet," we thought, "He's bought a gift for his wife or girl friend." Later we saw the same chap striding along Manyoni's main street, sporting the self-same hat cocked on his head at a rakish angle!

And, a pair of ladies' fur-lined boots with two-inch heels ended up on the diminutive feet of Yonna, our gate guard.

"What the heck, if you've got it, flaunt it!" seems to be the attitude.

Speaking of Yonna, the poor man suffered a terrible loss in the recent storm. Both his house and the Pentecostal church, where he is the pastor, collapsed. No one was injured, thank God; the family had been away preaching in the villages. When they returned, they found the rain-soaked mud structures lying in heaps on the ground.

Changing the subject, did you hear that Dave, Chris and Roshean are talking about coming to see us? Roshean's mom has offered to look after the kids, and Bro is checking out cheap fares for them. The prospect of their visit has us so excited we're already planning their safari.

Well, dear friends, do keep us in your prayers as you are in ours.

Love,

Leona and Cyril

****

To our sons Christopher and Dave and daughter-in-law Roshean:
Manyoni, Tanzania
July 4, 1991

Dear Chris and Roshean and Dave,

We are absolutely thrilled with the news that you three are coming to visit.

We see that Bro has booked you on Air Ethiopia. Your stop in Addis Ababa should be an interesting experience. But be forewarned. This type of airline offers cheap fares, but watch out for the "trade-offs". A friend of ours regularly flies with a budget airline within Nigeria that never allocates seats and consistently overbooks. The policy is; the first ones on the plane get the seats. So, if you're not nimble enough, you might find yourselves hanging onto "standing room only" straps! Just joking! We're sure the regulations stipulate that everyone will have to have a seat on an international flight.

Anticipating your visit has put a spring in our step and a song in our hearts. I've already planned your safari and have made application to the Bank of Tanzania for permission to pay for your lodgings in Tanzanian shillings. We'll try to take advantage of a little known provision that allows Tanzanian residents to pay the resident rate for visiting family members. It'll save you a bundle and we'll get rid of all our shillings before we leave.

Remember to get your yellow fever shot at least ten days before you're scheduled to arrive in Tanzania. It takes that long for the body to build up immunity to the disease. (Remember that the Armstrongs were very nearly tossed out of the country when they arrived on the eighth day. Bob used his Rotary connection to get them through, but since none of you are members of that august club, you'd better see that all your 'i' s are dotted and your 't' s crossed.)

A final recommendation! Don't forget to bring binoculars. Both the Moores and the Armstrongs failed to bring theirs, which was a shame. We managed to share ours, but it would have been so much better if we'd had more pairs for game viewing. You wouldn't want to miss a spectacular sight such as a lion stalking an antelope and moving in for the kill as we pass our one pair of binoculars back and forth. Can't you imagine the tugging and fighting over the binoculars if that were to happen?

Our safari with you will be our last. Our contract with the mission is coming to a close. We'll be heading home at the end of September travelling via the eastern route. When we arrive back in Canada, we will have encircled the globe. We'll stop first in India, then on to Thailand, Malaysia, Australia and New Zealand before arriving home in time for Christmas.

There is a group of Indian Fathers in Dodoma who've been most helpful to us in planning the India portion. They've arranged for one of their confreres to meet us in Bombay to direct our travels within India. We wanted to show Girish our appreciation for all he's done for us so we bought him a ticket to India; he'll be with us for the first few weeks. After India we'll move on to Bangkok where we'll stay at a missionary guest house, and in Malaysia we'll be guests of Mel and Luanne Johnson who hail from Whitehorse. In Australia we'll be with Uncle Dennis and the Aussie Lanes. Dad is really thrilled, as his sister, your Aunt Eileen, is going to be flying there from England. (It will be the first time in 20 years since all three of Dad's family will be together.) In New Zealand, we'll be visiting my niece Peggy and her family. (That's what they call "networking!")

But, back to your trip. We will, God willing, be at the airport to meet you. If we should not be there when you arrive, take a taxi out to the Kunduchi Beach Hotel where we will find you. Failing that, go to the Canadian High Commission offices. Bro will be here in Tanzania when you arrive. He and our good friends Jim and Anna Lamb will all be looking out for you.

We're so excited and happy about your coming that we can hardly concentrate on our work. See you in August!

Love,

Mom and Dad

****

To our son Greg and daughter-in-law Carolyn:
Dar es Salaam, Tanzania
September 18, 1991

Dear Greg and Carolyn,

Our safari with Chris, Roshean and Dave has come to an end. Tomorrow we'll be taking them to the airport to catch their flight home. All too soon they'll be gone. It was the first time any of our family had come to see us in Tanzania. It was marvellous for them to be able to meet our friends and see for themselves the work we've been doing.

It's been a godsend having them here. They've been amazingly supportive, especially when being dumped down headfirst into dealing with malaria - one of Africa's greatest challenges.

A few days before they were to arrive in Dar es Salaam, I began to feel poorly. I knew the symptoms of malaria: fever alternating with chills, diarrhoea, headache and general malaise. I'd had those signs before but always managed to ward off a serious attack by starting on a chloroquine regime. Everyone in Tanzania knows what to do. Indeed, the malaria treatment code, "4,2,2,2," is prominently displayed above the windshields of the cabs on many of the trucks and buses. As before, I began the regimen, faithfully taking the tablets as per schedule: four tablets immediately at the first sign of malaria; another two, six hours later; a gap of 24 hours, then two more, finally ending the treatment 36 hours later by taking the last two.

I had done all this, but I was no better. While we waited at the airport for the kids to come through the doors of customs and immigration, I paced the halls in the arrivals area feeling more and more unwell. Any moment now, I thought, the chloroquine will kick in.

I rallied a bit when our family came out to us all starry-eyed with excitement, but the full joy of seeing them was blunted by the inability to focus my eyes. We drove straight out to Jim and Anna Lamb's place where Chris, Roshean and Dave opened up their carry-on cases and withdrew the gifts they'd brought for the Lamb family: a necklace with a gold encrusted cross and dream catcher earrings for Anna, books and T-shirts for the girls and single malt scotch for Jim. I tried to join in the festive atmosphere, but was feeling sicker and sicker as the day wore on.

We left Jim's place after a few hours and checked into the Kunduchi Beach Hotel where Dad and I rested while our newly arrived family members romped in the warmth of the Indian Ocean.

By the next morning I was very ill indeed. But, I was not yet ready to give up. We were scheduled to leave for up-country, so several times I tried to get up and pack, only to be knocked back down on my bed by the disease. By late afternoon I could no longer shrug off the seriousness of my situation. I had begun to pass blood and knew that I needed medical attention. Dad passed the word on to the kids, helped me into the car and off we drove to the Lamb's house. God bless Jim! The dear man dropped what he was doing, took the wheel of our Isuzu and drove us directly into Dar to see his family doctor. Without so much as a knock on the door, Jim charged into the examining room at Sunni Muslim Hospital and interrupted Dr. Margaret Sheja who was with a patient. We waited anxiously in the outer room until she was free and could turn her attention to us. "I'm going to test both you and Cyril for malaria and infections," she said. It was a remarkably simple test. In moments she was back announcing that the results showed that both Dad and I were ill and needed to be hospitalized. "You, Cyril," she said, concern reflecting through her dark eyes, "are just coming down with malaria, but Leona is gravely ill. She has both full-blown malaria and an infection." I heard all this through the fog of fever.

Sunni Muslim is a small four-story hospital sandwiched in between cluttered *dukas* on a busy downtown street. There are no elevators, but, with Jim supporting me, I made the long and painful climb to the medical wards on the fourth floor. Dad was not as ill as I and was able to make it on his own. He was admitted into the men's ward and I into the women's ward across the hall.

While Dad was attended to by one of the nurses, Dr. Margaret herself took over my treatment. The malaria had progressed so far along I needed an infusion of quinine directly into my veins. While our treatment trays were being organized, Jim zipped back to the Kunduchi Hotel to pick up the kids and bring them to the hospital.

I don't know what was happening to Dad in his ward, but through my feverish haze I became aware that Jim, Chris, Roshean and Dave were standing by my bed as Dr. Margaret tried to find a vein. I have prominent veins and lab technicians have never had trouble before, but now, each time the doctor gave a poke, a huge purple bruise broke around the area. This happened at least six times until at last a connection was made into a vein and the quinine drip began.

Roshean was so sweet. "I'll stay here with you all night Mom," she said, then promptly fell into a dead faint. Chris caught her and laid her on the empty cot next to mine. Then, everyone abandoned me and surrounded Roshean. It was quite surreal! In a few moments Roshean came to and Dr. Margaret said to her very gently, "I don't think you should stay here, dear."

Everyone was advised to leave then and I was given a sedative. The nurses dropped the mosquito net down around my bed and left me there. The sedative did nothing. Nightmares plagued me and I tossed and turned trying to find some rest for my overactive brain and my body that was wracked with pain in every bone and muscle. In the morning Dad was discharged into Jim's care, but I would have to stay another eight hours because my quinine drip had been so slow and not enough had been absorbed by my body to take effect.

The daylight hours crawled by and a grey gloom settled over the ward. Occasionally, I would break through my delirium and mumble, "What's happening to my husband? Where's my family?" I was dimly aware of the staff moving about tending to other patients but not one came by to comfort me. Only in the evening, when Jim and the family came to pick me up, did a nurse come to my bedside to find that I was in a very bad state. My arm with the IV was swollen and red. The volume in the drip bag had hardly gone down at all. The quinine was being infused into the tissues instead of the vein. When Jim saw me still incoherent and so obviously ill, he made a very rash decision. "Unhook that thing," he said to the nurses, referring to the IV, "and get her clothes. I'm taking her out of here!" The nurses were dumbfounded but did as they were told. Roshean helped me dress. Chris supported Dad as we descended the four flights of stairs while Dave and Jim supported me. "Where are we going?" someone asked. "I'm taking Leona to Dr. Margaret's house," Jim replied, as we piled into the Isuzu Trooper. I remember that the road was appalling as we made our way across the city to the doctor's place.

My eyes and ears were now profoundly affected. I could no longer focus at all and my hearing came and went, but I recall arriving at the doctor's house next to a bar/disco. Music blared and lights were strobing into the dark night, and I wondered how the doctor and her family could abide living in a place such as this. She did not chide Jim for his impetuous move in taking me out of the hospital, but she took one look at me and said, “We’ll have to take her back.”

Dr. Margaret squeezed into the car with us. There were now seven of us in a vehicle meant to seat five. Chris and Dave volunteered to move to the back compartment and sat on the spare tire for the tortuous ride back to the hospital.

I was so ill by the time we got back I have no recollection of climbing the stairs to the ward. Dr. Margaret reconnected the IV and I spent the night under the mosquito net while her replacement, another gentle African doctor, sat by, monitoring the quinine drip. By morning I had improved, but I was still not ready to leave. I needed some nourishment at this point. Hospitals in Tanzania don’t provide food for the patients, so Jim drove to the Kilimanjaro Hotel where he bought a bottle of ginger ale and a tomato and onion sandwich and brought it back for me. How I relished that meal! What a simple joy it was to be well enough to sit up in bed and eat. Dr. Margaret came and ordered my discharge. “But before you go,” she said, “would you like a bath?”

“I would love a bath,” I said. The nurse led me into a tiny cement room with a drain in the floor and brought in a bucket of hot water that she set on the floor. I knelt down beside the bucket and dipped my head into the water and washed the dried sweat out of my hair and then proceeded to wash the rest of my body.

We went back to the Kunduchi for one last night. Then, three days later than scheduled, we continued on up to Manyoni. I remember saying to the kids, “I’ve spoiled your visit. This isn’t what was supposed to happen!”

They were so kind. “It’s OK Mom,” Dave said, “Even if we have to go back home now, the trip would have been a success. You and Dad are both well, and that’s all that matters.”

But, after that rather rocky start, their safari turned out to be just as spectacular as the others. (Chris and Roshean may wish to qualify that statement because, at several places we stayed, they were the ones to have the misfortune of being in situations where they were plagued by the peculiarities of African living.)

For example: in Dodoma, the seminary guest house was full so we had to stay, yet again, at the unsavoury Jamboree Hotel where Chris and Roshean, the newly weds, were booked into a twin bedded room. Only one of the beds was draped with a mosquito net but they had no trouble squeezing together under that. Not that it was any protection from the mosquitoes; there was a huge hole in the foot of it. To add to their misery, the halls were noisy with the twittering of the "night angels" as they prowled, clacking their heels on the concrete corridors, as they catered to clients who were attending a convention in the hotel. In the morning the kids were bitten and bleary-eyed. "Mom", Chris asked, "What kind of place *is* this anyway?" We explained that, normally, we'd be put up at the seminary but since that's not possible, they'd just have to endure, the same as us.

Their problems with lodgings continued. In Singida, while Dave, Dad and I stayed with our friend Lois, Chris and Roshean were hosted by a neighbour who was considerably less fastidious than Lois. The bed was clean, Roshean said, but the room hadn't been swept for days. Fuzz balls rolled about on the floor, and spider webs hung from the corners of the room like gossamer in a Halloween haunted house.

Then, at Gibbs farm they had to move to a different room when *siafu* (driver ants) invaded the first, and, at the Baobab Hotel in Tanga, bedbugs infested their mattress. (The hotel staff dealt with the bedbug problem by stripping the beds, dousing them with diesel, letting them air for a day and then putting them back into service.)

But, Chris and Roshean weren't the only ones having to adapt to less than perfect accommodations. While they were dealing with the diesel fumes in their quarters, Dave was being freaked out by a huge cockroach in the room he shared with us. He had never before seen such a creature. "Dad," he said, pointing to the brown vile insect that was crawling on the floor beside his bed, "What's *that*? It's enormous."

"Here, let me kill it," Dad shouted. Then, chasing after it, he knocked into furniture, fell over the bed and created a fracas such as could be heard throughout the hotel. When he finally cornered it, he brought his shoe down on it with three hefty thumps. Whump. Whump. Whump. "There, that's done him in!" he yelled triumphantly.

Meanwhile Chris and Roshean, overhearing the hubbub, were wondering what sort of crisis was going on in our room. Soon there was a light tapping on the wall and Chris asked tentatively, "Are you guys OK in there?"

We managed to cope well enough with the inadequacies of the Baobab Hotel, but, because we'd never visited Tanga before, it was something of a miracle that we were even able to find it. In spite of Dad's admonition that everyone hurry up and stop dallying when taking photos along the way, we found ourselves approaching the city in the dark. People were, as always, walking in the road accompanied by goats, cows and chickens. Roshean's sharp eyes were our best asset, and she was able to spot these things long before Dad could, allowing him to take evasive action. "There's a goat, Dad," Roshean would cry. "There's a person on a bicycle, Dad." And so it went, until we finally arrived on the outskirts of Tanga where there was a roundabout. We'd been told to take a right at the juncture and continue south to the Baobab Beach Hotel. When, through the feeble street lights, we saw what appeared to be a "Y" in the road, Dad made a choice. It wasn't until we were faced by an onslaught of vehicles, some without headlights or only one dim lamp, that we realized we were going the wrong way. Drivers expressed their fury by shouting and honking their horns. There was a squealing of brakes as rubber was peeled from tires and laid onto the pavement, but, with Dad's skilful driving, we found ourselves going up and over the grassy roundabout centre and exiting on what proved to be the correct road.

But, that wasn't the end of our miraculous journey - we still had to find the hotel. I never believed in angels, that is, not until then. (Actually, I'm still not *truly* sure that I believe in angels, but, if they do exist, this story shows how one might be useful.) When we were lost and confused, we stopped three times to ask the question, "*Barabara hi itakwenda Hoteli Baobab?*" ("Does this road go to the Baobab Hotel?") Twice we were told, "*Nenda tu.*" ("Just keeping going.") But when the last person we asked climbed in beside us and guided us to the hotel through the dark stands of palm trees, I knew that someone somewhere was looking out for us. Our "angel" happened to be an employee of the hotel. He had finished his shift for the day and was on his way home, but still, he willingly escorted us to the Baobab. He did not ask for compensation from us for taking him out of his way, but we did open our hearts and our wallets to this Good Samaritan.

Having said all that, the kids took things in stride and we shared many memorable moments. Escorting them to the game parks allowed us, once again, to rejoice, through the mirrors of their eyes, in the glories of the animal kingdom: the thrill of catching a glimpse of a lioness hiding in the grass over the remnants of her recent kill, the feelings of fear and fascination as a herd of elephants passed closely in front of our vehicle, and the tingle of excitement at seeing the gathering of the animals at the water holes.

It's hard to believe that our commitment to the mission is coming to a close. We've been here for three and one-half years and it's been an unbelievable experience, always challenging and never dull. At times it was so frustrating and difficult we were ready to leave on the next plane. Then, it would become so exciting and satisfying we'd talk of prolonging our stay. All in all, it's been a tremendous experience and we wouldn't have missed it for the world.

Right now, in the interim before our departure, we're living in a state of limbo. Our feelings are confused. We're leaving this life behind, but haven't yet re-entered our old familiar one. We wonder how we'll adapt to the safe predictability of the so-called "First World". I've heard it said that once a development worker has tasted the exoticism of this lifestyle he'll have a hard time settling anywhere; he'll be truly happy only when he is on a plane either coming or going.

Speaking of planes, we picked up our tickets at the travel agency today. God willing we'll be home in three months.

We miss all you guys so much.

Love,

Mom and Dad

****

To our friends and family:
Dar es Salaam, Tanzania
Sept 13, 1991

Dear Family and Friends,

In a few moments Bro will be coming to pick us up at Jim and Anna's house to take us to the airport for our flight that will take us bodily out of Africa. But we know deep down that there will be a part of each of our souls that will never leave this place.

It's strange what Africa does to you when you are about to leave it - how it tries to hold on to you, and you, to it. Commonplace things take on extraordinary qualities and friends, in their hearts, refuse to let you go.

On our last day in Manyoni, we walked through the workshops and classrooms taking pleasure in the improvements we'd helped to bring about. But, overshadowing our satisfaction are lingering regrets that, having come so far, all our work may have to be abandoned. In many ways, it has been burdensome, but now that the time has come for us to leave, we find ourselves fretting. We wonder what will become of our staff if the workshop is to be shut down. Where will they find work in this small town? If the school is closed, where will the students go for training? Bro has asked us to return and continue our work. "Have a good holiday," he said, "then think about it." We know that, should circumstances change, we could develop one of the finest training centres in the region, but it would take many more resources, both human and financial, to accomplish such a goal. In the meantime we're both burned out and desperately need to go home. There are new grandchildren we must get to know and reconnections we must make with the older ones. Perhaps we'll feel differently once we've had a break.

We've developed good relationships with our staff and it is hard to leave them. They held a short ceremony of goodbye in one of the classrooms. A note of sadness hung over all of us. Laurenti and Kimome spoke on behalf of everyone, thanking us for what we had done for them. They smiled as they presented us with gifts of carvings and cloth, but their smiles did not reach their eyes. Cyril responded by referring to them as our African family and told them that they had taught us much more than we had taught them. "We will never forget you," he said. I tried to make it into a festive affair by distributing Christmas sweets that I had found in the food container, but there was little pleasure in the humbugs and colourful ribbon candy. At the end of the program, the staff and students came forward to shake hands with us for the last time.

The Fathers and the Sisters hosted a special supper for us and gave us a most magnificent oil painting. But there was no joy in any of it. We were going home to a more affluent life, yet we felt only a dispirited heaviness.

Girish is not coming to India with us after all. He has discovered that he doesn't have enough money for internal travel in India. We gave him the international airline ticket anyway and told him to cash it in and use the money in whatever way he sees fit. It's the least we could do in repayment for all he's done for us. Taking leave from Girish was very hard. Our embraces were longer than usual. The men clapped each other on the shoulder and Girish folded me into his arms, not once, but again and again until it was time for him to go, and, when he left, Gemma came over with the children dressed in their Sunday best for a photo session.

On our last night in Manyoni, the moon was on the wane, its crescent shape suspended against the background of a billion stars. From our dining room window, the solar lights glowed from the four points of the cross on Manyoni Mountain, signalling that the work of the mission will continue, with or without our presence.

As we drove slowly out of town the next morning, we didn't recognize the stooped figure that was plodding along in front of us until we pulled alongside. It was our electrician Temaeli, who had hollowed out a special spot in our hearts. When we stopped beside him and leaned out of the window to say goodbye, we were astonished at the sadness in his face. His dark eyes were so clouded with pain that we, too, were overcome with sadness. He was silent for a few moments and then said in Swahili, "You are going away and I am grieving." There was no greater accolade that we could receive. "Yes, Temaeli," we replied, "we are grieving too."

I see that Bro has just driven into the yard and we must now take our leave from Jim. What can we say about Jim? We treasure his friendship so much. In caring for us, he emulated Christ's paradigm, "When I was hungry you gave me food, when I was thirsty, you gave me drink. I was ill and you comforted me. I was a stranger in a strange land and you welcomed me."

I will close on this melancholy note. Soon we'll be winging our way to another adventure, but the experiences of these last three and a half years will remain with us forever.

Love to all,

Leona and Cyril

Epilogue

Since our return to Canada we've often been asked, "In what ways do you think your work abroad has contributed to the people of Africa?" It was not until two years ago, when we returned to our old haunts with some of our family, that we could respond with any certainty. What we saw then banished any doubts about the contribution of the missions, and so impressed us that we felt honoured to have been involved.

The trade school that we helped revitalize in Manyoni is functioning well, and the hospital in Itigi and the nursing clinics continue to serve hundreds of sick people each day. Throughout the country, young men who'd been seminarians during our time of service, have since been ordained and have ably assumed priestly responsibility in the parishes.

And, from its headquarters in Dodoma, the Water Project, under the direction of Brother Anthony Canterucci and Father Tim Coday (formerly Brother Tim), the on-site manager, continues to bring clean water to areas where before there was none; a new English medium primary school, spear-headed by Brother Anthony, has opened, and children affected by AIDS are being cared for and educated at the Village of Hope under the direction of Father Vincenzo and the Precious Blood Sisters. There are no words to describe their work. In trying, one would fail to bring justice to the projects. Indeed, one of our sons, seeing the youngsters affected by AIDS flocking around Father Vincenzo said, "I have never before seen so much love."

Brother Anthony (Bro), at age 80, continues to travel to Tanzania twice a year, dividing his time between the head office in Toronto and the field office in Dodoma. Under his aegis, the number of partnerships lending moral and financial support to the mission continues to grow. As well as groups in Toronto, there are associations in Airdre, Alberta, Kamloops, B.C. and Yellowknife, N.W.T. Without their support, and the generous contribution of others, the work could not continue. Bro has maintained a solid faith in his mission even when, from time to time, resources dwindled. “It’s God’s work,” he often says, “And He knows how to keep it going.”

Ted Van der Zalm and his wife Miriam have settled in Niagara-on-the-Lake, Ontario. As co-founders of the charity “Wells of Hope”, they continue to serve the poor. For several months each year they leave their comfortable home and the charity’s headquarters in Canada, and, demonstrating astounding self-sacrifice, travel with their children to Central America where they supervise the building of schools and the drilling of water wells to provide clean drinking water for the Guatemalans.

Ana Hook and her family have retired to Italy after spending 20 years in Tanzania, working initially in the field of health care and later as managers of the Water Project. Dr. Lillian Lome has retired in Toronto while Maureen Forsyth and Geoff Hayes continue to work in the field of world development. Alan Kreutzer (formerly Brother Allan) lives with his second wife Joyce in Kansas. (His first wife, Sandy Notley, passed away many years ago at their home in Canada.) Bibi Lois Swanson is retired at her home in the U.S.A. and, from her home in Ontario, Blanche Hinton continues to work as a teacher of the deaf as well as operating her own touring company. She is an active member of Rotary International. The Van den Herk family, after serving in Tanzania for three terms, has returned to farming in Canada.

Fr. Francis Bartoloni has risen to the position of Moderator General of The Society of the Precious Blood. He is headquartered in Rome. Father Dino continues to serve in Tanzania while Fathers Gianni (John) and Domenic have been assigned to parishes in Italy.

Girsh and Menoj Vishani live in Dar es Salaam with their families where Girish holds the position of Branch Manager of Simba Trucking Co. Ltd. When we last heard of Baldwin, he was clerking in a jewellery store in Dar es Salaam, while Laurenti, Kimome and Alex and Darcy Isinika continue to live in the Singida region.

Father Bill Fryda M.D., the charismatic leader whom we met at Swahili Language School in Musoma, is the co-founder and Medical Director of two of the most modern hospitals in Kenya. The original St. Mary's Mission Hospital is located in the Karen district of Nairobi while the other, a branch of St. Mary's, is situated in the Rift Valley near Lake Elementita. In 2003, Father Fryda was a recipient of the Mayo Clinic Alumni Association Award for his work in Africa.

Father Joseph Tham M.D., who was a medical student at the time we first met in Tanzania, has since completed his medical training. He served as an emergency room physician in Toronto before going on to become a priest with the Legionaries of Christ. Based in Rome, he is the holder of advanced degrees in Philosophy and Theology.

We are sad to say that our lives have been diminished by the untimely passing of our special friend, Jim Lamb. His wife Anna and the girls still reside in Dar es Salaam.

Although our home is now in Vernon, B.C., Cyril and I continue to satisfy our yearnings for involvement in development work. We have served on short-term projects in Kenya and Sri Lanka, and, as the local representatives of Save-a-Family-Plan, India, have twice travelled to that continent. My husband often quotes the motto of the Christophers, "It's better to light a candle than to curse the darkness." Our whole family has been enriched by our associations with all these wonderful people and projects, and we feel that, together, we have helped light one small candle.

Leona Lane
June 2009